HABIB TANVIR

HABIB TANVIR

Towards an Inclusive Theatre

―――――――――――――

ANJUM KATYAL

SAGE   www.sagepublications.com
Los Angeles • London • New Delhi • Singapore • Washington DC

First published in 2012 by

SAGE Publications India Pvt Ltd
B1/I-1 Mohan Cooperative Industrial Area
Mathura Road, New Delhi 110 044, India
www.sagepub.in

SAGE Publications Inc
2455 Teller Road
Thousand Oaks, California 91320, USA

SAGE Publications Ltd
1 Oliver's Yard, 55 City Road
London EC1Y 1SP, United Kingdom

SAGE Publications Asia-Pacific Pte Ltd
33 Pekin Street
#02-01 Far East Square
Singapore 048763

Published by Vivek Mehra for SAGE Publications India Pvt Ltd, typeset in 11/13.5 pt Minion by Diligent Typesetter, Delhi, and printed at Saurabh Printers Pvt Ltd, New Delhi.

Library of Congress Cataloging-in-Publication Data Available

ISBN: 978-81-321-0951-8 (HB)

The SAGE Team: Shambhu Sahu, Shreya Chakraborti, Nand Kumar Jha and Rajinder Kaur

To my father,
the late Mumtaz Ahmad—my doorway to a world.

Thank you for choosing a SAGE product! If you have any comment, observation or feedback, I would like to personally hear from you. Please write to me at contactceo@sagepub.in

—Vivek Mehra, Managing Director and CEO,
SAGE Publications India Pvt Ltd, New Delhi

Bulk Sales

SAGE India offers special discounts for purchase of books in bulk. We also make available special imprints and excerpts from our books on demand.

For orders and enquiries, write to us at

Marketing Department
SAGE Publications India Pvt Ltd
B1/I-1, Mohan Cooperative Industrial Area
Mathura Road, Post Bag 7
New Delhi 110044, India
E-mail us at marketing@sagepub.in

Get to know more about SAGE, be invited to SAGE events, get on our mailing list. Write today to marketing@sagepub.in

This book is also available as an e-book.

CONTENTS

FOREWORD

Anjum Katyal's book on Habib Tanvir's ideas, and his rich and varied practice, is an elegant and timely reappraisal of one of the greatest artists of modern India. It takes us through his readings and conversations, through text, music, performance and theatre history.

In order to find entry points into Habib Tanvir's vast body of work, a few signposts may need to be placed. When writing about him, the words popular and traditional, modern and secular immediately come into orbit. The important thing to emphasise is that these are *contested* categories and the degree of radical energy we draw out from them is dependent on the historical contexts within which they function. Further, that as categories they must not obscure and over-define the work; that we as audience must constantly revise our understanding of them in the contemporary moment where they are deployed; that we must side by side revise our notion of the contemporary itself, when it is understood through these self-same categories. In other words, we should allow the work in its contemporary rendition to destabilise the categories.

One of the markers of the traditional is an element of unchangeableness. Traditions are handed down to be preserved, as it were; their connection with the past is their principal value. However, that value is relative to the mode of transmission—whether the transmission is done with impelling force or with ease and informality; with ceremony, as for ratification, or as an active process of dialogue and change; within the urgency of practice or with the drive of an upholder. Habib Sahib both assembles and takes apart traditional devices and conventions in the *process* of play-making, causing a rupture in the modernist sense and yet sustaining a course through the traditional *by* use and handling.

Tradition and modernity are oppositional concepts too familiar to be stretched; the word modern, possibly the most apt description of Habib Sahib's work, is more elastic as it is invested in innovation. It foregrounds the most 'up-to-date' constituents of the present as separated from those that establish continuity with the past.

If we take the concept 'modernity' with this cargo of meanings, then Habib Sahib's work complicates it by cross cutting the traditional modern binary with *contemporary* forms of the folk and popular. Now the popular is what people *do*—their ways of eating, singing, talking, dressing, dancing, worshipping—referring, therefore, to relationships and processes, as well as objects and images.[1] Beliefs and values shape the popular and these in turn are expressed by particular aesthetic strategies and conventions—by the nature of formal choices taken towards art-making.

While popular culture might be that which is produced *by* the people as a part of their everyday life, the symbolising power of popular cultural work often creates a 'public' with a political understanding—even a space for resistance. One way or another, definitions of popular cultural work are never neutral; they are always entangled with questions of *culture* and *power*. In looking at Habib Sahib's commitment to political activism and especially to secularism, such an understanding of the popular is quite critical.

'Popular culture' is sometimes used interchangeably with 'everyday' culture. The term everyday is important precisely for its taken-for-granted qualities. But it is also a *boundary*[2] word, readable only when compared to something that is not everyday, that is, extraordinary or out of the way. Habib Sahib works with the *ordinariness* of theatre-making, derived from the popular forms of Chhattisgarh; he attempts to revalue it—revalue the commonplace, that is—and the artwork that is grafted within it. The workaday and the familiar become remarkable and strange once their taken-for-grantedness is disrupted by transfer to literary and performative spaces; into other and new narratives and stories. The cultural translation of Shakespeare's *Midsummer Night's Dream* as *Kamdev Ka Sapna* by Habib Sahib comes to mind. *Kamdev* is a translation, not an adaptation, and the difference is important to mark. Translation as we know is the process of shifting meaning across cultural boundaries. And it can raise, often in very urgent ways, questions of interpretation and meaning, even destabilising assumptions of originals within literary hierarchies. In an adaptation, which *Kamdev* I believe is not, one text is absorbed into the other with no trace or residue visible; *Kamdev*, on the other hand is like a palimpsest, where the original is visible under the overwriting.

Habib Tanvir's journey through the major concerns that occupied artists of the 1950s, 1960s and 1970s as citizens of a newly independent India— identity, nation and democracy—as well as his vision for a more egalitarian

and equitable society underlined by justice, freedom of expression, modernity and socialist collectivity with a stake in art practice, have been defining
forces in modern Indian theatre practices.

Anjum Katyal's illuminating study is keenly attentive to the way Habib
Tanvir gave value and tangibility to cultural forms; that he sought to open a
radical space in a society that is becoming rapidly consumerist. Her research
allows us to traverse the complex landscape that he himself tracked.

Anuradha Kapur
Director, National School of Drama (NSD)
New Delhi, July 2012

Notes

1. See Michael Payne and Jessica Rae Barbera (eds), *A Dictionary of Cultural and Critical
   Theory* (Chichester, UK: John Wiley and Sons Pvt. Ltd., 2005), pp. 553–555.
2. Tony Bennett, Lawrence Grossberg and Meaghan Morris (eds), *New Keywords: A Revised
   Vocabulary of Culture And Society* (Malden, Massachusetts: Blackwell Publishing, 2005),
   p. 116.

ACKNOWLEDGEMENTS

Habib Saab has generated such a wealth of goodwill and esteem that my task of seeking help was made easy as soon as the subject and purpose of my research was disclosed. Everyone I approached while working on this book was unhesitatingly generous with resources, materials, time and conversation. Thanks are due to: Nageen Tanvir, who gave me her full support, providing me access to materials and photographs, and contributing her own memoirs and observations in response to a request from me; Mahmood Farooqui, who in an act of incredible generosity allowed me access to his work in progress, a first draft of his English translation of Habib Saab's memoirs; my friends and former colleagues at Seagull, who responded promptly to all requests for material; Vikram Iyengar, for lending me books and invaluable resources; Sameera Iyengar, for her very useful feedback and criticism. I am also grateful to Natya Shodh Sansthan, where I spent hours looking up material on Habib Saab with the warm cooperation of Pratibha Agarwal; Javed Malick and Samik Bandyopadhyay for their helpfulness; and Sudhanva Deshpande, who is as much a Habib fan as I am, for his insights. For the photographs, I am indebted to Avinash Pasricha, for his prompt and kind permission to use his stills of Naya Theatre productions; to Naveen Kishore for the use of his portraits of Habib Saab; to the archives of Natya Shodh Sansthan; and to Nageen Tanvir for photographs from the Naya Theatre files.

Anjum Katyal
April 2012, Kolkata

INTRODUCTION

Making Space for the Oral Tradition in Indian Theatre Today

One of my favourite Habib Saab stories (and he was quite a raconteur) is about a brief encounter on his European odyssey, when he was travelling through Europe in the mid-1950s, seeing theatre, doing odd jobs and barely managing to make ends meet. One evening in Nice, as he sat on the beach with hardly any money left in his pocket, a young Algerian lad approached and kept pestering him for a souvenir—his last 10 pound note, his fountain pen—till Habib asked him if he could sing. He said yes.

> I said, 'Would you like to hear a song?'
> 'Yes'.
> 'D'you promise to give me an Algerian song?'
> He said, 'Yes'.
> I said, 'Then I promise to give you an Indian song.'

> He sang me an Algerian song. I liked it. I liked the lilt of it. I learnt it and then I sang to him a Chhattisgarhi folk song. He liked it. So I took some time learning his song and writing it and he took his time trying to learn my song—I don't know if he still remembers it or not—and the night passed. It was time for the train, four in the morning and I shook him by the hand and said, 'Now you've got a souvenir from me and I've got one from you and we're none the poorer for it, in fact we're richer. Goodbye.'[1]

This little anecdote has stayed in my mind. So much more than just an amusing tale about a random encounter, I feel that it speaks volumes about the man, and his philosophy of culture. By offering to exchange songs as souvenirs, he gives a value and tangibility to cultural forms—particularly ephemeral ones like songs and oral narratives—that are largely disregarded, especially in our current consumerist society. By exchanging a nugget of our own culture, he seems to suggest, we exchange a valuable part of ourselves. And this is a true gift: we spend time over the process of exchange, thereby bestowing more value on it; we make an effort in both giving and receiving (learning) it; and the gifting enriches both parties equally. This kind of cultural exchange is also lasting—years later Habib Tanvir introduced the very same Algerian song in a production.[2]

Songs, and the oral tradition of which our folk performance forms are an integral part, remained central to Habib's theatrical journey right to the very end of his life.

ॐ

Habib Tanvir (1923–2009) was one of India's best-known modern[3] theatre directors. *The Oxford Companion to Indian Theatre* describes him as follows: 'Hindi and Urdu playwright, director, actor, manager, poet, and one of the most important theatre personalities of post-Independence India'.[4] He is best known for his work with Naya Theatre, the repertory formed by him and his wife and professional partner Moneeka Misra, with actors from Chhattisgarh, which started functioning as a professional company around 1972, after which Habib Tanvir's plays were mostly performed by this troupe of Chhattisgarhi actors who had largely been trained in the local Nacha performance form.

However, Habib Saab's true importance to Indian theatre, in my opinion, does not lie in his personal achievements as an actor or a director, playwright and manager, though these were remarkable enough to justify the sobriquet 'renaissance man'. Indeed, theatre activist and scholar Sudhanva Deshpande, writing three days after his death, calls him just that:

> Habib Tanvir was a renaissance personality. There was nothing he could not do in theatre—he wrote, translated, adapted and evolved plays; he was a master director, a superb actor and a good singer; he wrote poetry and songs; he could compose music; he was a designer; he was manager of his company Naya Theatre, which he ran first with his wife Moneeka (and single-handed after her death) for exactly fifty years; he was a critic and theoretician; more, he was a seer, a guru for generations of younger theatre artistes. In all this, and through his prodigiously prolific theatre career spanning some sixty years, he remained an artiste with a deep social conscience and engagement, a public intellectual who never shied away from taking a stand and lending his name to progressive and secular causes.[5]

There are several towering Indian theatre personalities who, like Habib Tanvir, have produced work of a very high standard, milestone productions in India's theatre history. His name will certainly be part of any 'who's who' of Indian theatre by these criteria. But to my mind that is not his most valuable or significant contribution to the history of Indian theatre.

What makes Habib Saab's contribution so invaluable and irreplaceable is his intervention in the most fundamental discourse of theatre in independent India—the whole question of direction and form. He entered the world of theatre at a critical point, just as India gained independence. His contemporaries, major practitioners and theorists were engaged in giving a shape, an identity, to Indian theatre. On the one hand, there was the colonial legacy of Western-style proscenium, modernist and avant-garde theatre; on the other, the Orientalist-led rediscovery of ancient Sanskrit texts and traditional performance forms.

Urban India adopted the proscenium with enthusiasm, regardless of political persuasion or theatrical style. From the popular Parsi and Company theatre to the politically leftist theatre of Utpal Dutt in Bengal, the Western-style stage came to dominate theatre in the cities. The popular Parsi and Company theatre troupes also toured extensively in the small towns and rural areas, thereby, familiarising audiences there with the conventions of the proscenium theatre.[6] Parallel to this, individual stalwarts turned to traditional performance forms. Sanskrit theatre as laid down by the Natyashastra, was one discovery. (Habib also did Sanskrit classics like Sudraka's *Mrichhakatikam* and Visakhadatta's *Mudrarakshasa*.) Another area of exploration was the rich legacy of regional performative traditions to be found all over the country. From the Nacha of Habib's homeground, Chhattisgarh, to the Tamasha and Lavani of Maharashtra, the Bhavai of Gujarat, Yakshagana of Karnataka, Koodiyattam of Kerala, Therukoothu of Tamil Nadu, and the Chhau of Orissa—the list is as varied as it is colourful. Closely connected to these are performer-training systems and martial arts disciplines—like the Manipuri Thang-ta or Kalaripayyat in South India. Arguably the Indian People's Theatre Association (IPTA), out of their interest in people's culture, was the first to explore these 'folk' forms and bring them into their theatrical presentations in a sustained way. Later, these became grist to the mills of theatre directors in search of ethnic forms of expression. The outcome of this trend was the loosely termed 'roots theatre' movement. Typically, 'theatre of the roots' utilised aspects of training or presentation taken from one or more of these traditional systems in the service of a 'modern' theatre which was usually the vision or artistic expression of an individual director.[7]

Both these dominant parallel trends in modern Indian theatre—the Western-looking and the ethnic-looking—were far removed from the folk theatre that was still vibrantly alive in the Indian countryside. These folk theatre forms were of, by and for the rural and semi-rural populace, and travelled a separate circuit all their own. Closely linked to the robust oral culture of Indian village life, they had evolved over centuries and continued to adopt from and adapt to contemporary reality—whether this meant satirical skits on current affairs, topical references to local scandals or the introduction of popular Hindi film songs into their performance routines. They were subaltern forms, brimming with irreverent digs at the status quo and subversive wit and humour. However, as the rural economy weakened and collapsed, folk actors and groups found their survival threatened. Precious oral heritage slipped into oblivion as songs ceased to be sung, dances ceased to be danced and rituals ceased to be performed. Invaluable skills and indigenous knowledge, as important a part of India's cultural heritage as the Sanskrit scriptures the nation-state so zealously preserved, gradually grew extinct, largely unnoticed by the cultural mainstream.

Habib Tanvir recognised the value of this oral cultural heritage. He spoke often on the subject:

> The educated lack the culture which ... the villages possess so richly though they are illiterate ... being more than compensated by the rich oral tradition of our culture and who therefore are the more cultured.

> The rural sophistication is not understood by the urban people and vice versa. But I find the villager much more sophisticated ... in many, many instances. In the arts they are much more sophisticated.

> I believe in the viability of the rich forms of the rural theatre in which they have a tendency to incorporate the most topical, the latest local happening, the thematic and formal flexibility by which we cannot claim this is how it was performed 200 or 2000 years ago.... I believe that it is possible to usher in progress without demolishing this culture. This environment should be preserved, this ... rural environment most conducive to the fullest growth of the folk theatre form, because this community life which is so rich in its cultural expression can be transformed to a progressive community in which this expression remains.[8]

In fact, at the time when Habib began his career, 'fo'k' was not a term in common use. As theatre critic and scholar Javed Malick points out, it was

> neither the fashion nor the passion of India's contemporary stage. Far from being the all-inspiring catchword that it later became in Indian theatre, it

was a neglected and greatly devitalised category. Tanvir was one of those who pioneered the revival of interest in folk performance traditions and made it into a significant and influential category.[9]

Several of his peers were also excited by the riches of the folk performative tradition. However, rather than use it, like they did, as a resource for images, motifs, idioms and elements to be transformed into a theatre of his own design and making, Habib chose to shape his own theatre around the presence of the folk performer, who is, literally, the embodiment and vehicle of oral performance culture. The folk performers are in themselves 'endangered archives'. He has said, time and again, that he was not running after folk forms as much as running after folk actors; with the actors came the forms. Another way of saying it was that the owners of the tradition brought it with them; it was not taken from them for the use of others.

Yet his was not folk theatre, although, since he frequently used material such as folktales, folk songs and rituals in his productions; it is often mistaken for an attempt at it. But this would be a misreading of his work. As Javed Malick clarifies, 'Tanvir's fascination with the folk is not motivated by a revivalist or an antiquarian impulse.'[10] Sudhanva Deshpande further insists:

> On Habib Tanvir's theatre, it is quite common to hear two views. One sees a development of the IPTA legacy in him, the other sees him as a practitioner of 'folk' theatre. Both are incorrect. IPTA sought to build an all-India network of revolutionary cultural groups in close association with the Communist movement. Habib Tanvir, after his early years with IPTA, has never again done that kind of work. Certainly in his theatre *practice* there isn't even a whiff of IPTA; while IPTA used 'folk' forms essentially as carriers of revolutionary ideology to 'the masses', Habib Tanvir has fashioned a popular modern theatre, borrowing elements from rural dramatic traditions that has more often than not been utopic rather than revolutionary.[11]

Habib himself emphasised: 'And howsoever other people would like to characterize it, my theatre was, and still is, modern and contemporary.'[12]

Indeed, Tanvir brought the whole of his education and experience to bear upon his theatre—from his early exposure to touring Parsi theatre companies and all-night Nacha performances in Chhattisgarh, to his literature college course, to his IPTA years in Mumbai, his training at the Royal Academy of Dramatic Art (RADA),[13] the Bristol Old Vic and the British Drama League in the UK, his exposure to Brecht and the Berliner Ensemble, and the range of Indian theatre he observed and critiqued. 'I thought you can do nothing worthwhile unless you went to your roots and tried to reinterpret traditions and used traditions as a vehicle for transmitting the most modern and contemporary messages. Which means intervening in the tradition creatively.'[14] As a result, his was a modern theatre; but one which had the space in it for folk actors, who brought with them a whole culture and aesthetic rapidly being marginalised by mainstream theatre in India. This was the oral tradition—improvisational, non-linear in approach to time and space, collective in practice. It is this oral tradition that made Tanvir's theatre so unique.

To me, this is the greatest importance of Habib Tanvir's theatre legacy. His trial and error pursuit of a satisfactory theatre form, carried out over several decades, can be seen as a sustained and serious exploration of how one could create a modern theatre integrated with an age-old yet equally contemporary oral culture, not just as an 'exotic' imported element but as an integral part of its form and content. He achieved this in his Naya Theatre work with Chhattisgarhi actors; together, he and the actors shaped a theatre that was both critically acclaimed and hugely popular (his iconic *Charandas Chor* is still in demand, even after his demise). They travelled the country and the world, and everywhere his productions were accepted as modern, not folk, theatre. In a theatre environment divided between two dominant approaches, Habib opened up a third way. Indeed, this was his vision:

> If it is attempted to close this gap between the village and the town … above all in the realm of art, then we will begin to think in terms of a true indigenous form which is good enough for modern India whether in the cities or in the villages. After all we are trying to bridge this gap in terms of development in industry, agriculture. In terms of culture also we have to come to grips with what are the roots and not always remain in the urban vacuum which has been created in the last few decades.[15]

So, he says,

> In my plays I take up the important issues of our times while working with people who are linked to the soil, people who are open minded and unin-hibited. And it was the interaction of these two elements that gave birth to a new theatrical idiom.[16]

His respect for this oral culture led him to a collaborative mode of inter-action based on an attitude of mutual respect. Javed Malick stresses this aspect of Habib's approach:

Tanvir is careful not to create a hierarchy by privileging, in any absolute and extrinsic way, his own educated consciousness as poet-cum-playwright-cum-director over the unschooled creativity of his actors. In his work, the two usually meet and interprenetrate, as it were, as equal partners in a collective, collaborative endeavour in which each gives and takes from, and thus enriches, the other.[17]

Javed Malick sees examples of this in the way Habib 'fits and blends his poetry with the traditional folk and tribal music, allowing the former to retain its own imaginative and rhetorical power and socio-political import, but without in any way devaluing or destroying the latter'[18] and also in the way he 'allows his actors and their skills to be foregrounded by eschewing all temptations to use elaborate stage design and complicated lighting'.[19] To me, Habib's way of developing a scene with his actors also exemplifies this collaborative process; he would give them free rein to improvise, watching and guiding until the moment when he would step in and 'freeze' the sequence with his directorial touch.

As we move towards an increasingly globalised cultural reality that has no time or place in it for oral traditions—which, as I have mentioned, are typically collective, participatory, improvisatory and resistant to regulation—Habib's intervention gains a haunting significance. For those who are engaged with envisaging a way forward—socially, culturally and economically—which is more inclusive, and benefits the majority, his theatre is a wedge holding open a space of possibility, a foot in a door that is steadily closing. He has shown that it is possible to envisage and practise a form of cultural expression that includes the oral culture of the Indian majority as part of a modern sensibility. He has shown that the folk actor can confidently perform in and make a major contribution to modern theatre, in terms of both form and content. In the brochure for his breakthrough production *Gaon Ke Naon Sasural Mor Naon Damad*, he asserts:

> The two hours' duration of the play in itself stands for a new direction. It implies that an oral theatre improvised by illiterate folk actors without the aid of a well considered text written by a playwright also has possibilities of holding its own.[20]

After Habib, it is no longer possible to maintain that the folk and the modern cannot co-exist, in cultural practice, without the former becoming merely an exotic import for the latter.

ℰᏼᏨᎡ

We have spoken of the oral tradition in Habib's work—what are these elements of orality that he incorporates?

Let's begin with language. Growing up in Raipur, Tanvir was exposed
from an early age to the robust and colourful Chhattisgarhi dialect. A poet
and writer, he always had a keen interest in language, particularly the language of the common man. This fascination deepened during his years with
the IPTA and Progressive Writers' Association (PWA).[21] Yet Tanvir did not
just lift the language and use it to write dialogue, just as he did not just lift
folk material and fashion plays from it. Rather, he was interested in working
with folk actors who embodied the language, which informed the quality of
performance they had to offer. This becomes clear when he describes how
he met the actors who were to become the core of Naya Theatre; he selected
them all for their outstanding talent, stage presence, acting prowess and
their impeccable comic timing.[22]

It was the actors, then, who became central to his kind of theatre. And
they brought a whole oral performative tradition with them. His was a
work to be shaped by and with these actors, using their training and their
experience of the oral cultural heritage.

Improvisation is central to the folk oral performance forms, where there
is no written script and, therefore, no fixed authorship. The actor contributes
his dialogue, inserts little bits of stage business, brings in topical references,
interacts with the audience and plays to the gallery. By incorporating two
fundamental principles into his theatre—the native language and the freedom to improvise—Tanvir ensured that the actors gained agency.

Improvised theatre is also collective theatre—another characteristic of
the oral tradition. The performance belongs to those who make it; there
is no single author. Tanvir's practice of collective improvisation is clearly
delineated in his description of how he works:

> We work like this. I put a story across to the group members and they think
> it over. The next time round we go over the storyline and each one puts in
> a word for an elaboration or a nuance he thinks should be fitted in at such
> and such a point in the course of the play. This is something I've always tried
> to do—get the actors to move the play in certain directions.[23]

Another aspect of the folk oral culture that Habib Tanvir incorporated
in his work was the non-linear treatment of time and space, in direct

contrast to Aristotle's stipulated unities of time, space and action. He talks of his discovery of fluid, flexible time and space when he began to plan *Mrichhakatikar*.

> You see, I've learnt many things from watching Nacha, although, of course, from *Mitti ki Gadi* in 1958 I'd come to a very simple kind of stage set . . . and learnt to have the stage set functional, very economical so that we remain mobile, for artistic as well as economical reasons. The architecture, set design, were also affected by the kind of awareness I gained in regard to the importance of the actor related to space and the relation of time to space and to actor and to action. All these things, I think, gave me very simple forms, like a rectangular platform with just one tree, to which I came after a few shows.[24]

He talks elsewhere of how he discovered the magical simplicity of an actor making a round of the performance area to indicate a journey or a new locale; of how it is the actor's body that defines space and time in performance as opposed to sets, lights or scene divisions.

Tanvir's productions are characterised by subversive social comment through wit and humour, another folk characteristic typical of the oral tradition. His seminal *Charandas Chor* abounds in searing indictments of the hypocrisy and corruption of the rich and powerful, including the falsely pious figures of priests and gurus. *Ponga Pandit*

> focuses on the cheeky intelligence of a *bhangan* (sweeper) who enters a temple and counters the disdain of the reigning priest with native shrewdness. One by one, she touches all the objects, which the priest immediately declares 'polluted'. So she walks off with them, delivering her clincher: she can build her own little temple with the discarded idols—she does not need him anymore![25]

This 'hilarious attack on casteism'[26] has been performed by dozens of Nacha companies over the years; yet, in the wake of rising Hindutva right-wing violence post Babri Masjid, Tanvir's production was repeatedly attacked on the grounds of being anti-Hindu.

Prime amongst the oral elements in Tanvir's plays is his use of song. Fascinated by the sheer wealth and variety of traditional folk songs intrinsic to every aspect of daily life in Chhattisgarh, Tanvir's love of music led him to gather a treasure trove of these, many of them on the verge of growing extinct, as even the Nacha, catering to popular demand, was eschewing these traditional songs for Hindi tunes. Their inclusion in his plays has ensured them a healthy survival.

The songs in a Habib Tanvir play, performed live by musicians and actors, punctuate the performance. Invariably based on folk melodies and rhythms, they use indigenous instruments and are delivered in the characteristic vocal style associated with folk songs. He also combined his own lyrics with traditional folk tunes.

ℰↄℭℛ

Habib often spoke about his long journey towards the crystallisation of his characteristic theatre form. It would be misleading to create the impression that he found his form in a moment of epiphany or that it presented itself to him fully fashioned. The entire process of trial and error, of experimentation, failure and lessons learned, took almost half a lifetime. And everything fed into it—his life experiences, his political beliefs, his literary passions. The structure of this book keeps this process in mind. Starting with early influences and exposure, it traces the different phases, influences and experiences of his life and work until he arrived at what he felt was his true form, with *Charandas Chor* in 1975.

Chapter 1 looks at his childhood and growing years and his early exposure to different forms of theatre and performance, especially the vibrant Chhattisgarhi language and culture. Chapter 2 studies his years in Bombay, his engagement with the film industry and his stint in the media, his involvement with Urdu poetry and the PWA, and his hands-on experience of doing theatre as part of IPTA. Chapter 3 begins with his decision to eschew film for theatre and his relocation to Delhi, and ends with his first production of *Agra Bazaar*. In Chapter 4, we follow him to the UK and then Europe, a period that was a major learning and growing phase for him. Chapter 5 deals with his return to Delhi and his production of *Mitti Ki Gadi*, the beginning of his gradual movement towards theatre with Chhattisgarhi actors. Chapter 6 covers the intervening years till his breakthrough play *Gaon Ka Naon Sasural*, filled with a variety of developments, from the formation of Naya Theatre to marriage and fatherhood, and a stint in the Rajya Sabha. Chapter 7 focuses on *Charandas Chor*, and the realisation that he had finally found his true theatrical form.

Thereafter, each chapter takes up an important aspect of his work in theatre. Chapter 8 is devoted to understanding his relationship with his Chhattisgarhi actors. In Chapter 9, we examine the way in which he handled classic and literary texts, both Indian and international. Chapter 10 focuses on his theatre with folk material, especially folk tales and folklore. In Chapter 11, we consider his use of music, song, ritual and dance; finally Chapter 12 talks of the political side of Habib and how it inflected his theatre.

Notes

1. Habib Tanvir, '"It Must Flow"—A Life in Theatre', *Seagull Theatre Quarterly*, 10, June 1996 (henceforth *STQ*), p. 14.
2. Habib Tanvir, *STQ*, p. 19. 'One of the plays I chose was Moliere's *The Bourgeois Gentleman*, in which in the Turkish scene.... I used the Algerian song, which I'd learnt from that Algerian boy.'
3. A word here about my use of the term 'modern' throughout this book, a contested term due to Modernism being recognised as a movement and a moment with distinct allocated characteristics, manifesting differently in different regions of the world, and indeed within a country. I use 'modern' in the loose, broad sense of common usage—to indicate 'not traditional, not folk'.
4. Ananda Lal (ed.), *The Oxford Companion to Indian Theatre* (New Delhi: Oxford University Press, 2004), pp. 472–473.
5. Sudhanva Deshpande, 'Habib Tanvir and his Red-hot Life' in *Pragoti*, http://www.pragoti.org/hi/node/3456, accessed on 27 May 2012.
6. Indeed, Habib Tanvir has vivid memories of watching such plays as a child in Raipur. See Chapter 1 ('Growing up in Raipur, and Early Influences').
7. For a comprehensive study of 'theatre of the roots' see Erin Mee, *Theatre of Roots: Redirecting the Modern Indian Stage* (Kolkata: Seagull Books, 2008).
8. 'Habib Tanvir Interviewed' by Rajinder Paul, *Enact*, 87, March 1974. [Reproduced in *Nukkad Janam Samvad*, Focus on Naya Theatre (henceforth *Nukkad*), April 2004–Mar 2005, p. 87].
9. Javed Malick, 'Refashioning Modernity: Habib Tanvir and His Naya Theatre' in Neeraj Malik and Javed Malick (eds), *Habib Tanvir: Reflections and Reminiscences* (New Delhi: SAHMAT, 2010), pp. 15–16.
10. Javed Malick, 'Introduction to Habib Tanvir', *Charandas Chor*, translated by Anjum Katyal (Kolkata: Seagull Books, 1996/2004), p. 7.
11. Sudhanva Deshpande, 'Upside-Down Midas' in *Nukkad*, p. 15.
12. Habib Tanvir, 'In Conversation with Shampa Shah' in Neeraj Malik and Javed Malick (eds), *Habib Tanvir: Reflections and Reminiscences*, p. 142.
13. Royal Academy of Dramatic Art, United Kingdom.
14. Habib Tanvir, 'In Conversation with Javed Malick' in Neeraj Malik and Javed Malick (ed.), *Habib Tanvir: Reflections and Reminiscences*, p. 104.
15. 'Habib Tanvir Interviewed' by Rajinder Paul, p. 86.
16. Habib Tanvir, 'In Conversation with Shampa Shah', p. 142.
17. Javed Malick, 'Habib Tanvir: The Making of a Legend' in *Nukkad*, p. 12.
18. Ibid.
19. Ibid.
20. Naya Theatre brochure for *Gaon Ka Naon Sasural, Mor Naan Damad*, Triveni Garden Theatre, 11–15 April 1973.

21. A progressive leftist creative organisation that had a major influence on the formation of modern Indian arts and literature in the 1940s.
22. For an account of this, see Chapter 5 ('Coming Home to *Mitti Ki Gadi*').
23. Habib Tanvir, 'The World, and Theatre, According to Habib Tanvir' in *The Telegraph Colour Magazine*, 17 April 1983, p. 6.
24. Habib Tanvir, *STQ*, p. 29.
25. Sameera Iyengar (ed.), *On the Road with Naya Theatre*, Prithvi Theatre Yearbook (Mumbai: Prithvi Theatre, 2006), entry for 17–30 June.
26. 'Trauma of Our Times', *The Hindu*, 27 August 1993. Also, in Iyengar (ed.), *On the Road with Naya Theatre*, entry for 19 June.

CHAPTER ONE

GROWING UP IN RAIPUR, AND EARLY INFLUENCES

A young Habib in *Rustom-o-Sohrab*. From the Natya Shodh
Sansthan archive, courtesy Naya Theatre

'*Duniyaa, makkar-o-abla fareb, duniyaa*! Oh world, this treacherous and deceitful world!'

This was a line from a play, written by our Persian teacher Mohammmed Ishaq Saheb, being directed by the drill master at our school. The title of the play was 'Pearl of Poverty, alias The Polishwalla,' and I played the title role of the polishwalla. I was in the second year of primary school at the time.[1]

This was Habib Tanvir, reminiscing about his early tryst with the stage. Ishaq Saheb, who later became Habib Tanvir's brother-in-law, had written the play in the style of the Parsi theatre, and Master Samiullah also tried to direct it in the same style.

Being a drill master and a bodybuilder, he gave us movements which were very athletic and on every word, you'd have a gesture to accompany it. *Duniyaa*— put your fist on your forehead—*makkar-o-abla fareb, duniyaa*—move two steps forward. I found no fault, at that time, with that kind of direction, because I knew no better. I enjoyed it.[2]

He elaborates:

I was told to enter from stage left, walk sideways while speaking this dialogue and exit from the right. I had to walk on my toes with my heels raised, and speak in a loud and quavering voice. Now that I look back on it I feel it was completely appropriate that a play written in Parsi theatre style should also be performed in that vein, that is to say in a declamatory voice with melo-dramatic gestures. What I can't make out is why he asked me to walk like a wrestler, except for the fact that the director Master Samiullah was himself a bodybuilder and so that walk came naturally to him. I had seen him walk-ing exactly like that. Anyway, I shouldn't complain about it since I won the Thakur Pyare Lal Singh Best Actor Silver cup for this play.[3]

Young as he was, this was not Habib Tanvir's first time on stage. Earlier that year he had performed in a short extract from Shakespeare's *King John* in English. He had played Prince Arthur in the scene where

Hubert … comes to take the prince away to put out his eyes, and the prince suddenly pleads—if you had a grain, a speck of dust in your eye, how would you feel? It was a small piece, but very moving and I enjoyed it.[4]

He was awarded first prize for English acting and won another silver cup. 'Everyone at home was delighted.'[5]

Habib Ahmed Khan (he adopted the pen name Tanvir later) was born on 1 September[6] 1923 in Raipur, Chhattisgarh, into a large family. His father was from Peshawar, a religious man who did not approve of music and performance. His mother's family was from Raipur, and his maternal uncles were fond of both music and poetry. Raipur, as Tanvir states,

is more or less a kind of capital of Chhattisgarh, which consists of six districts. It's a large region: Raipur, Bilaspur, Durg, Rajnandgaon, Raegarh and Bastar. So, it is ethnically compact—ethnically and linguistically. The dialect spoken by and large is Chhattisgarhi, which is a dialect of Hindi.[7]

He grew up surrounded by this tongue, which later became the language of choice for his theatre.

Raipur was, in the days of his childhood, a small town surrounded by villages, 'where the line between the town and the country was far from clearly defined';[8] in fact, the links between town and country were intricate and numerous. Village men and women supplying milk, curds, vegetables, eggs, fruits, etc., visited houses every day, often over generations, leading to close relationships; many town dwellers owned agricultural land or had relatives who did so and, therefore, frequent visits to the villages were common. 'Although Tanvir's immediate family did not have direct connection with the countryside, several of his uncles and grand uncles did. It was through these that he had his first exposure to the rural life and its songs and music.'[9]

His memoirs describe a relaxed childhood in a large, rambling house filled with siblings (of the 11 children his parents had, 7 survived into adulthood), grandmothers, aunts, uncles and cousins. Vivid thumbnail sketches bring them to life in a few quick strokes—his keen director's eye for unusual characters, replete with physical and behavioural idiosyncrasies, leads him to recall a parade of personalities in affectionate detail. Clearly, he was a sharp observer of 'characters' even as a child. For example, his account of Rangeela of Raipur:

> He used to be a madari[10] but had set himself up as a Doctor, with a clinic at home, complete with a board saying, 'Doctor Rangeela'.… He was quite an actor. He could make people laugh with his dramatic ways. He would explain the advantage of having a bald head compared to a hairy one by saying that in a fight your hair could be caught by your opponent, whereas if your head was bald, there was nothing to grip. He would act out both parts himself. He had thick, curly hair and would clutch his locks with one hand, pretending to be in pain, rising up on his haunches and making dreadful grimaces of protest. Similarly, he would play out the part of a bearded versus a clean-shaven man. When he had gathered a sizeable crowd and they were enjoying themselves he would suddenly open a *pitari* (lidded cane basket) and begin to show off his collection of snakes and spiders, saying, what a pair of snakes this is, see, these are their properties, and so on and so forth … he would take off on lizards and *girgits*, on *sande ka tel* (natural oil) and cures for impotency and finally he would state the prices of different medicines and the crowd would begin to disperse. But he always found a couple of buyers.[11]

Amongst immediate members of his family, there was the irrepressible Bhaijan, his brother Zaheer, who was a major influence in his life:

> Bhaijan was an incredibly interesting man. He used to compose poetry under the pen name of 'Vashi' or 'Savage.' The title suited his personality to a tee.

He was very free spirited and could not stick to anything. He would change his job and even his profession at the drop of a hat. He was very witty and would have all of us in splits all the time. It was this comic strain that probably helped him survive everything.[12]

The account of Bhaijan's various failed business ventures is described in hilarious detail:

One day he got a brainwave about a new business and he started an agency for assorted goods. In no time the house was full of samples of swatches of cloth of all kinds for men and women, shirts, suits, saris, blouses. Samples upon samples, cloth upon cloth and tin boxes all over the house, with cards carrying the company's name and address. None of his friends had the means to buy these clothes, strangers refused to, and even relatives and family members showed no interest. Eventually he went to Ammijan who, indulgent as ever, paid advance money for some samples; and of course the delivery never happened! She just smiled like she always did and said, 'Never mind Zaheer, the money will come'.

The agency was changed. Buttons, buttons upon buttons. Of all kinds, colours, shapes, sizes. Buttons for jackets, for overcoats, for ladies' blouses, for kurtas. Bhaijan would roam around with samples of buttons but he failed to find a buyer, not even Ammijan. Eventually they were all returned to the supplier.

Then it was the turn of watches and clocks. The trunk could not contain them all so they spilled over on to tables, beds, almirahs, shelves. Wrist watches, pocket watches, time pieces, alarm clocks, wall clocks, the house was overflowing with them. Prospective buyers were lured by the music of different alarms. Often many wall clocks would strike simultaneously, their din shaking the entire house. Amma would shout, Zaheer, what is this ruckus, you have turned the house into a museum. People would come to look at the clocks but no one would buy. Again, it was Ammijan who fell into the trap and ended up buying a double alarm timepiece.[13]

These descriptions of personalities and experiences from his childhood bespeak a thorough enjoyment of the farcical and the absurd, a trait that was manifest in Habib Tanvir's productions as well. His robust sense of the comic was clearly nurtured on the colourful characters who surrounded him throughout his growing years.

It was Bhaijan who introduced him to theatre. He used to take part in plays when Habib was a child, usually playing women's roles in amateur productions. There was a tradition of a group of friends mounting an annual production in Kalibari, and Habib made a point of going to see these when he was in school. They were usually in Urdu.

> They belonged to what we call the Parsi theatre tradition, because of the professional companies run by Parsis, doing predominantly Urdu drama. There was a whole crop of playwrights that this movement had given rise to; they toured all over India. Many of them originated in Lucknow, then travelled to Calcutta, Amritsar, Lahore, Bombay, all over the country.[14]

His first experience of a play is worth recounting in the detail in which he remembers it. As he says, 'This was my first ever experience of theatre and it so captivated me that I have not been able to come out of its spell.'[15]

The occasion was the annual Durga Puja theatrical offering at Kalibari, and the play was *Mohabbat Ke Phool* (The Offerings of Love), a staple of the Parsi theatre repertoire.

> Even before I went inside, I was mesmerized by the atmosphere outside the hall. There were innumerable hawkers, there was an enormous crowd and a band playing with great gusto. By the time the band stopped playing it was late at night. The band moved inside and along with them the crowd poured in. I too followed. The band settled into the orchestra pit and began to play a kind of overture. Then the curtain began to rise. First we saw coloured and bejewelled feet, then bright multi-coloured costumes and then finally beautiful, heavily made-up faces. The curtain was rising to the beat of the music and behind it we saw a row of actors singing the traditional opening tune of the Dhrupad Vandana. These days the curtains usually part sideways to reveal the stage. I have always preferred it the older way, when curtains rose up from the ground and disappeared.... When I first experienced the stage in childhood and the curtain that rose so magically and so majestically, I was completely taken by it. Bhaijan was playing the role of the heroine and our neighbour Lutfullah was playing the hero Janbaz. When the hero is bound in shackles and thrown into the dungeons and the heroine starts wailing for him, I was so affected that I started crying and hiccupping loudly in the audience. There was another trick that wholly captivated me. In the wings was a man holding a long iron rod with which he would strike hard at an iron receptacle which contained gunpowder. There would be a big blast and voila! The whole scene on the stage was changed! The sets were made of painted curtains, a garden was depicted by slanting rows of flats as wings, with painted flowers and trees, a palace was depicted by a painted backdrop. The lighting too was quite adequate—even spectacular, given the times and limited resources.

I recall seeing a scene where a cave was depicted by a clever placement of rows of flats which were then lit in a way that made it seem really dark and cavernous. The 'street' was usually placed right in front, down stage, rows of houses painted on either side with a road in their midst. Often a comic scene would be played out on the street. These usually had nothing to do with the main plot, but they were quite marvellous. You would be in the middle of a serious scene, overwhelmed with grief, and suddenly there would be a blast, the stage would revolve, the scene would change to a street, the curtain would rise up on a roller and a comic scene would begin. The viewer, who may have been crying at the sad scene, would now begin to laugh.

The stage must have been quite deep too, because behind the street curtain there might lie five more such curtains, each depicting different locations and scenes. There was a revolving turntable-like platform on the stage which rotated with the wings and the curtains. It was nothing short of a spectacular act of sorcery to hear the blast and see the scene change so dramatically.

Anyway, the play got over, the hero and the heroine were united, and at the curtain call all the actors came together in a delightful formation and sang a song. There were two intervals in between. As soon as they began, hawkers selling tea, lemon soda and peanuts poured in, and their cries and movements would create another spectacle.[16]

This festive atmosphere was also to be found in the many *mela*s (fairs) for which the region was known.

Chhattisgarh is full of fairs of all kinds but some of them are really old, like Rajam ka mela, Dungargarh, Ratanpur, Shivri Narayan. I went to these fairs when I was young, and I have been to them lately—but they just do not have that same charm. Earlier the antics of *chhappan chhuri*, the circus, magic shows, roundabouts, bioscopes, stalls of food, jewellery, toys, the cattle fair, clothes, combined to turn these fairs into cultural centres. Now they have lost most of their colour.[17]

In an interview with theatre scholar Javed Malick (also his nephew), when asked how come he developed an interest in folk forms, he reminisces:

As a child, I had often accompanied my uncles to villages in Chhattisgarh. I used to listen to their songs and music. I had even learnt many of these songs, some had stayed in my memory automatically and some I had made an effort to learn because I liked them and wanted to learn them.[18]

Clearly the lively local culture made a lasting impact on the young Habib, and much of his aesthetics of theatre—spirited, musical, colourful, dynamic, earthy—has its roots in his childhood in Chhattisgarh.

We already know that he first fell under the spell of theatre in Raipur, but another artistic pursuit that was to be a lifelong love affair—poetry, especially poetry in Urdu, along with a complementary fascination with words and language—can also be traced back to his formative years in his hometown. 'I became acquainted with New Poetry in Raipur itself. As teenagers we would go to listen to *mushairas*[19] on the radio at Company Bagh. These were regularly broadcast on Lucknow or Delhi radio.'[20] It was an exciting time for Urdu poetry; there was a strong sense that a new poetic movement was underway. Poets such as Majaz, Jafri, Jazbi, Ali Jawwad Zaidi, Jan Nisar Akhtar, Faiz and Makhdoom were making waves. With his close friend and constant companion Aziz Hamid Madani, who later went on to become a celebrated poet in Pakistan, Habib was in the thick of this heady atmosphere, as he recounts with relish:

> Oblivious to hearth and home we would wander the streets of Raipur for days and nights on end, arguing about everything under the sun. The topics ranged from poetry and literature to discussions on Hitler and Mussolini. When we returned home we would be severely rebuked. In those days radios were not common enough to be found in every house. To listen to the news about the war, people would gather at tea stalls or panwallahs, wherever a radio was playing, and debate about who would win the war. 'Arrey bhaiyya, Hitler took Poland in minutes, France too is gone, he controls all of Europe and is now moving towards Sweden. England cannot be saved now. He will rule the whole world.' Meanwhile *mushairas* continued to be organized and people participated in them with the same gusto and enthusiasm. The stench of gunpowder and corpses trapped in barbed wire would permeate some of the poetry; to some extent the war also cast its shadow on these poems.[21]

Habib brings alive the atmosphere of the *mushairas* in his usual vivid style. A gentleman called Abdus Salim, who wrote under the poetic title of Kaif, would often organise these poetic assemblies in his house. He held the post of *munshi*[22] in the commissioner's office. Kaif Saheb would host weekly *mushairas* at his place and preside over the gatherings. Habib, Madani and a certain Yawar were regular participants and would read or recite their new writing. Sometimes, Kaif Saheb would give them a *tarah* or rhyming scheme for the next week's gathering, and they would all try to compose something accordingly. There would be tea and snacks for everyone, followed by long conversations and arguments over the rival merits of poets from Mir and Ghalib to Majaz, Makhdoom and Jafri. Remarkably, although Yawar was in his mid-30s and Kaif Saheb well into his 40s, the two 16-year-old lads were treated as friends and equals, and the age difference never affected the atmosphere.

Habib often organised *mushaira*s at his own home too, and Madani's father Hamid Saheb, a former *tehsildar* (revenue administrative officer), himself a poet, would host them at his place. Habib recalls:

> Most of the Ghazals I wrote at that time have been lost. They were not good enough to be preserved anyway. There is one *sher* which remains in my memory
>
> > *Guzari raat, aankhon mein shuaa-e arzu lekar*
> > *Ummeed-e yak nigah e lutf par kar di sehar maine.*[23]

This practice of *sher-shairi* was not restricted just to private gatherings. At that time, Chhattisgarh College in Raipur, established in 1940, was a centre of *mushaira*s; a visiting professor from Lucknow, Sadi Hyder, himself a fine poet, took the initiative in organising local and all-India *mushaira*s at the college.

Habib remembers first meeting Sardar Jafri, whose poetry he greatly admired, at one such event.

> I was already under the spell of his poetry; now I also became taken with his personality. This attachment kept growing, and when I moved to Bombay and he began to guide me in the art of poetic composition, an entirely new chapter got underway.[24]

A third great life-long interest—cinema—can also be traced back to his childhood in Raipur. 'I was a great filmgoer', he says, 'right from my childhood'.[25] He recalls seeing silent movies and also watching films in a tent, a mobile cinema, and then in Babulal Talkies, the first cinema hall in town. Babulal, as he puts it, 'was quite a character'.[26]

> He began his life in a mobile cinema, moving around in a tent and showing films; and we used to go in without tickets. Some naughty boy would cut the tent and those openings allowed us in, or sometimes we would duck in between the ropes, from below. Just as we used to sneak into the circus, we did to the cinema as well. But then he built a building and in that auditorium he showed these silent films. Babulal had his full orchestra outside. And also there were no fixed timings. He'd sell tickets till the house was full. He'd print the tickets himself and he'd stand at the gate and sell the tickets himself, he didn't trust anyone else. He'd order the band to stop when the house was

full, they'd move in and so would he. He'd get the doors all locked, sit in the corner watching the film with the audience and improvise—he was a great improviser. Firstly they'd play the music for a silent film whenever the occasion arose, for example, for the chase on horseback—they'd play la-di-da-di-da-da-da and so on and Babulal would go 'Faster, faster, c'mon you bastard, you sonofabitch, I'm getting late, c'mon now.' Then he'd say, 'C'mon kiss her, *chumma-chati ka mauka aa gaya hai. Dekh bhai chumma-chati ho rahi hai*' (it's time for a bit of kissing and cuddling. Look, look, they're kissing now). And many times he'd make up any kind of story he wanted. It was so hilarious. Many people went more for the sake of Babulal than for the film. And then later on came the talkies and then we'd already started making such beautiful films, perhaps better than we do now. By and large they were wonderful. New Theatres, Bombay Talkies and Prabhat Cinetone, Saagar, even so-called stunt films—they were great fun: Nadia in *Hunterwali* and so on. But Saagar did very good socials with Motilal—Motilal was a great actor. Prabhat would do mythological, historical films produced by Shantaram, Master Fatehlal etc., with very good actors like Jagirdar, Chandra Mohan, Shanta Apte. New Theatres had a galaxy of wonderful directors—Barua and Nitin Bose, and composers and very, very good actors, including the glorious singers K. L. Saigal and Pahari Sanyal, K. C. Dey, Very good actors and wonderful films—in-depth, allegorical and beautiful: *Manzil, Devdas.*[27]

With all these preoccupations, Habib Tanvir still managed a first division in his matriculation exams. The principal of Laurie Municipal High School, Mardhekar Sabeb, made a rare visit to his home to celebrate the good news and created quite a stir:

This was the first time that the headmaster of Laurie school had visited our house. People at home were already overjoyed with my results and this visit added another layer of excitement. After tea and refreshments Mr Mardhekar began to address my father while wholly ignoring me. The boy is bright, he said, he should apply for the ICS; he has got a distinction in Botany, he also has good grades in Maths, he should opt for the Sciences because if he works hard he can get 99 or even 100% marks in those subjects whereas he will never get such high grades in the Arts, nobody can. This year a new college, Chhattisgarh College, is opening in Raipur. Habib should just apply there.[28]

After he left, Habib was under tremendous pressure from his father to join Chhattisgarh College, opt for science and appear for the ICS exam. But Habib had other plans. He wanted to study arts at Morris College, Nagpur University, which 'was a very good college at that time, with a good

reputation'.[29] So he defied both parental pressure and his teachers' advice
to follow his own conviction and went off to Nagpur.

> There I took arts and my dramatic activities continued off and on through
> my college days. For my post-graduate studies I went to Aligarh, to do my
> MA in Urdu. But I didn't go beyond the first year. I began to lose my divi-
> sion because I began to be less inclined to go in for ICS or for any of these
> bureaucratic lines—I thought I'd be a teacher. And later on even that didn't
> interest me. I wanted to join the films.... I was enamoured of the cinema
> and in Nagpur I would also see all the foreign films. That's why I wanted to
> go into cinema.... This [was] 1944.[30]

Growing up in Raipur and its environs imbued in him a close familiarity
with the local Chhattisgarhi culture. He had sat through all-night Nacha and
Pandvani performances; enjoyed the vibrant energy of the *melas*; was steeped
in the rhythms and nuances of the dialect. Years later, as his creative quest led
him on the search for a theatre language, these early, formative experiences
came to the fore; but for the present, they remained a largely undigested and
untheorised—albeit fundamental—part of his cultural construct.

Notes

1. From the English translation of Habib Tanvir's Urdu autobiography, chapter titled 'The
   Teachers of Laurie School', translated by Mahmood Farooqui (Forthcoming).
2. Habib Tanvir, *STQ*, p. 4.
3. 'The Teachers of Laurie School'.
4. Tanvir, *STQ*, p. 4.
5. 'The Teachers of Laurie School'.
6. There is some confusion over his exact birth date; some claim it is 23 September.
7. Tanvir, *STQ*, p. 3.
8. Javed Malick, 'Refashioning Modernity: Habib Tanvir and His Naya Theatre', in Neeraj
   Malik and Javed Malick (eds), *Habib Tanvir: Reflections & Reminiscences* (New Delhi:
   SAHMAT, 2010), p. 16.
9. Ibid.
10. A *madari* is a traditional term for someone who bred and performed with monkeys.
11. From the English translation of Habib Tanvir's Urdu autobiography, chapter titled
    'Massaheb in Bilaspur', translated by Mahmood Farooqui (Forthcoming).
12. From the English translation of Habib Tanvir's Urdu autobiography, chapter titled
    'Bhaijan', translated by Mahmood Farooqui (Forthcoming).
13. Ibid.
14. Tanvir, *STQ*, p. 3.
15. From the English translation of Habib Tanvir's Urdu autobiography, chapter titled
    'Kalibari Theatre', translated by Mahmood Farooqui (Forthcoming).

16. Ibid.
17. From the English translation of Habib Tanvir's Urdu autobiography, chapter titled 'Massaheb in Bilaspur', translated by Mahmood Farooqui (Forthcoming).
18. Tanvir, 'In Conversation with Javed Malick', p. 103.
19. This is a type of Urdu poetry gathering, where poets recited and shared their work.
20. From the English translation of Habib Tanvir's Urdu autobiography, chapter titled 'Raipur ke Mushairey', translated by Mahmood Farooqui (Forthcoming).
21. Ibid.
22. This is a type of secretarial post.
23. From the English translation of Habib Tanvir's Urdu autobiography, chapter titled 'Raipur ke Mushairey', translated by Mahmood Farooqui (Forthcoming).
24. Ibid.
25. Tanvir, *STQ*, p. 5.
26. Ibid.
27. Ibid.
28. From the English translation of Habib Tanvir's Urdu autobiography, chapter titled 'The Teachers of Laurie School', translated by Mahmood Farooqui (Forthcoming).
29. Ibid.
30. Ibid.

CHAPTER TWO

THE BOMBAY YEARS

Habib with his troupe in 1982.
Photo courtesy Avinash Pasricha.

Habib Tanvir's fascination with movies inevitably led him to the capital of cinema, Bombay. He recalls how 'in Aligarh I got myself photographed in different poses for the films'.[1] Bombay beckoned but he did not have the wherewithal to get there on his own; so he resorted to a stratagem:

I saw an advertisement for the navy: they required officers. There were to be several tests: the district level interview, the provincial level interview and the final one, which was in Lonavla, beyond Bombay. I was hoping that I'd get through the district and provincial levels, and that if I had to fail, it would be at the end, so I could get close to Bombay. In those days, for these interviews you were given an intermediate railway pass for a return journey, which was valid for one month.... I passed the Raipur and Nagpur tests and in the final I was alright in other respects—I.Q. and things—but I couldn't build a bridge for my troupe to cross the river—I was given 10 minutes and the rope and many other gadgets were placed in front of me. I could use any of them, but I kept on thinking of various ways and then time ran out. So, having failed, I went to Bombay.[2]

Which is what he wanted all along.

This was 1945. Bombay was brimming with promises and possibilities. The film industry was a nascent world of chance and opportunity, and some of the country's most creative minds—writers, poets, directors—were part of it. Habib was soon enough drawn into it:

> I did many jobs in Bombay—but to begin with I went to see *The Picture of Dorian Grey*, in Metro cinema. I was sitting there in the restaurant and talking about the book, which I'd read, and there was a man sitting across at another table watching me intently. He got up and came up to me and said, 'Well, I've been listening to some of your conversation'. He liked my face and he felt that I'd be inclined to acting in cinema. He said 'Are you interested?' I said, 'Yes, I've come to Bombay for that.' And he booked me in the lead role for the film *Aap ke Liye*. The director's name was Suryam. So I began as the leading man in this film.... It didn't have a public release at all, I think.[3]

However, acting was not the only thing the young Habib was doing to support himself in the big city. He talks about Soho House, which belonged to a gentleman from Uttar Pradesh called Mohammed Tahir, who was very fond of *shairi*.

> I was writing poetry and I sang my poems—I sang quite well—and he was fond of *mushairas* he'd organize them. So he took my help as secretary in his office, to help him organise *mushairas* and look after his correspondence.[4]

Mohammed Tahir had an ammunition factory; the war effort was still in full swing. Habib worked as the supervisor, and daily contact with the workers, most of them from eastern Uttar Pradesh, allowed him to pursue his fascination with language.

> [T]hey'd speak their dialect and they had a great facility for turning English words into Indian words—Indianizing them: like 'the *tapiya* has been made, now I have to make the *bottomiya*'—the 'top' and the 'bottom'. So

my interest was also literary when I'd talk to these people. I was drawn to dialects, because of their richness; I was amazed to find, both in Urdu and in Hindi, after independence, when it came to lexicons and dictionaries and coining words which were needed: like air-conditioned compartment, I still cannot pronounce it, in Hindi, it's a very long word, same in Urdu, but the Bombay coolie simply called it *thandi gadi* (cool coach)—'*Kahan jana hai, saab? Thandi gadi mein chalenge?* (Where d'you want to go, sahib? To the cool coach?).' And I thought for a tropical country, calling an air-conditioned coach *thandi gadi* was the most appropriate thing. Language is constantly getting coined by people who use it, who need it, who make their living off it. For words connected with horse and saddle, every part has a name, but who has given the names? Those who make those things. You go to the ironsmith, he'll give you all the names connected to the horse's hooves. Our scholars have taken recourse to books to coin words, an artificial, arduous and futile process, instead of going to the people and learning. I'm mentioning all this because it became the basis of my theatre.[5]

As he puts it, he soon got 'picked up' by Zulfiqar Bokhari, at that time station director, All India Radio (AIR), Bombay, who liked his voice; he ended up acting, writing and producing musical features and programmes for women and children, 'though as a casual artist'.[6] He lived in a small room beside Bokhari's flat in the AIR building on Queen's Road.[7] Shama Zaidi, Bokhari's niece, who is a scriptwriter, designer, documentary filmmaker and theatre worker, remembers the young Habib of the time:

I don't know whether he learnt anything about radio broadcasting while on the job, but it certainly whetted his appetite for becoming an actor. And like many who were influenced by Zulfiqar mamu, Habib adopted his style of accentuated dialogue delivery, something he was to retain throughout his life. For a while Habib copied mamu's 'afro' hairstyle as well.[8]

Of all the programmes he did, film reviews were his favourite, and they turned out to be quite popular. However, his youthful enthusiasm led him to 'dissect the films rather ruthlessly',[9] and this had an unexpected outcome:

Baburao Patel was then the editor of *Filmindia*. It had a very large circulation, all over India. It was a reputed monthly, very prestigious. And Baburao Patel was considered quite a critic. But he had a very interesting way of writing. He had a discerning mind and was perceptive—he would appreciate minute things and he'd write absolutely frankly, without pulling any punches, totally ruthlessly and funnily. Anyhow, he was a friend of Bokhari's and in those days Bokhari threw many parties.... Baburao Patel, at one of these parties, meeting me for the first time, said, 'Oh, so you are Habib Tanvir!... Do you know that you're leading a dangerous, risky life?' I said, 'How come?' He said, 'You don't know these filmwallahs. These directors and film-producers are goondas, hooligans, murderers, thieves. They can knock you off, kill you and you wouldn't even know who did it, if you go on like this with your reviews—under whose protection? Bokhari's? Bokhari can't defend you. The only man who can defend you is I, because I'm the goonda of goondas. When these people come to me, sitting in my office, I open my drawer, take out my dagger and put it on the table like this, and say, "Now talk." So they're afraid of me.' And it was a fact. He was really quite violent and militant. What he was trying to say was, come to *Filmindia.* So an appointment was made and I did go there and I was the first assistant editor of *Filmindia*—of which I was quite proud—and the last.[10]

This was not his only stint in journalism. He reminisces:

I was doing freelance journalism, which took me into various, fields—book-reviews for the *Illustrated Weekly of India,* whose editor was Schaun Mandy, an Irishman and a very good journalist and writer.... I was the editor—if you please—of a magazine as far removed from my subject as a textile journal. I was also slightly connected with the Burma Shell magazine. I was *also* the editor of a weekly in English called *Box Office.* This was owned by Badri Kanchwala, a Gujarati.... He ran it for more than a year and I remained on it, as an editor. I'd sleep on the table in the office sometimes. He would treat me to Scotch whisky, to dinners, never paying my salary. He'd laugh—he was a jovial man—and say, 'What d'you need a salary for? You have a tin of cigarettes—555—great luxury, and Scotch whisky, good dinners—food—what d'you want money for?' You never felt offended by the man. He was quite a joker. He'd laugh, enjoy himself. There was also another daily news-paper, where also I had a similar kind of life; I was proof-reading galleys and dealing with the compositors and sleeping on the table.[11]

Shama Zaidi recalls yet another editorial assignment: 'Habib edited the English periodical of the Bombay Youth League, which he sold on the pavements of Bombay as well.'[12]

In the years between 1945 and 1953, apart from the above jobs, he wrote scripts for and produced advertising shorts, acted in feature films in various character parts, and wrote songs, scripts and dialogue for films. He was also an active member of the IPTA and PWA. These were fertile and formative years, and he was continuously storing away new experiences in his receptive brain. He talks about his first viewing of a dance performance:

> When I first went to Bombay.... I was quite amazed by a dance programme I saw. On an open stage in a huge area, two dancers appeared, holding a six foot square curtain which they carried to the centre of the platform. They stood still, holding it taut. Somebody, positioned behind the curtain, was shaking it. He first showed us his golden painted fingernails by displaying them above the curtain, then he stirred the curtain with his hands for a while, then he lifted it slightly and revealed two feet for a quick moment. We saw a pair of grey-haired feet, laden with silver ornaments. Then, as the apparition jumped up, above the curtain we caught a glimpse of a bunch of grey hair, which vanished as quickly. Then he lifted the curtain sufficiently for us to glimpse his legs and his waist, covered similarly with grey hair, with a beautiful golden string tied around his waist. Playing around with the curtain like a child, he suddenly let it drop to reveal his face for a moment, and we caught a sight of his red lips, fair, ruddy cheeks, bright dark eyes, white brows, gold crown and grey tresses. This disappeared quickly too, until eventually he pulled the curtain and threw it aside, while the two dancers made a quiet exit. In front of us was an extremely handsome man, scratching his grey beard like a monkey. This was Hanuman! Painted white, with shades of golden and red. And the artist was the famous Kathakali dancer from Kerala, Vallathol.
>
> Vallathol took some twenty to twenty-five minutes to reveal himself fully. Why? I think that if he had shown us his full get up right at the beginning we would not have appreciated the beauty and majesty of Hanuman as much.... Therefore he showed us different parts of Hanuman before revealing himself fully so that we became gradually accustomed and prepared to witness the full glory.... Anyway, the Hanuman depicted by Vallathol stood still for a long time scratching his beard. Having taken in his whole persona my eyes were now riveted on his face and beard. Then gradually he raised his eyebrows, rolled his eyes and began to move slowly around the stage. The entire dance program took at least two hours to complete. When Hanuman was standing still, the focal point was his face; before that it was the crest of his crown, then his feet, then his waist and eventually his face. A constantly changing scenario where the artist could shift the focal point of his being playfully and at will. In a sense this dance programme was an entire manual of theatre training for me. Salute. Valatholl was my first Guru in theatre.[13]

This lesson learned about the focal point on stage, which he compared to the focal point in a painting, was later applied in Naya Theatre with his actors. There were other lessons too:

Bedekar was a great director of the Shantaram and Prabhat days and he was directing *Lokmanya Tilak*. I played the role of the jailer who was looking after Tilak and helping him with letters in a clandestine fashion. In one scene, after he'd read a letter, the jailer takes it, tears it and burns it, to efface all evidence. I did what I was told. And when I tore the letter, and threw the pieces into the fire, Bedekar exclaimed, 'Oh Habib, for God's sake, you're taking the fire out of the shot.' I said, 'I thought you said tear it and burn it.' 'Yeah, but not that quick. Do it very delicately, throw it in the fire very, very slowly.' I still remember this. He was a great director, and these things came to mind when I started directing, these were the hints that helped me.[14]

Soon after arriving in Bombay, he joined the newly formed PWA, as a poet. This organisation, formed in 1936, consisted of the best contemporary writers and poets in the country at the time, a veritable who's who of the literature scene. Committed to progressive left-oriented and nationalist ideals, the group had a great influence on new writing in the country, in terms of language, themes and form. And the young Habib fitted right in:

At that time we'd gather at the house of Sajjad Zahir, whom we called Bannebhai. He was a very great critic in Urdu: weekly meetings would take place at which writers would read new stories, poems—whatever they'd written. So it was a lively literary session every Sunday and I'd go and recite my poems, which were liked very much.... I'd travel around U.P., Ahmedabad, take part in all-India *mushairas* and because of my voice and my poetry, I was quite popular.[15]

Within a short time, he also joined the IPTA. Formed during the Quit India Movement in 1942, the IPTA had its formal inauguration in 1943–1944, just before Habib came to Bombay. Considered widely to be the cultural wing of the Communist Party of India, the IPTA was formed to coordinate and strengthen all progressive tendencies that had so far manifested themselves in the performing arts; the objective was to bring theatre to the masses with the aim of building awareness about social responsibility and national integration. At the time, the IPTA was made up of outstanding artists, and the list of members reads like a hall of fame of India's leading actors, musicians, writers, singers and dancers. Zohra Segal, the veteran actress, was also part of the IPTA at the time. In her memoirs, she says:

A central committee organized the running of the Association and nominated a president and vice president every two or three years. We all met in the evenings after our regular professional activities, and such was the zeal of its members that no one grudged the extra hours of work devoted to IPTA. Sometimes, if we were lucky, we performed in regular theatres but most of our performances were held in large halls, because they were cheaper to hire. A great number were performed anywhere on the streets or alleys, wherever an audience could be assembled … the Bombay IPTA had utilised the folklore of Marathi theatre, using 'tamasha' and 'pawada' as forms of expression … the themes of IPTA's songs and plays were radical in nature and left-oriented, inspiring and uniting us to action.[16]

Shama Zaidi remembers Habib

telling us how they used to stage street plays by pretending to be a pickpocket and a policeman quarrelling. The crowd which collected had no idea that this was just a play and by the time they found out and the real police arrived, the actors melted away.[17]

This kind of theatre, 'agit-prop plays done on an improvised stage in the open-air for thousands of workers'[18] was very different from the Parsi theatre he had grown up watching. It was more collective, developed out of improvisation, communicating a strong social or political message. He reminisces about those years:

There was, near the opera-house (which no longer is the opera-house), a beautiful theatre made in the British days in which Raj Kapoor used to perform. Across the road there was a smallish hall, where the IPTA used to function every evening, and there I was acting under the direction of Balraj Sahni and Dina Pathak … first under Balraj Sahni's direction and then under Dina's and some of the younger people like Mohan Sehgal, we collectively improvised plays. There was one Rama Rao, who was the general secretary from South India, and he thought of a simple idea about a middle-class office-going man who lived in Borivilli and had to come all the way into central Bombay to his office. And this little line we gradually whipped up into a full play. Mohan Sehgal directed it. It was called *Jadu ki Kursi*. It was a hilarious comedy—a satire on social and political condi-tions. Balraj played the lead and never again have I seen Balraj in a comic role—at least not in any film. He had great comic talent, a deadpan face and he'd just speak and bring the house down. We were all given the liberty to improvise on our roles. I was the judge, and I decided to stammer. It was a full-fledged play, with no script yet. There was an IPTA conference in 1949 in Allahabad. We went with this play and it was a great success, like in Bombay and elsewhere.[19]

Another work he remembers is a street play called *Shantidoot Kamgar*. 'I wrote and directed it. We did it in chawls. It wasn't a hell of a play, but it was good enough for the occasion, it propagated peace and agitated the workers to strike for better wages etc.'[20] There was another play 'about the Dogra regime in Kashmir, in which Balraj played the role of Kashmir's revolutionary poet'.[21]

There are other memories of that period, recounted in his trademark tongue-in-cheek style:

At the IPTA conference in Allahabad in 1948, I was also acting in a tragic one-act play written by Vishvamitter Adil, an Urdu poet and writer of stories.[22] He had adapted it from some Chinese play. The subject was the Telengana movement in Andhra Pradesh. I was the old man whose son gets shot. And then I wail and weep in a long speech, a tirade. And for many weeks it went on. Balraj was directing it. In Allahabad again, we had a last rehearsal which went on till 2 at night. The next day it was to be performed. Balraj wasn't satisfied; he was angry. He came up to the stage and hit me hard on the face—a big slap. All his five fingers left red lines on my cheek, and tears came to my eyes. And he screamed, 'Say the lines now.' And I wept and said the lines, then he hugged me and said, 'Now you'll never forget it. That's how it should be.' I was in my twenties, playing the role of an eighty-year-old man and then I had to cry to boot. All of which was not happening. So I did ask Balraj, 'Was it one of your methods of direction?' He said, 'Yes. It's called muscle-memory.' I remember that muscle-memory to this day.

Immediately on our return, there was to be some kind of protest and a procession in which the PWA and IPTA both had to march to all the working-class areas. We were given the mandate to continue with slogans and marching and if the police stopped or attacked us, not to fight or surrender, but to save ourselves and continue as far as possible. Everybody was arrested—Balraj, Dina, Sardar Jafri. One of the boys was killed by a bullet and somebody was injured. I was hit by a lathi on my wrist. I went and started living with Vijay Kishore Dubey who was a student at that time, in his hostel just near the YMCA at Colaba. I shared his room. There was a great search on, 'Where's Habib?' One day Surender Ahuja, who was in the IPTA and a great friend of mine, came and said, 'So here you are; but where were you?' I said, 'Here'. 'Why?' 'I'm underground.' 'Who asked you to go underground?' 'We were asked to protect ourselves and it appeared to me only logical to save myself from the police by going underground.' 'And what's this bandage?' 'I got hit with a lathi.' 'Why not show it to a doctor?' 'For the same reason, I'll get caught.' He said, 'What delusion. Nobody is looking for you. They had a list of all the prominent leaders and they've caught them. IPTA is defunct, you've got to work. The Party, from inside the jail, has said to catch hold of Habib and keep the organization going.' And that's how I then became the organizer, the secretary of IPTA, the playwright of IPTA, director-actor of IPTA, collecting boys, re-assembling them for two years—1948–50. And they spent two years in jail. All of them came out with colitis—Dina, Sardar Jafri, Balraj. Because of jail food. Anyway, that's another story.[23]

Amusing anecdotes aside, Habib's appreciation of the IPTA was deep:

IPTA [was] an all India movement. It was a powerful and popular movement. Spread across the nation, from Lahore to Kanyakumari, from Calcutta to Bombay, it was a force to reckon with. All our best brains were involved in it—all our most creative people in the field of music, dance and theatre. It could raise lakhs of rupees in aid of the famine stricken people of Bengal in 1942–43 and produce Uday Shankar's *Immortal India* and Bijon Bhattacharya's *Nabanna* (which became the basis for K. A. Abbas's film *Dharti ke Lal*) in the following years. Like many others I too was deeply influenced by this movement.[24]

By the early 1950s, the IPTA was a spent force. For some time after the breakup of the IPTA, Habib continued to do theatre with the J. J. School of Arts and other groups.[25] But in 1953–1954, he decided to leave Bombay and shift base to Delhi.

Habib had come to Bombay seeking a career in films. But he left Bombay with his eyes firmly fixed on a career in theatre. He explains the reasons behind his decision:

I left Bombay and went to Delhi with the sole intention of getting out of the way of temptation to act in films, because by then I'd come to the conclusion that in the cinema of those days there was no autonomy for the artist—you could not act the way you wanted, nor direct the way you wanted. The producer, who had no artistic sense, who was only a money-bag, a financier, would meddle in the work of the director, actor, writer, everyone; and I thought, even as an actor, doing a role, there is a certain social comment that you can bring to bear upon that character. But that kind of autonomy wasn't given.

There used to be quite a discussion on this. A few progressive writers—Rajinder Singh Bedi, Krishen Chander, Ismat Chugtai, Ali Sardar Jafri, Shailendra—were going into films as script-writers, poets—Balraj as an actor, Mohan Sehgal as a director. So the discussion in Bedi's house or in Ismat's house would revolve around this. Can we change things? I felt that we couldn't be effective. Many years later when the subject cropped up while talking to Balraj he almost admitted, yes, you're right.... Look at Balraj's films—they're all commercial films. As an actor he could change nothing. He could hold his own as an actor, because he was such a good actor. But giving more autonomy to the writer and director and with Balraj in it, it would have made a big difference. Anyhow, right or wrong, I was convinced that I had something to say. And for what I had to say, in aesthetics, in the performing arts, as well as what I had to say socially, politically—the medium was not the cinema, it was the theatre. This was a very clear realization in the early fifties, which brought me to Delhi.[26]

Notes

1. From Habib Tanvir, *STQ*, p. 5.
2. Ibid., pp. 5–6.
3. Ibid., p. 6.
4. Ibid.
5. Ibid.
6. Ibid.
7. Ibid.
8. Shama Zaidi, http://www.naachgaana.com/2009/06/14/remembering-habib-tanvir/, 2009, accessed on 27 May 2012.
9. Tanvir, *STQ*, p. 6.
10. Ibid., pp. 6–7.
11. Ibid., p. 7.
12. Zaidi, http://www.naachgaana.com/2009/06/14/remembering-habib-tanvir/.
13. From the English translation of Habib Tanvir's Urdu autobiography, chapter titled 'Kalibari Theatre', translated by Mahmood Farooqui (Forthcoming).
14. Tanvir, *STQ*, p. 7.
15. Ibid.
16. Zohra Segal, *Close-Up: Memoirs of a Life on Stage and Screen* (New Delhi: Women Unlimited, 2010), p. 114.
17. Zaidi, http://www.naachgaana.com/2009/06/14/remembering-habib-tanvir/.
18. Habib Tanvir, 'Janam Comes of Age', in Sudhanva Deshpande (ed.), *Theatre of the Streets: The Jana Natya Manch Experience* (New Delhi: Jana Natya Manch, 2007), pp. 68–70.
19. Tanvir, *STQ*, pp. 7–8.
20. Ibid., p. 8.
21. Tanvir, 'Janam Comes of Age', pp. 68–70.
22. This was *Deccan Ki Ek Raat*.
23. Tanvir, *STQ*, p. 8.
24. Neeraj Malik and Javed Malick (eds), 'In Conversation with Javed Malick' in *Habib Tanvir: Reflection and Reminiscences* (New Delhi: SAHMAT, 2010), pp. 105–106.
25. In 1952, he directed *Jaalidar Parde*, his adaptation of a Soviet play, *The Feminine Touch*, for the J. J. School of Arts.
26. Tanvir, *STQ*, pp. 8–9.

CHAPTER THREE

NEW DIRECTIONS: DELHI AND
AGRA BAZAAR

A tender moment between father and daughter—Habib as *patangwala*, and his daughter
Nageen as Nazir's granddaughter in *Agra Bazaar* (1978). Photo courtesy Naya Theatre

As Habib journeys to Delhi to begin a new phase in his creative and
professional life, having decided to dedicate himself to theatre, it is a
good time to survey the theatre in India to which he had been exposed
till date.

We already know that he was familiar with the Parsi theatre tradition,
and as a child was spellbound by the extravagant effects, gimmicks, elaborate
sets and melodramatic acting style of that theatre; he enjoyed the fairground
atmosphere of the entire theatrical experience, and the sense of drama and
spectacle that infused it all. Mythologicals, historic plays, social dramas, epic

love stories seeped in tragedy but interspersed with comic interludes—he lapped it all up.

Alongside were the dynamic, living folk forms of his home state. All night performances of Nacha with their songs, dances and humorous skits stayed in his memory—particularly, the songs and music. This fascination with folk songs was reinforced in Bombay through his experience with the IPTA.

> We got familiar with folk-forms like Tamasha and Lavani, Bhavai, the folk songs of Gujarat. The IPTA Konkani squad had a lovely music-squad and Konkani music was very vibrant, I liked it very much. The group was very strong. I love music and so all this was worth watching.[1]

He also began to actively gather folk songs: 'After my association with IPTA I collected more songs consciously.'[2]

Habib clearly credits the IPTA with his trajectory towards traditional and folk performance forms: 'The IPTA provided my first schooling in theatre, especially in the folk forms of performing arts.'[3] In fact, in his opinion, it was the IPTA that 'made the first big organised effort to align the theatre with the peasantry and the new Indian working class whose cultural base once again was rural and agrarian'.[4]

He also appreciates that tradition in the hands of contemporary artists is always an interpretation:

> My background in IPTA had given me an insight into the richness of our cultural history. I felt that our classical tradition does not have continuity through this interruption of centuries, it lives only in books and tombs, except when it is resurrected by great dancers like Ram Gopal, Uday Shankar, and Rukmani Arundale. These artists were interpreting the tradition creatively and imaginatively.[5]

At the same time, in Bombay he encountered another kind of theatre—proscenium plays in English. He says:

> The English language theatre ... was, in one way or another, connected with colleges and universities and produced plays (which included Shakespeare, Shaw, and Ibsen) with and for the urban, upper-class, educated people. Many theatre persons came from this kind of background. For example, Alkazi came from St. Xavier's College in Bombay, where he was associated with student drama in English.[6]

By the late 1940s, Habib had already begun to develop a critique of certain types of theatre:

> I had already developed a certain distate for this kind of theatre as well as for proscenium theatre in general. In IPTA, we had produced Ibsen and admired the work of Stanislavski in Russia and that of the Actor's Studio in New York. Despite all this, I now think in retrospect, that somewhere deep down I was beginning to feel that all this was not quite right, not really our kind of theatre. Gradually, I came to recognize that we cannot really go very far by imitating the West. I thought that this kind of imitative theatre, with its severe limitations, could not help us to be creative, to do anything new or startling, or to interpret plays in a manner that is really meaningful.[7]

He preferred some of the experiments he had seen in these years:

> [D]uring this time, Jaishankar Sundari of the Parsi theatre days, who was a great impersonator of female roles ... and Dina Pathak, who too has a background of IPTA and *bhavai*, were invited by Rasikbhai Parikh to do a workshop at Ahmedabad University. In an interesting experiment, Parikh had, thus, brought together a traditional performer and a theatre-person with a modern attitude to life and theatre. Together, they did several dramatizations, including some Bengali classics like *Biraj Bahu*. One of the remarkable things they did was to introduce us to the *bhavai* tradition—for example, in their production of *Mena Gurjari* which Dina produced. These productions were big hits and were even travelled to places like Delhi. These productions may not have created exactly a furor all over the country but they did possess enough life and dynamism to be talked about in many important quarters.
>
> At about the same time in Calcutta, Sombhu Mitra, who too had come out of IPTA, carried on a very genuine theatre—in a most profound sense, a theatre which was very analytical of life and was presented most artistically. He produced *Raktakarabi* in the early 1950s. This, to my mind, was the most outstanding of all the productions.
>
> .... Utpal Dutt, on the other hand, had an English theatre background from the college days. In the early 1950s, he switched over to Bengali productions. In 1954 he came to Delhi with two productions which I saw. One was Michael Madhusudhan Dutt's *Ekei Ki Bole Sabhyata* and the other was a Bengali adaptation of Gorky's *The Lower Depths*. The latter, although in the Western tradition, was so well done that I find it unforgettable to this day.[8]

It is fair to say that as he launched into serious theatre activity in Delhi, he had already been exposed to the major strands of theatre activity in India at the time—from the socially committed IPTA, performing on the street, in public spaces and also on the proscenium, to the elite, niche English language theatre; from the varieties of folk theatre to the group theatre of Bengal. He had also been exposed to experiments across these genres.

Habib started his life in Delhi at a school run by a German educationist, Elizabeth Gauba, whom he had known for many years. According to Habib, she was a good friend of Jawaharlal Nehru, Indira Gandhi and Krishna Menon, and received the active encouragement of Krishna Menon to set up her school, applying experimental and progressive methods which combined Montessori methods with her own concepts. Habib comments: 'It was a very good system in which to teach children, she'd get them to play a lot, to do some clay-modelling, painting, write their dreams, write about their elders—I've seen the children's paintings, clay-modellings, their dreams and stories, and they were fantastic.'⁹

Habib had been invited to come and do drama with the children.

> I was given a room, and gallons of tea, the whole day I'd drink tea without sugar and milk—she was a good cook and she'd make very good soups and feed me like a mother. Very loving woman, energetic, capable of laughing such a lot, wonderful sense of humour, but with very strong ideas about things, very perceptive, but nonetheless, very strong ideas. Anyhow ... I'd sit there with the children all around me, in her drawing room, telling them folk tales and the one to which they responded the most, I'd turn into a play.¹⁰

The first play to come out of this approach was *Gadhey*, based on a folk tale common to Aesop, India and Turkey. The dialogue incorporated the children's dreams and stories, and the stage design used their paintings. It was based on the theme of a children's town.

> Elizabeth had a way of doing things—school-teachers were involved and children were involved, there were shops selling handicrafts, sweets, tea, everything, on the lawn, on the stage when the play was done; and at the gate I suggested a sign, 'Welcome to children's town.' The theme of children's town was—we want our own government.¹¹

As we see, not only was he already favouring folk tales over other kinds of children's stories, but he was also politicising the children over issues like a government of their own!

This was a period when Habib devoted himself to children's theatre. Not so surprising, when one thinks of the essential purpose of the IPTA's work which was to educate and change, in the broad sense. Nor when one

considers his stated reason for moving away from cinema—that he felt he
had something to say, and that theatre gave him more of a chance to say it
his way. Working with children offers an enormous potential for effecting
change and the freedom to communicate one's own ideas. He went on to
do more plays with children. *Har Mausam Ka Khel* was based upon 'a little
essay by Mirza Farhatullah Beg; a story about seasons personified, and the
various advantages of each season'.[12] Another children's play was *Doodh
Ka Gilas*, in which 'the ingredients of milk become different characters and
they dance, there's a strong atmosphere of unity. Then the milk splits and
it's a different kind of dance. A child who doesn't like to drink milk dreams
all this'.[13] Yet another, called *Chandi Ka Chamcha*, was about 'hygiene and
civic sense in a highly metaphysical sense, a comedy'.[14] He says, 'I wrote 6–7
plays for children and they were published.'[15]

It was at this juncture that he got involved in working towards his first
major theatre production, *Agra Bazaar*, written and staged in Delhi in 1954,
with students and teachers of Jamia Millia Islamia University and villagers
from the neighbouring Okhla.

I consider this to be one of Habib's most important productions. It
reflects his fundamental concern with the beauty and value of the culture and
language of the common man. In this piece, already, 20 years before he came
to crystallise his own unique style, his work was exhibiting characteristic
features: a fluid structure with interwoven narratives, humorous sequences,
live songs and music, a local flavour in the setting and the language. He was
already using folk tunes from his childhood and Chhattisgarhi songs in this
production.[16] Although he says, 'In 1954 when I produced *Agra Bazaar*, I was
neither familiar with classical Sanskrit drama nor with Bertolt Brecht. Nor
did I possess a deep enough understanding of folk styles of performance,' he
claims that 'the genesis of what eventually developed into my characteristic
style was there in *Agra Bazaar*' which contained 'that fundamental feeling
which has been active in my theatre from the outset'[17] and which, he states,
was one of the three milestones in his theatre career.[18] 'I think already by
1954, in *Agra Bazaar*, I had established my signature.'[19]

Let's take a look at the whole process of how he evolved this play.

It all started when an old friend from his Aligarh University days, Athar
Parvez, a writer who was teaching at Jamia Millia, approached him with
a request—the Jamia Millia chapter of Progressive Writers' Association
wanted him to come up with a feature to celebrate Nazir Diwas. Nazir
Akbarabadi, whose anniversary was being marked, was an 18th century poet,
said to have been born around 1735. He died in 1830 at the advanced age

of 95, having lived through close to a century. Habib had been interested in his poetry, but it was not until he began reading everything he could about Nazir that he found his interest growing into a deep fascination:

> I went and lived in Jamia with Parvez and there'd be food and a hookah and gallons of tea and I writing, reading, writing; reading all of Nazir's verses, all that was written about him, very little documented as hard facts. The one thing that did emerge was that the poetry of Nazir was spurned by the critics of the day who hardly considered him a poet, because they didn't like the people's language that he used; they thought it vulgar language because it was colloquial. It's fantastic, beautiful language; but they didn't like it. So in history books of Urdu literature he is brushed aside in two or three lines while lesser poets and writers get pages after pages. He was a man of great humility and never bothered to get his things published or collected. He was known to respond to anyone wishing to get something written; maybe a vendor saying *tarbooz pe kuchh likh dijiye* (please write something in praise of the watermelon we sell). So he would, and they'd sing it and sell their fruit. And all of it is beautiful poetry. Nazir wrote about swimming and kite-flying tournaments; he wrote about all the indigenous flora and fauna of India. If you want to, you can trace them through Sanskrit literature, or through Nazir's poetry. Most Urdu poetry repeats Irani flora and fauna, at best trees which are found in Kashmir. Nazir has *motiya, chameli, genda,* all Indian flowers; *tota, maina, baya, gilehri*—all these animals and birds; references to all the religions—Guru Nanak, Hazrat Mohammed, Ali, *Baldevji ka mela,* Ram—a very eclectic, open-minded man. True poet. Very sensual, very amorous poetry with some unprintable words, but beautiful, calling a spade a spade—that sort of poetry.[20]

One can immediately see why this subject gripped Habib's imagination as it did. Here was a people's poet, an artist who put his creativity at the service of the common man, just as Habib himself had spent years trying to do, with both the IPTA and PWA. His own interest in dialects and the language of ordinary people found an echo in the poetry of Nazir. In order to write *Agra Bazaar,* Habib read up on the vocabulary of daily life in Delhi:

> I looked up Mirza Farhatullah Beg, a writer of Delhi writing in Delhi language or Ahmed Shah Bokhari, who wrote *Dilli Ki Galiyan*—beautiful language.... And *Dilli Ki awazen,* the sounds of Old Delhi, the sellers, the vendors, the *katora-bajane wala,* the *jeerapani bechne wala* (the man who plays the *katora,* the vendor of cuminwater), they all have musical calls; there's a book called *Dilli Ki Awazen,* it has all these things, *kaun kaise bolta hai, kaise pukarta hai* (who speaks in what way, who calls out in what manner). And then you go to

Old Delhi and hear this language. And a lot from the people's language, that I heard then, has gone into *Agra Bazaar*. Therefore it has that vigour.[21]

Nazir was marginalised by the elite both in his own time and in the later histories of Urdu literature, Habib feels, because he gave value to the colloquial language of the man on the street. He praises him as one of India's most important Urdu poets, and certainly Urdu's most 'Hindustani poet'.[22]

During his life no writer cared for him and, for more than a century after his death, no critic ever mentioned him. But he was kept alive by the common people for nearly two hundred years and his poetry, transmitted orally from generation to generation, continued to survive. People preserved their inheritance with great love and care. Even today Nazir's poems can be found on the lips of mendicants, vendors and others in streets and bazaars throughout India. This is the greatest drama of Nazir's life and work, as well as the most interesting chapter of our literary history.

It was this aspect of Nazir's poetry that I wanted to focus on. So I chose it as the subject of my play.... I wanted to highlight the fact that Nazir's love of the ordinary people has immortalized him.[23]

Habib's leftist background made it imperative for him to situate Nazir in his historical context:

I found that it was possible to reconstruct the entire socio-cultural history of that period on the basis of his work. I also realized that it is difficult to fully appreciate his poetry without its political and social context.... Our books on literary history tend to leave out the political conditions of a period entirely or, at best, make perfunctory references to them. Similarly our political histories do not tell us much about the literary and cultural aspects of life. It is wrong and misleading to see these two aspects of our collective existence as two absolutely separate categories.[24]

He decided to locate his play in the year 1810 when Nazir was already 75 years old but still had about 20 years left to live. Habib felt that historically this was an important period of transition. It was the year the famous Urdu poet Mir died; Ghalib was an adolescent of 14—these were the two most celebrated Urdu poets of the time. Politically, Mughal rule was defunct; British power was in the ascendant.

There was widespread plunder and anarchy in the country.... Urdu poets were fleeing Delhi and Lucknow was fast emerging as an important literary centre…. The process of the decline of Urdu poetry … had already set in. At the same time, Urdu prose was registering remarkable growth. In Calcutta's Fort William College, recently established by the British, the work of translating and publishing was proceeding in full earnest…. The old social structure was crumbling. There was anarchy and political turmoil everywhere. The economic condition of the common people was steadily deteriorating…. One can understand the depth and authenticity of Nazir's poetry better by viewing it in the context of these social and political developments. This is why I found it more appropriate and meaningful to set the play in the early nineteenth century.[25]

An important decision Habib took as a playwright was to let Nazir remain an absent presence, the central character who is never seen on stage.

I didn't bring Nazir on stage because I felt—this became my inspiration—that there wasn't very much known about his life, except some anecdotes, but his poetry pervades the country, so let it pervade the stage. Poetry everywhere, which has his presence, but not the man.[26]

In his preface to the first edition, written in April 1954, soon after the first performance, he says,

I wanted to present him and his poetry as immortal. I also wanted to preserve the legendary aspect of Nazir's personality. Therefore, it was only by keeping him offstage that I could establish him as the greatest hero of Urdu literary history. It would have been very difficult for any actor to convincingly represent this character on the stage.[27]

In his attempt to show the contrast between the affection and respect awarded to Nazir by the plebeian populace and the disregard shown to him by the educated elite, he conceived of the 'the Book-seller and the Kite-seller who help the play move forward and whose shops become the two opposing poles of the marketplace':[28]

So I went about producing a bazaar in which I created two poles, the kite-seller's shop with conversation about kites in colloquial, spoken languages, and the bookseller's shop where poets and critics and historians gather and speak an ornate literary language, spurn Nazir and uphold Ghalib, Mir and others; and the vendors who sing his poetry because they obtain it from him and their wares, which were not selling, immediately get sold when they begin to sing the songs of Nazir.[29]

Instinctively, Habib was inclined towards a fluid structure for his production, so much so that 'when people read the play, they said, "Where's the play?"'[30] He elaborates on his discovery of a flexible theatrical form:

> It was just movement on stage—and the openness of the play, its form, the singing of the Nazir songs, came to me first as a feature. There was not enough material on Nazir to do anything more than just a feature. So I decided on collecting a few poems, the best, and making a feature of it with a thin narrative to describe Nazir; and I suddenly arrived at a dramatic form. Then I worked further on it, brought it to Delhi and it became a play. Now, that gave me great flexibility of form.[31]

He says that after a month of research, he wrote the play in a week's time; with the active help of members of the Jamia Millia they had the production ready after just one week of rehearsal.

> Those who participated included not only the teachers, students and children of Jamia but also some persons from the city of Delhi, and men, women and children from surrounding villages. Local groups from Tughlaqabad, Badarpur and Okhla, together with a goat and donkey, also participated.[32]

He describes how this came about:

> The neighbouring Okhla villagers used to come and sit and watch rehearsals on the open air stage. So one day I told them that instead of watching from there, they could go on the stage and sit and watch, because *bhalu naach ho raha hai kabhi, kabhi bandar ka tamasha ho raha hai* (because at times there was a performing bear, or a monkey dance). So they did that, that's how they became part of the play.[33]

Habib says that this experience made him 'even more aware of the potentiality and the inherent richness of the folk theatres of this country'.[34]

The first production of *Agra Bazaar*, done on the Jamia Art Institute's open-air stage, was only about 40–50 minutes long. When it was received enthusiastically, they decided to present it in New Delhi. A show was held at the Ramlila grounds in front of an audience of thousands.

> The same villagers appeared on stage when the play was performed at the Ramlila Grounds in front of thousands of spectators. Jamia's real paan-seller in the role of the Paanwala, the real tailor in the role of the Tailor, and the silent presence of a donkey in front of the Potter's shop throughout

the play was very effective. An addition to the realistic atmosphere of the performance was provided by the quiet and patient donkey who produced a whole lot of dung on stage. Now the stage had both the colours and the smell of a traditional bazaar.[35]

Over time *Agra Bazaar* evolved into a full-length play:

I wrote into the play more and more nuances—the *kotha* was introduced, a *goonda* (ruffian) was introduced, prostitutes and an inspector. At first it was a skeleton, then it developed into the full two hour version in which Nazir is talked of, he's here, there, but never comes on stage.[36]

Every time the play was revised, Habib made changes in the plot and the characters, in an attempt to convey more of Nazir's oeuvre:

The first Urdu edition of the play published in 1954 by Azad Kitabghar offered the original 50-minute version that was staged in Jamia. In that version the plot was entirely centred on the Kakri-seller who finds it difficult to sell his kakri until he gets Nazir to write a poem on it. He sings this poem and does brisk business. Gradually, another strand was added to the play which concerned a prostitute and a Police Constable. This also produced three other characters—the two cops and the Rake. The character of the Horse-trader Manzoor Hussain survived but all his dialogues were jettisoned. He became dramatically more effective as a mute figure who had lost his mental balance after being robbed by highwaymen and who was passionately in love with the Courtesan. However a new character, Beni Prasad, was needed to tell Manzoor Hussain's tale. The two eunuchs, Kariman and Chameli, were also added later. They arrive at the Potter's door to sing and dance to celebrate the birth of his son. This becomes the excuse for bringing in Nazir's poem about Lord Krishna's childhood days. New and appropriate dialogues had to be written for the two eunuchs which perhaps made the scene even more interesting.

The third strand of the plot is located in the conversations at the Bookseller's shop. It relates to major changes that were taking place in the nineteenth century in printing and publishing, and in the language of public and literary discourse. It also focuses on the implications of these changes for the material conditions of the Urdu and Persian poets, writers and publishers. A new character, Ganga Prasad, was added to represent these changes more fully. This hectic activity of the marketplace forms the backdrop against which Nazir wrote. His poetry, his life, the source of his livelihood, namely tutoring, was closely connected with this environment and his poetry reflects this. The play is nothing but a portrait of all those aspects of that marketplace. My purpose was to provide a comprehensive picture of Nazir's work.[37]

Agra Bazaar has remained one of his most popular productions. 'It was taken up by some ladies of Delhi like Anis Kidwai and Qudsia Zaidi, and we took it to Aligarh. It went on and on.'[38] It was revived by popular demand every decade.

Habib has stated that it was his dream of establishing a professional theatre—in which the practitioners could subsist through theatre alone, and work on theatre full time—that led him to Delhi:[39] 'My endeavour to establish a professional theatre had already begun with *Agra Bazaar*.... The success of *Agra Bazaar* on the Jamia Millia stage further intensified this desire and I actively began to look for ways of realizing my dream.'[40] Professor Mohammed Mujeeb, vice-chancellor of Jamia Millia, was himself a playwright and used to direct plays. He had founded the Jamia Drama Society and promoted an interest in theatre among students and teachers. He offered Habib full support in his endeavour. Kalam Sahib, director of Jamia's Arts Institute, was also of great help. The rehearsals were held on the Arts Institute's open-air stage, as was the play's first show. However, negative forces were at work:

> Jamia Millia also had gentlemen with long beards who wielded considerable influence and power. These mullahs and maulvis were opposed to theatre and even Mujeeb-sahib had to often keep quiet in front of them so that the play could be staged. Kalam-sahib was an important ally. However, for some unknown reason even he turned against me. A whimsical person by nature, he was suddenly overcome by the strange suspicion that I was trying to replace him as Director of the Arts Institute. Thus a valuable supporter and ally turned against us and became our enemy. This made me give up the idea of establishing a theatre in Jamia and instead I founded 'Okhla Theatre'. M. S. Sathyu even designed an impressive monogram, and we had a seal made. Okhla is situated on the banks of the river Jamuna and Jamia Millia is adjacent to Okhla village. This proximity made Kalam-sahib object to Okhla Theatre too and I had to give up that idea as well.[41]

This was when he received support from Begum Qudsia Zaidi who came up with a solution; it was her drive that led to the formation of Delhi's first professional theatre group, the Hindustani Theatre. By now, he had received the offer of a training scholarship abroad:

> I got a scholarship under a scheme for further training in theatre, of about Rs 300 per month, meant for further training inside the country. And I didn't consider that there was any training inside the country which I needed. I had a long experience in theatre already by that time—at least nine years.

The sole institution which had the semblance of a school was Alkazi's, in Bombay, and I didn't consider it had a lot to teach me. I felt that where Alkazi had learnt from was where I should go, to RADA. To my rescue came the British Council. The passage became a problem. Zakir Hussain was the vice-chancellor of Aligarh University. I'd known him, he knew my poetry and plays. He was a great help to young people, and I was, of course, in a way an ex-Aligarh student. So from some funds for old boys he gave me passage money.[42]

The future looked bright; first his trip to study theatre in Britain, and then, on his return, Begum Zaidi's Hindustani Theatre, his dream of a professional company finally realised.

Begum Zaidi said to me, 'What d'you need for professional theatre?' And I said 'First of all, some plays. We don't have enough plays to keep perform-ing. We need at least twelve.' She said which ones? So I said, 'Three Sanskrit classics—*Mrichchakatika, Mudrarakshasa* and *Uttarramacharita*…. I gave a list. I took some classics from abroad. And of course there was one Chinese play thrown in, a melodrama, historical. 'Alright. You will get trained in two years, in 2 years these translations will be ready. How big should a repertory be? We calculated, about 12-15. She decided how much it would need, and said, I'll collect the money, so many lakhs of rupees. She knew all the big-wigs…. So at the end of two years—she went on writing to me, saying, I'm ready. She herself translated all the twelve plays. A woman of great dynamism. She said, we have twelve plays, 2-3 lakhs of rupees for the organization called Hindustani Theatre and you must come.[43]

But before Habib returned he first passed through a new and rich phase in his learning process—in Europe.

Notes

1. Habib Tanvir, *STQ*, p. 7.
2. Neeraj Malik and Javed Malick (eds), 'In Conversation with Javed Malick' in *Habib Tanvir: Reflections and Reminiscences* (New Delhi: SAHMAT, 2010), p. 103.
3. Habib Tanvir, 'Journey into Theatre' in *Nukkad*, p. 101.
4. Habib Tanvir, 'The Crisis of Identity and the Question of Authenticity in Theatre'. Paper presented at the seminar on Perspectives of Contemporary Indian Theatre organised by the Sangeet Natak Akademi on 17–19 December 1984, New Delhi. In *Nukkad*, p. 115.
5. Tanvir, 'In Conversation with Javed Malick', p. 104.
6. Ibid. p. 106.
7. Ibid.

8. Ibid. pp. 106–107.
9. Tanvir, *STQ*, p. 9.
10. Ibid.
11. Ibid.
12. Ibid.
13. Ibid.
14. Ibid.
15. Ibid.
16. Habib Tanvir, 'Preface to the Revised Edition: Some Excerpts' in *Agra Bazaar* (Kolkata: Seagull Books, 2006), pp. 18–19.
17. Ibid. p. 8.
18. Ibid.
19. Tanvir, *STQ*, p. 11.
20. Ibid. p. 10.
21. Ibid. p. 9.
22. Tanvir, 'Preface to the First Edition' in *Agra Bazaar*, p. 2.
23. Ibid. p. 3.
24. Ibid. p. 4.
25. Ibid. p. 5.
26. Tanvir, *STQ*, pp. 10–11.
27. Tanvir, 'Preface to the First Edition', p. 6.
28. Ibid. p. 3.
29. Tanvir, *STQ*, p. 11.
30. Ibid. p. 10.
31. Ibid.
32. Tanvir, 'Preface to the First Edition', pp. 6–7.
33. Tanvir, *STQ*, p. 11.
34. Tanvir, 'Journey into Theatre', p. 103.
35. Tanvir, 'Preface to the Revised Edition: Some Excerpts', pp. 11–12.
36. Tanvir, *STQ*, p. 11.
37. Tanvir, 'Preface to the Revised Edition: Some Excerpts', p. 16.
38. Tanvir, *STQ*, p. 11.
39. Tanvir, 'Preface to the Revised Edition: Some Excerpts', p. 9.
40. Ibid. pp. 9–10.
41. Ibid.
42. Tanvir, *STQ*, p. 12.
43. Ibid. p. 13.

CHAPTER FOUR

ENGLAND, EUROPE AND BRECHT

Habib in *Hirma Ki Amar Kahani* (1985).
Photo Avinash Pasricha, courtesy Naya Theatre

Habib joined the two year course offered by the Royal Academy of Dramatic
Art (RADA), only to find, after just one year, that he had had enough.

> I felt that it had no relevance for me. I discovered that language is connected
> with speech, which is connected with movement and therefore, quite simply,
> a change of language makes a change of movement and character and cul-
> tural ethos. We slur our words like the Spanish do and our movements, our
> gestures and hand movements differ from North to South. RADA teaches
> that movement starts from the spine. Indian movements do not start from
> the spine. Ours is a more rounded culture in every sense of the word. I had

to sit in some classes trying to correct my 'w'—as you know, we tend to make no difference between 'v' and 'w'.[1]

Habib approached the head, 'a great authority on Shakespeare, a very respected old man' with his request that he terminate his studies, but met with resistance.

> He wouldn't hear of me leaving the school. I said I've learnt enough and gained a lot. If I learn more, stay longer and spend more time, I'll get stilted as an actor. I'll go back to pursue my activities, not in English, but in my language; and in my language all the rules and principles applied here will not work.[2]

However, Habib could not prevail. 'He said, you come from across seven seas to this country, to a time-honoured institution with a long tradition and you want to break our rules? Nobody leaves in the middle. We can't give you any certificate.'[3]

Habib wanted to spend his second year studying production, which RADA did not offer, at the reputed Bristol Old Vic Theatre School. But it was a struggle trying to make this happen, particularly since the Indian Embassy, which dispensed his scholarship, backed RADA against him. He had one sympathiser—a lady in the British Council Drama Cell who understood his position and supported him. Then came a stroke of luck—the principal retired, and a new person joined—John Fernald,

> who was a very good director of the Arts Theatre Club, who had produced the first production of *Waiting for Godot*. He saw my point at once and after the first year test, gave me a very good chit, and I went to the Old Vic Theatre School.[4]

Finally, he was in an educational environment that stimulated him and, consequently, learned a lot that felt relevant, that he could apply and that remained influential in his theatre practice.

> There I enjoyed every minute of my stay. They taught us mask making, stage-craft writing, production. Duncan Ross, who later went to America, was also a very good producer, a very articulate man and a great teacher. One day he said, succinctly, in very lucid, terse language, 'Production is telling a story.' I got the full meaning of what he was trying to say. To this day I quote it and I believe it couldn't have been put more simply but more comprehensively. Telling the story is all the game in production. If it falters, it means the

production is faulty, you've failed to tell the story. If anything is coming in the way—costume, light, decor, anything—you've failed to tell the story. He would talk a great deal beyond class time to three of us; the other two were Israeli boys, older, like me—I was almost 30 by that time. These two boys from Tel Aviv were married, with children and had put in work in theatre over a number of years. The other girls and boys in this school were teenagers. Duncan Ross was a mature man in his 50s by then. So his head would pan almost always to the three of us because he got the most response from us. Most of it was going over the heads of the other children. The way he'd dissect Lorca, the way he'd talk about a play, just talking—it was wonderful. For example, he'd say … You just want to read a play and in one reading if it gives you a certain kick, if you get something from it, then that's your play— whether well known or not, you do that play. In producing that play, if you enjoyed the first reading, that's the kind of experience you want to transmit to your audience watching it for the first time. So you've read it, now you show it. But in this showing of it, unless you can transfer that experience, you've not managed to succeed. After many rehearsals you tend to forget the first experience. The thing to do is to hark back, go back to the first response and try to capture it in the production. That was another fine point. Thirdly he said, decor or sets or anything coming in the way of the progression of the story is out. You should see what facilitates the progress of the play. That alone is the best set and lighting and costume, nothing else.[5]

For Habib the director, with almost a decade of theatre under his belt, these were invaluable lessons which he continued to apply to his work throughout his life.

On the whole, the experience in England reaffirmed for him that his path lay in returning to the traditional culture of India and revisiting its performance forms with a fresh eye.

My absence from the country for about three years in the mid-1950s, when I was studying theatre in England and observing the theatres of Europe, made me acutely conscious of the fact that India needs to fall back upon its traditions in theatre in order to evolve a new type of theatre which will be both authentic and contemporary. That to my mind is the crux of all cultural renaissance. You draw strength from the old, inject contemporary consciousness into old cultural patterns and thereby produce the new. It is like a chemical process which results in a qualitative change flowing from the mixing of two known quantities.[6]

After completing his two years in theatre school, Habib decided to postpone his return to India in favour of hitchhiking through Europe, watching

European theatre as he went, with the ultimate aim of meeting the great Bertolt Brecht whose work he had encountered in England. 'I was doing all kinds of things, grape-picking, ushering for a circus, writing for radio, singing in nightclubs and earning my way.'[7] His travels included visiting Jean Vilar and Maria Cesares in Paris—'Jean was a great Communist Party man and a great leftist actor and director with a company. Maria Cesares was his wife. I saw their festival.'[8] He went to Avignon in 1956 to attend the youth drama festival, picking grapes to earn the money to do so. He made enough to finance a trip to Spain; more importantly, he met a lot of young people from across the world, who had assembled there. 'I made friends with them and took down their addresses, which helped me in my hitchhiking.'[9]

Nice, Trieste, Belgrade, Zaghreb, Dubrovnik, much of Yugoslavia and then Budapest, in Hungary—in all these places he was seeing the local theatre and building connections with young artists and theatre workers. Intending to stay in Budapest a week at the most, he ended up spending three months there. The story is best heard in his own words:

> There was a regulation in those days, that you could only use hard currency, that means dollars, pounds sterling, marks—western money—for anything beyond the border. Inside the border you could buy with and spend only local money. I was earning only local money; it could not be changed into hard currency. I had no access to my bank in London. I couldn't get out of Budapest .... There came a time when I dried up. I had nothing to write about. By now I'd come to know lots of students, theatre people, journalists and radio people. One of them was Itala Bekes. She was a very good singer, dancer, actress, and mime artiste. She came up with the idea that if we could cook up a number interesting enough to be shown in a nightclub, it might be taken up by a chain of nightclubs. Budapest was full of booze and nightclubs, with lovely wine and beautiful gypsies, music, guitar-players, very cozy places. So I said alright, let's see. So she, her brother and myself concocted an idea, a very simple idea—we go to see a western film in a cinema house, there's a queue. At the end we come to know the house is full, we can't go in. Frustrated, we begin to imagine what's going on inside. She does some mime and I sing my Indian song. So we concocted this 20–25 minute piece. And we presented it in a nightclub. It succeeded and I came in for more money than I could imagine, but my problem wasn't solved.[10]

He turned to the Indian embassy for help, but there was no solution forthcoming from that source:

> I went to Rehman, the Ambassador, in Hungary—hailing from Agra, speaking very chaste Urdu. I'd met Rehman in a theatre when Sitara Devi had come

and presented Kathak; Vilayat Khan had come and presented his sitar recital at the same time, and on these occasions I'd just met him briefly. But I was a nonentity. So I went specially to meet him in his office with my problem. Hearing my problem his response was candid and official, 'Well, there's only one way you can be helped—we can give you a passage back to India, free, we'll confiscate your passport which you may not get again. You'll have to first declare yourself a destitute. That's the only help the embassy can offer.' I said no, it was too high a price.[11]

Unexpectedly, he got a lucky break. A touring puppet theatre from Bratislava, the capital of Slovakia, arrived. He found them wonderful puppeteers, made friends and began to visit them every day. Suddenly it occurred to him that they could help him—after all, they'd be going back to Bratislava.

> I asked them how to do it and they told me. Now I had the other problem of what to do with my money, the Hungarian money. It'd be no use in Czechoslovakia. There were no machines in 1956 that you could invest in, cameras or gadgets. It was by and large an agrarian country. Not even good enough clothes to buy.[12]

So he decided to throw a big party. By now he had a wide circle of friends comprising students, journalists and actors, and he invited them all to a big hotel to drink the best and most expensive Hungarian wine: 'It was a Hungarian name which literally translated into oxblood. We had some wine and some dinner and all the money was gone. In acknowledgement of how much they'd done for me.'[13]

Three days after his arrival in Bratislava, 'there was a large exodus of people from Hungary and I came to know that the revolution had happened, the Soviet intervention had taken place. Had I stayed three days longer, I'd have got stuck for several more months!'[14]

His next stop was Prague where he saw plenty of theatre.

> I saw a wonderful puppet show in Prague of Tagore's *Post Office*. And many lovely musicals by many eminent directors. I saw Jean-Louis Barrault. A great mime, before Marcel Marceau's time, and a great actor. He's written a beautiful autobiography in which he mentions that the Egyptian Book of the Dead inspired him just as yoga did and he talks of actors conserving their energy like a cat does before pouncing on her victim. And his experience as a young man wandering onto the stage after the show and finding himself on Volpone's bed, alone, everyone gone—and he spends

the night on stage on Volpone's bed. He loved the smell of greasepaint. So, this was Barrault.[15]

These meanderings through Europe about a decade after the Second World War gave Habib invaluable first-hand exposure to some of the most innovative, avant-garde theatre of the time. Europe, particularly Eastern Europe, took its performing arts seriously. Theatre outside the English language mainstream, in different European languages, seen in such concentrated doses within its own cultural and performative context—this was an invaluable learning experience for any keen theatre worker and for someone of Habib's interest and talent, even more so.

Finally, he made his way to Berlin—only to find that Brecht had died a few weeks previously. He could not meet the great man, but he could experience Brecht's theatre:

> His productions were all there and I saw them all. I saw the rehearsals done by two very eminent directors who directed together, special disciples of Brecht. Ekkehard [Schall] the actor, Brecht's son-in-law, a great actor, was already there. He's still the best of their actors. Ernst Busch was the cook in *Mother Courage*, a great singer and a wonderful actor. I was there for eight months in Berlin, met all the actors and actresses, sat in their canteen, discussed many things, saw *Caucasian Chalk Circle*, some Chinese one-act plays, *Mother Courage*, the whole gamut, except *The Good Woman of Schezuan*. I did not see that because it was not in the repertoire at that time. Of course I did meet Elisabeth Hauptmann and also Helene Weigel. She was doing the role of the mother.[16]

Habib stayed on in Germany for several months, seeing theatre and travelling. At the time there was no wall, and he says it was quite common to work in the East and live in the West. It was a bohemian life: 'I was sleeping on the pavement, sometimes in the canteen, or in some club or travelling with friends'.[17] One such friendship was to last many decades: A friend who was a minor actress introduced him to Nele, the daughter of Hanning Schroeder, a music composer for a film company, and Cora, who also worked with music. The family befriended him and offered him a cosy attic room in their house to sleep in. 'I'd get up in the morning and have breakfast with them, and then leave for the day for the East.'[18]

Theatre remained a constant, as did a concern with the political. He was writing for a theatre journal. 'We had great political discussions about communism and there were people belonging to the left among my circle of friends, newspaper journalists and actors etc. who were already against the regime, talking a great deal against the constraints they felt.'[19] He also continued to see lots of good theatre. At the time, he says, the best theatre was happening in the East, and people not just from the West but also from across Europe and the world, would come to see shows there.[20]

As Habib hitchhiked all over Germany—Nuremburg, Heidelberg, Munich, Vienna—he was being urgently sought by Khwaja Ahmed Abbas, the well-known Indian filmmaker. Abbas was in Moscow, making a film on a character called Afanasi Nikitin who had visited India and written a travel story. The film, *Pardesi*, was in Hindi. A Russian actor, Strezhenov, was playing the hero and Nargis was the heroine. Abbas had sent a telegram to the Embassy in London:

> [T]hey'd told him that I'd left for Europe. So he cabled all the embassies and in Berlin I got one of the telegrams, asking me to wire back. I did. He sent me a pre-paid return flight ticket for the air passage. I flew from Berlin to Moscow where I was for three months, working in Mosfilm Studio as the director of dubbing, and giving the voice to Strezhenov.

It was an excellent opportunity to see theatre, and he did—'Mally theatre, the Bolshoi theatre, Gorky theatre, Meyerhold's theatre.'[21]

Apart from watching theatre, Habib was pursuing a parallel aim throughout his wanderings through Europe. 'I was trying to produce *Mrichchakatika, The Little Clay Cart*, the Sanskrit classic.'[22] He had already identified this text by Sudraka as the next play he wanted to do, after *Agra Bazaar*. 'I found that play very attractive. Something drew me to it irresistibly'[23] and 'I was producing *Mitti Ki Gadi* all over Europe on paper. I must've produced on paper something like twelve sets at least, drawings,' he says.[24] Meanwhile, he tried his best to interest producers in Europe in the play:

> I'd tried to sell the idea in Belgium, in Germany, and also Poland … in Krakow I met Kristina Skuszhanka. She was the head of a very good theatre, and she got interested and said, 'By the time you come back from Moscow, we shall have the new translation ready.' They had a Polish translation, but a rather outdated one. In Warsaw I'd met a man called Mikoleitis; he was interested in translating it and undertook to do so. By the time I returned to Warsaw, it was done. But then suddenly he said, 'I want to be a co-producer.' He had no theatre experience, none at all; he had just an ambition that he should be considered co-producer and not just the translator and he wanted the lion's share of the money, which wasn't palatable to Skuszhanka, or to me.

It was downright cheating. So it never happened. But I did produce a small scene from *The Little Clay Cart* for television in Warsaw. In Germany I went to Rostok. Hanning was born in Rostok. I went and met his people there, saw the theatre; and there a director got interested in my proposition. He said, 'Yes, why not. But why just one play? Why don't you take up a job of a director here, and do it.'[25]

One would have thought that he would have jumped at the offer, a chance to stay on in Europe where he was leading such an interesting and stimulating life, but Habib was sure by now that it was time for him to go home.

I was clear in my mind that culturally I belonged in India. If you're dealing with words and culture, you belong where you come from, because that's where you'll be your most creative. And also, of course, I'd met people and observed enough to know that I was about to overstay my time. I'd seen people who'd stayed away close to three years, finding it exceedingly difficult to get readjusted to India.[26]

So, after three long years in Europe, years crammed with invaluable experiences, exposure, learning and growth, Habib returned to Delhi, where Hindustani Theatre was awaiting him. Adjustment was not easy, as is only to be expected: 'It took me not less than a year and a half to really get reconciled. I was out of my depth with every little thing.'[27] It must have helped that he was able to plunge straight into the project he had already been conceptualising during his wanderings in Europe—*Mitti Ki Gadi*.

Notes

1. Habib Tanvir, *STQ*, p. 12.
2. Ibid.
3. Ibid.
4. Ibid.
5. Ibid., pp. 12–13.
6. Habib Tanvir, 'Journey into Theatre' in *Nukkad Janam Samvad* (7: 23–26, April 2004–March 2005), p. 103.
7. Tanvir, *STQ*, p. 13.
8. Ibid.
9. Ibid.
10. Ibid.
11. Ibid., p. 14.
12. Ibid.
13. Ibid.

14. Ibid.
15. Ibid., p. 14–15.
16. Ibid., p. 15.
17. Ibid.
18. Ibid.
19. Ibid.
20. Ibid.
21. Ibid.
22. Ibid.
23. Ibid., p. 13.
24. Ibid., p. 16.
25. Ibid., pp. 15–16.
26. Ibid., p. 16.
27. Ibid.

CHAPTER FIVE

COMING HOME TO
MITTI KI GADI

A moment from *Mitti Ki Gadi*—with the legendary Fida Bai.
Photo courtesy Avinash Pasricha

On Habib's return to Delhi, Begum Zaidi, who had impatiently awaited his return for a year, promptly gave him *Mitti Ki Gadi* to direct for Hindustani Theatre. As a young man in his 30s, Habib was by now amply qualified to launch into his professional career. He had already familiarised himself with a wide range of theatre. Not only had he seen the best of theatre within India, that too, not just in one style but across the spectrum, he had also seen, close up, the work of Berliner Ensemble and many highly talented European directors. He had received training in theatre both through direct experience and also from highly reputed institutions in the UK. He was more than ready.

He had returned with a developed perspective on the theatre direction he wished to take:

> Europe further brought me back both to the classical Sanskrit tradition and the folk theatre forms of Indian drama. It appeared to me that many new and vital patterns of Indian drama could easily be evolved through an understanding and utilization of these two strains of Indian theatre. I blended the two in my first experiment with Sanskrit drama, Sudraka's *Mrichchakatika*. I adopted it to a musical Hindi form called *Mitti Ki Gadi*. That was in 1958. In my production of this play I used folk tunes, folk theatre techniques and harnessed the services of actual folk artists of Chhattisgarh in order to project these in all their vividness and authenticity. This was my first involvement with the folk artists of Chhattisgarh.[1]

We already know that he had been working on this production and had tried to interest European producers in it; the play had been an active part of his creative preoccupation for almost a year.

Mitti Ki Gadi can be considered another major milestone in Habib's theatre journey for several reasons. Firstly, struggling to design his production led him to realise one of his most important lessons about traditional Indian dramaturgy—that it follows a completely different approach to time and space from the Aristotelian unities, which had been accepted as the classic norm to date. ('I must've produced on paper something like twelve sets at least, drawings, and every time it obstructed the flow of the story. But my reading of the play never produced this obstruction.'[2]) This basic realisation shaped his whole approach to direction and design. Secondly, he introduced Chhattisgarhi actors in this production for the first time. From here on, these two features would be an integral part of his theatre. Thirdly, this play led to his strong belief that the classic and the folk traditions are not two separate streams but instead are intertwined, feeding off and into each other; that there is no such thing as 'high' and 'low' art or the greater and lesser traditions, as cultural scholars of the time would have it.

Talking about the fluidity of movement through time and space that characterised traditional Indian theatre, he says:

> There is a clash between Bharat Muni's dramaturgy which is followed by the Sanskrit playwrights, and the Poetics and Aristotle's theory of the three unities.[3] Many Western scholars of Sanskrit—and I dare say great translators, through which medium alone I got these classics, because I do not know Sanskrit, and Hindi translations by and large were lousy till then—when they

commented on those plays, praised the authors as Mahakavya writers, with great poetic imaginations, a great command of words. Only somewhere you found a subdued apology—the poor chaps did not know their dramaturgy, because they failed to see the unities. That was bad enough. It was much worse when you came across books written by Indian pundits echoing the apology because they knew no better either. For all their knowledge of Sanskrit grammar and language, they had no clue as to what was going on, because they had no contact with theatre. And what do I read? I find, in the very first act of *Mrichchakatika*, which is divided into ten acts, the stage-manager, the sutradhar and nati talking, introducing Charudatta; and Charudatta comes from outside somewhere and goes into his house, some scene takes place there. The scene continues on the road. Suddenly you find Vasantasena the courtesan, with Shakara and his retinue all over the road and somehow—without break of scene—she comes to the exterior of Charudatta's house and slips into the house—things going on outside the house, also inside, in and out—that's scene one. Scene two, a gambler's being chased, and he goes out on the road, comes back and, moves into a *mandir*, becomes a *murti* on the pedestal, they chase him, fool around and he again gives them the slip and runs into Vasantasena's house, talks to her and she comes out and hears the shouting—all one scene. The locales haven't been changed.

Duncan Ross had taught me an important lesson: it must flow. So I made those scenes on paper and everything seemed to obstruct the play because how could you have a very swift set for a particular locale and move on in the kind of fluent manner in which you read the play? And I wanted the play to come across exactly as I read it, not with those obstructions. So I ended up, after removing this, that and the other, with a bare, circular platform. This gave me space enough on the stage for the exterior and enough for the interiors, which was the circular platform on stage with a diameter of about twelve feet. And the play just flowed. I didn't have to explain the scene changes. Initially I used to hang things, which would keep dropping and going up to suggest a locale. Later on I thought it was fussy, I removed it.[4]

Even more specifically, he pinpoints one concrete example of how elastic the treatment of external time and space is:

[I]n a scene in a court of law the judge asks a witness in the court to go to the garden to see if there is the dead body of a woman. The man runs in a little circle and in the next line says—I have been to the garden and indeed there is a dead woman's body lying in the garden ... you can see that the time sense is broken, action is broken and space is broken. But he is right there on stage.[5]

Fluidity of time and space was not the only feature of the Sanskrit drama that led him to dispense with elaborate sets. There was also the poetic and descriptive language that made him question the need for the pictorial representation of locales:

> In the play the vidushaka goes into Vasantasena's house and you see nine courtyards, one is painted with all kinds of beautiful pictures, in another *angan* there're monkeys and horses and cows and he describes them all. In the third, wonderful things are being cooked and he describes the smells. So each *angan* has a description. Suddenly he comes to the eighth or ninth *angan* and he finds a huge woman seated there, and he finds out that this is Vasantasena's mother. And he wonders how she managed to enter the house. And then he comes to the conclusion that she was already seated there and the house was built around her. Now, such beautiful descriptions, what will we do?[6]

Habib had always given great importance to language, and his response to the wonderful poetry of the Sanskrit text was to allow it to shine forth, to showcase and highlight it by removing anything redundant or competitive that may reduce its impact:

> And also I felt another thing, quite candidly. I felt that the descriptions of the Sanskrit poets who wrote these plays are so vivid and so beautiful, so graphic, that in your imagination, before your mind's eye, any kind of picture of which you are capable can be thrown up. One differing from the other, in the auditorium, in the audience. Now that liberty, that faculty, will not be given full play if you paint the scenery on the stage. I find it presumptuous to paint, to translate the words in terms of paint. Either you'll fall short of the description or you'll exceed it. In either case, art has mastered poetry. And as one says in Urdu, '*yeh zyada hai, yeh labz zyada hai*' (this is redundant, extra). The poem, the two couplets, must be terse—one word added for the sake of the metre is bad art. We know it from Shakespeare, from the great painters—what one line, one stroke can do, many cannot. Therefore, to have both painted and verbal descriptions is meaningless. And to have a painting as a substitute is to have a poor substitute, because it deprives the viewer of access to the work. At least I thought so.[7]

This is a major aesthetic choice, from someone who grew up spellbound by the elaborate painted scenery and sets of Parsi theatre productions. Of course, freeing his theatre from the constraints of backdrops and scenery also moved it a step closer to his next major directorial decision—that of using folk actors as the backbone of his theatre. Folk theatre throughout

India has always been highly mobile, free of dependence on technology and anchored in the body of the actor. The actor moves freely in space and time, unfettered by the logistics of set changes. By moving away from painted scenery Habib moved even closer to the aesthetics of folk performance.

As he explored this Sanskrit classic, he began to realise that Sanskrit drama, too, was an actor's theatre:

> So ... going by the internal evidence and the reading, I arrived at the con-
> clusion that there were neither curtains, nor machinery, nor a revolving
> theatre in the classical theatre days. There was utter simplicity—it was an
> actor's theatre. Whether the actor danced it out or acted it out. Otherwise
> you would not get instructions like, actor enter, seated on a throne. How
> will you manage that? Actor enter supine, lying on a couch. How? Only a
> dancer can do it. Or a kuchipudi curtain behind which the actor moves in
> rhythm, on drumbeats, rhythmically, and that by itself is a visual spectacle
> because the curtain is beautiful and behind it they reveal the actor, which is
> what I did in my *Mudrarakshasa*.[8]

On his return from Europe in 1958, he went home to Raipur to meet his family, before plunging into directing *Mitti Ki Gadi*. Here, with all the experience and sophistication acquired through his theatre exposure to date, from Brecht to IPTA, he rediscovered the folk forms of his childhood.

> It was summer. I heard that there was to be a Nacha on the grounds of
> the high school where I was educated—Nacha is a Chhattisgarhi form of
> secular drama. It was to start at 9 o'clock. I saw it all night through, which
> is the usual duration for a Nacha. They presented three or four skits. There
> was Madan Lal, a great actor, Thakur Ram, another great actor, Babu Das,
> a very good actor too, Bulwa Ram, a glorious singer: and what comedians,
> these fellows, like music hall comedy. They were doing *chaprasi nakal, sadhu
> nakal* (take-offs). I was fascinated. I went up to them and said—would you
> like to come to Delhi and join me in a production? They were happy to do
> so. So I enlisted Bulwa, Babu Das, Thakur Ram, Madan Lal, and Jagmohan,
> who was on clarinet.[9]

What is interesting about this account is his almost instinctive recogni-tion that the talent and facility these actors possessed would be an asset to his planned production. His response was to their competence as actors; he was able immediately to compare them to international standards ('like music hall comedy'); and he knew that there was a place in his theatre for their skills. This was just the beginning of his involvement with the folk

actors of Chhattisgarh—on the very same trip he developed his relationship
with them further:

> Then I was to go to Rajnandgaon to speak on Indo-Soviet friendship or
> something. There they wanted to know about my European tour. I described
> my Hungarian travels and sang a Chhattisgarhi song as an illustration. At
> the end a dark man with squint eyes and a short, grisly black beard, came
> up to me and said, 'Come to my house.' This was Lalu Ram. He liked the
> folk songs. I went to his house. He offered me *ganja*, we shared *ganja*, and he
> heard many songs from me. He sang many, one of the best singers in Chhat-
> tisgarh, glorious voice. The session went on all night. So I enlisted Lalu Ram
> as the sixth member of the troupe.[10]

A characteristic that marked Habib's relationship with the folk actors he
employed is already evident in this reminiscence about his first encounter
with Lalu Ram, which is an element of mutuality—a two-way exchange.
Habib accepts hospitality, he spends time, he shares songs, he gives as well
as receives. And the bedrock of the link between him and these actors is
respect for their artistic prowess, a genuine appreciation of their evolved
talent. Without overly romanticising or idealising their relationship, one can
still recognise that it was not just a one-way process, where he, the urban,
sophisticated director, condescends to offer an opportunity to obscure
rural performers to be part of his experimental production. The dynamics
are totally different here—there is a sense of excited discovery and genuine
respect for proficiency and a willingness to learn and exchange that mark
Habib's interaction with these actors. He selects them for their outstanding
talent, stage presence, acting prowess and their impeccable comic timing.

> These six came to Delhi and participated in *Mitti ki Gadi*, with Bulwa and
> Lalu Ram playing *chandals* and singing at the top of their voices, Jagmohan
> playing the clarinet, Madan Lal playing the gambler, Thakur Ram playing
> Sarvilaka.[11]

Mitti Ki Gadi was his first professional offering to the world of theatre
post his return to Delhi, and he was already breaking taboos, which inevitably led to a few brickbats.

> I simplified till the play moved without a hitch. The pundits all attacked
> it. The Sanskrit scholars said, this has been done in *lokdharmi* and the play
> belongs to *natyadharmi*—that means that I did it in folk style and it should
> have been done in the classical style.[12]

Nevertheless, Habib was convinced that the pundits had got it wrong; there was no clear divide between the two styles: '[A]t the time *Mrichchhakatika* came to be written, it was more predominantly in Prakrit, using plebeian characters such as the gamblers, the jewellers and all the other rogues of that play.'[13] He felt that 'the manner in which these people mixed, the *ganikas*, the merchants and the other ordinary people' was a clear indication that Sanskrit drama was not sealed within the royal court but was accessed by the commoner as well.[14]

Despite the criticisms, Habib had a clear grasp of what he saw in the play and a clear vision of how to communicate it. Comedy, circularity, repetition, rhythm, these are the qualities he aimed for:

> *Mitti ki Gadi* is a *prahasan* (farce) and many critics have criticized the play for its lack of harmony and mixtures of rasas, saying that it doesn't work; it is not a romantic story, it is not another gambler's tale, it has got the jewellery thing travelling around, and so many strands of stories and the play doesn't have that kind of unity of rasa. But the play works. It has a certain harmony—when I read it, I felt it was harmonious. It has a circular mood, like the nine courtyards of Vasantasena, nine public squares where Charudatta is taken, and it is repetitive—the same announcement made again and again. So I got a feeling that the treatment in music and elsewhere—let's take the example of music—is repetitive. Hardly four or five or six words in a line, sung for two hours, several hours, all night, in classical singing. Develop the raga and you get everything that you want, not so much through the words, although the words also help a bit, though they're just an aid. But the repetitiveness of it, cumulatively, finally, casts a spell on you—if you're so inclined. Keeps you riveted. So that repetition is important.[15]

However, after *Mitti Ki Gadi*, his stint with Hindustani Theatre came to an end. Begum Zaidi had already expressed her disapproval over his introduction of village actors into the production, as Habib relates in his trademark humorous style: '[W]hen she saw these folk actors, she blew her top. "Are these the actors you are going to present to Zakir Saheb?" she asked.[16] "[F]or God's sake, theatre demands young handsome faces, not these strange creatures!"'[17]

Now she had another reason for displeasure. She wanted him to direct *Mudrarakshasa*, another Sanskrit drama, next. After all, that was the plan chalked out before he left for England. But Habib was unwilling: 'I said to her that it is a tough play and I require another five years' experience as a director to do it. I produced that play in 1964. Six years.'[18] So, as Habib puts it, 'After *Mitti Ki Gadi* I was thrown out.'[19]

Notes

1. Habib Tanvir, 'Journey into Theatre', p. 101.
2. Habib Tanvir, *STQ*, p. 16.
3. In his *Poetics*, Aristotle outlines the three unities of time, space and action which were adopted as the cornerstone of western classic dramaturgy.
4. Tanvir, *STQ*, pp. 16–17.
5. Habib Tanvir, 'Indian Theatre' [Lecture on 6 March 2000 in Berlin] in *Nukkad*, p. 67.
6. Tanvir, *STQ*, p. 17.
7. Ibid.
8. Ibid.
9. Ibid.
10. Ibid.
11. Ibid., pp. 17–18.
12. Ibid., p. 18.
13. 'Habib Tanvir Interviewed' by Rajinder Paul in *Nukkad*, p. 86.
14. Ibid.
15. Tanvir, *STQ*, p. 18.
16. Dr Zakir Hussain, then governor of Bihar.
17. Habib Tanvir, 'My Subversive Allies in Theatre', *Frontline*, 22 Aug 1997. In *Nukkad*, p. 113.
18. Tanvir, *STQ*, p. 18.
19. Ibid.

CHAPTER SIX

NAYA THEATRE AND OTHER MILESTONES

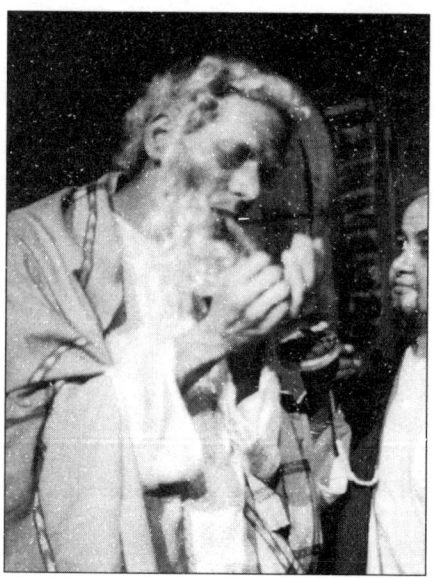

Habib and Moneeka Misra in a production from their
pre-Naya Theatre days. Photo courtesy Naya Theatre

Meeting Moneeka Misra was another major milestone in Habib's life. She
herself was trained in theatre and joined Begum Zaidi before Habib returned
to replace her. Initially, there were fireworks—best related in Habib's own
words:

> Begum Zaidi ... could wait no longer. She went around looking for a
> director.... She located Moneeka Misra, who at that time was working under
> Kamaladevi Chattopadhyay in Bombay Natya Sangh, teaching the students
> acting. She'd just come back from Colorado, having done her MA in Theatre.
> She jumped at the idea and came and joined at the proud salary of Rs 200
> p.m. The first play Begum Zaidi wanted to produce was *Shakuntala*. She did

it. This was 1957. I was still in Europe. I came in the summer of 1958. By then Moneeka had finished her second play, *Charlie's Aunt*, translated by Begum Zaidi as *Khaled ki Khala*. And when I came, Moneeka was thrown out. Thrown out is the right phrase. She went from pillar to post, weeping and crying and meeting Committee members. I'd met her briefly in Delhi at a party, just briefly. I was given my job. And I produced *Mitti ki Gadi*. Monica met me when I was working on it—very angry. She thought I was responsible for getting her thrown out. She was full of accusations. She was railing at me and I said no, I don't think I'm responsible, but shall we talk about it over a cup of tea? She said alright, and we went to Alps on Janpath. It was a cosy restaurant and in those days you could sit over a cup of tea for several hours and it was still the same charge. So we sat for several hours drinking gallons of tea for several days, sorting this out, till we fell in love. But that is another story…. Anyway, after *Mitti ki Gadi* I wouldn't take up *Mudrarakshasa*, so I was thrown out. Moneeka helped me, since we were both in the same boat. By then we'd really became friends. She found a garage in Janpath and that's where we started Naya Theatre with 9 members.[1]

And thus, Moneeka and Habib started their theatre company, Naya Theatre (which was registered later in 1964). With this began a period of struggle to make ends meet and continue with theatre at the same time. Some years later, they got married. The next 13 years see Habib, with Moneeka at his side, undertake a wide range of productions, from original scripts to adaptations of international texts to classical plays. In its very first year, Naya Theatre produced three plays: *Saat Paisey*, which was a dramatisation of a Czech short story, written by Habib and directed by Moneeka; *Jaalidar Pardey*, Habib's revival of an adaptation of a Soviet play he had first directed in 1952 in Bombay; and *Tambaku Ke Nuksanat*, written by him. In 1960, Habib directed *Phaansi* in which both he and Moneeka had roles—adapted from an English one-act play.

The decade of the 1960s saw him take on Moliere (*The Bourgeois Gentleman* as *Mirza Shoharat Beg*), Brecht (*The Good Woman of Schezuan*), Shakespeare (*The Taming of the Shrew*), Garcia Lorca (*The Shoe-maker's Prodigious Wife*), Goldoni (*Servant of Two Masters*) and Oscar Wilde (*Lady Windermere's Fan*). It is interesting that in this period Habib directed a series of plays in English—for example, the above-mentioned Brecht, Shakespeare, Garcia Lorca, Goldoni, Wilde and, in 1964, *The Signet Ring of Rakshasa*, P. Lal's transcreation of Visakhadatta's Sanskrit classic *Mudrarakshasa*. He was doing these plays for colleges such as Jamia Millia and St Stephen's College and for drama teachers' camps sponsored by the Ministry of Education and working with the most talented actors of the time in Delhi—Sushma Seth,

Aftab Seth and Roshan Seth amongst them. He also worked in Urdu—notably *Shatranj Ke Mohre, Mirza Shoharat Beg*, Aga Hashr's *Rustam Sohrab* and, in 1969, his own play on Ghalib, *Merey Baad*. This was the same year in which he was recognised by the Sangeet Natak Akademi with an award for his work in theatre.

After *Agra Bazaar, Merey Baad* was the next play researched and written by Habib on a major Urdu poet. In his introductory note in the play brochure, he mentions his research, listing the scholars whom he consulted for details on Ghalib's life, and says, 'I have adhered to facts throughout; and such liberties as I have taken for dramatic necessity are minor.'[2] His aim was to demystify the legendary figure, depicting him with all his human frailties and qualities, focusing not just on 'chronicles of life and Ghalib's genius' but trying to 'interpret events and establish a relationship between the artist and his environment'.[3] The students and teachers of Jamia Millia formed a major portion of the cast, and Habib himself played Ghalib, choosing not to sing but rather recite the poems in order to emphasise the thought behind the poetry.[4]

The decade of the 1970s began with his revival of *Agra Bazaar* for the Sangeet Natak festival on the occasion of the award ceremony, this time with an almost totally Chhattisgarhi cast.

> I called all my Chhattisgarh actors....They came and participated in the bazaar scene, and I got the music compounded with many strains of music including Chhattisgarhi folk tunes and it became much richer....The play again was so popular, that it went on and on. Twenty shows—I went on getting dates and extending it. It had a momentum. Then the Information and Broadcasting Ministry took on the play for twenty shows in Punjab/Kashmir and twenty in U.P.[5]

In 1971, he participated in the Congress (I) election campaign with his poster play, *Indra Lokasabha* and, later that year, presented another poster play, *Kushtia ka Chaprasi* on the Bangladesh Liberation War; no doubt this revived memories of the earlier IPTA experience of short propaganda street plays.

Through these years, Habib held different day jobs—as a producer at the TV Centre, as a freelance writer and reviewer for the *Statesman, Patriot, Link* and *Mainstream*. In 1964, his daughter Nageen was born; in the same year, he joined the Soviet Information Centre, Delhi. The job lasted till 1972; soon after, he was nominated to the Rajya Sabha. With the modest benefits that came with this position, he found that Naya Theatre could turn professional; they could afford to pay the cast and crew a small salary. 'By 1972 we had become professionals, in a small way, with our own momentum.

There was a Department of Culture subsidy for professional theatres, and in 1973 we got it.'[6]

Meanwhile, his interest in folk performance culture remained alive. He continued to work with Chhattisgarhi actors, presenting their stock comedies. He explored the Pandavani form, with its *Mahabharata* subject matter:

"Arjun ka Sarathi" was the name of a short piece of half an hour which I rehearsed for timing, saying you must talk only of *geet updesh* and for half an hour; combining it with ritual which was not usually presented on stage in Chhattisgarh but in temples, and with the singing of fascinating songs with intricate, changing rhythms. Seven songs coming one after the other, blending into one another, a fascinating experience in the temples, during the weeklong Ramsatta festival, when these women start singing from their homes and go to the temple. Ramsatta had some lovely ritual tunes. I got all these women, eight or twelve of them. Then there is a ritual song which is on Shiva-Parvati, called Gauri-Gaura (Gauri is Parvati and Gaura is Shiva). Songs are sung around the idols of Gauri and Gaura. Intricate rhythms, with one song flowing into the other. It's beautiful. That was launched as 'Gauri-Gaura' with 'Arjun ka Sarathi' and a half hour skit, 'Chaprasi'. This became an instant success in Pandavani, which enabled me to present Mahabharata in Pandavani in many drawing rooms, and then in Karol Bagh, in the open, the *sampurna* Mahabharata, for a number of days. Though they would sing and recite in Chhattisgarhi, yet the ordinary householder men, women and children thronged the park where we were showing it.[7]

By now, on the subject of traditional folk theatre, Habib had begun to advocate the benefits of a workshop approach, in which someone like him, an 'outsider', could function as a catalyst and not as a teacher.[8] He explains:

There was a time when I was so young and foolish that I thought one could go out to the villages and impose one's ideas upon the people. However, experience taught me that the only viable method was to work in coopera-tion with them on the basis of an exchange of ideas and joint improvisation and experimentation. This results in a mutual process of learning and leads to innumerable creative things.[9]

This was the method he employed when he was invited by well-known folklorist Komal Kothari to do a workshop in Rajasthan, on the Khayal form. He was clear that the folk artist has 'nothing to learn from us about acting or improvisation'.[10] There were other areas where inputs could be useful, however, with regard to content, simple lighting innovations, costumes, etc.

A major milestone in his development trajectory was the Nacha workshop held in Raipur from 6–18 March 1973, in his own words: 'One of the best I've had.'[11] This workshop was part of an informal education programme of Nehru Youth Centre, a pilot project under a new scheme of the Union Ministry of Education. Habib felt that it 'yielded exciting results not only in the villages of that region but also in some metropolitan centres including Delhi, where the Chhattisgarhi dialect, a special form of Hindi, is not spoken at all and hardly understood'.[12]

The Raipur workshop was to be followed by two similar programmes in Gujarat and Rajasthan over the next few months. It was a large gathering:

> Some forty folk artists, both professional and non-professional, including people from ordinary walks of life, from Raipur, Durg and Rajnandgaon formed the nucleus. In addition, about twenty urban youth and thirty to forty rural youth attended the Workshop as observers for varying periods of time.[13]

Thakur Ram, Madan Lal, Bulwa Ram, Lalu Ram, Brij Lal, Devi Lal, who were the core of his Chhattisgarhi actors' team, took part. Fida Bai, who was to become his charismatic lead actress, was discovered at this workshop. Several Nacha groups came as observers, participated, left or stayed at will. Professors of anthropology from the university were present, as well as scholars and theatre experts like Surajit Sinha from Calcutta, R. P. Nayak, an authority on Madhya Pradesh tribals and part of the Madhya Pradesh government, and Komal Kothari.

The objectives of the theatre were two-pronged:

> The director's task was to demonstrate for the benefit of urban observers the efficacy of the simple techniques of acting, stagecraft, make-up, improvisation, stylised movement and dramatic projection of the theme through music, dance and mime, inherent in the *Nacha* theatre of Chhattisgarh. The rural actors were to be helped to draw more deeply from the songs, tunes, dances, rituals, costumes and other cultural resources of their own community life rather than from either the alienated urban cultural forms or the commercial films.[14]

The method employed was 'mutual discussion and exchange of ideas and practical tryouts more or less on a collective basis'.[15] Activities included a make-up session led by Thakur Ram, who, according to Habib,

> used to put some white chalk on his face and look very good as an old man, and he was also very good with jewellery, and with tying his turban, quite an

artist in his own right in these things. So I asked him to conduct the workshop on make-up, how to use coal, chalk, all the local, inexpensive things, and teach the city boys one indigenous way of making up.[16]

Improvised lighting was another session, this time led by Habib himself:

> I would take a dalda tin and put a bulb in it, to show them the difference between a flood and a spot, and I told them, if you have nothing else, you can use this, and that by itself is a kind of spot since it controls focus, which is all a spot does, and the reflection of the white tin inside will increase the light. You can increase it more by adding reflectors, or put a lens on it.[17]

There were talks, discussions and demonstrations by veteran folk artists and urban intellectuals on various subjects including dance and music in Nacha, acting in folk comedy, book-keeping and carpentry; and practical classes in mime, movement and improvisation, *lathi*,[18] and fencing.[19]

Habib describes the Nacha performers and the form from a sociocultural perspective:

> The typical *Nacha* actor is usually a peasant, an agricultural labourer, a village artisan or a shop-keeper. He is also a semi-professional actor in the sense that in his spare time he travels about with his band of actors and musicians unfolding his repertoire of small musical comedies in all-night performances for the benefit of a most receptive rural audience all over the region, usually on a commissioned basis, which proves quite lucrative. The more successful parties give an average of 200 performances in a year. These are spread out in a concentrated form between harvest times, during which the actors tend to their vocations on land and in shops. The typical actor is a versatile artist, with a natural gift for singing, dancing, acting and playing instruments, which he polishes to perfection in the course of his experience. He does not have to be taught movement, voice projection, singing or acting. Being illiterate, he is of necessity an improviser of his own dramatic story and characters. Collective functioning in drama comes naturally to him due to the compulsions of his community life. Sometimes an individual evolves the story but more often a play is a collective product in the fullest sense of the word.[20]

The workshop was production oriented; one of the tasks in hand was to create an improvised play in the Nacha form, to be presented as public performances. Habib went about making his interventions in the established conventions of the Nacha, both in terms of form and content. Firstly, in addition to the experienced Nacha actors, he decided to include 'a sizeable group of housewives and other rural peoples … who had

never before appeared on the stage but who had the experience of singing and dancing in the temples, fields and homes as part of the process of
worship and daily work'.[21] Not only did this mean that the custom of men
doing women's roles was abandoned, it also meant that traditional songs,
dances, rituals 'and other artistic expressions of the village community
life'[22] which were not part of Nacha could be introduced which, Habib
felt, 'contributed to the enrichment of the basic plot and its situations'.[23]
Aesthetically, he also added authentic regional folk costumes and essential
props needed for the dramatic situations; both these theatrical elements
were usually non-existent in Nacha. In terms of building content and
structure, he decided to adopt a combination of directorial direction and
collective improvisation:

> A situation was discussed and developed, its characters were evolved and
> fixed, then roles were distributed to match the characters, and the rest was all
> improvisation. The dialogues got crystallised through rehearsals, and songs
> were altered or re-written to suit the situation wherever necessary. The result
> was an entertaining musical comedy about a rich old man marrying a young
> girl and in the end losing her to a poor but clever young rogue, her lover.
> The actors' electrifying improvisations and witticisms turned it into a social
> satire of some depth. It was christened with a long and funny title reading
> like a proverb '*Gaon Ka Naon Sasural Mor Naon Damad*'.[24]

This play was, in many ways, a precursor to *Charandas Chor*, considered to
be the apogee of Habib's form.

The content of the play came out of local folk material. After watching
several Nacha comic skits, three were selected to be welded into a single
narrative. These were stock comedies—*Chheri Chhera, Budhwa Bivah* and
Dewar Dewarin.

The first is set in the Chheri Chhera festival when, traditionally, young
boys collect donations of fruits, vegetables and grain which they carry to the
riverside and cook into a youth community feast. Two spirited young lads
encounter two young women and a lively flirtation takes place, with repartee
and song and dance. The second skit is about an elderly man who approaches
the father of a young girl for her hand in marriage, making it appear that
he is acting on someone's behalf—till he arrives as the bridegroom at the
wedding, holding the bride's father to his commitment and whisking away
his young prize. This is a hilarious satire and a strong musical. The third skit
is a spoof on the Dewar tribe by the Dewars themselves. 't portrays how the
Dewar male relatives of a married girl show up at her 'usband's place and

cause such an uproar that they are able to run away with the girl who will gain them a tidy bride price every time they get her 're-married'.[25]

None of these skits had a clear dramatic end. Habib interwove them, added four intermediary scenes and created a 'collage', including some additional characters and suitable songs and dances. The result was a two-hour-long production that could stand as a full-length work. The story was as follows: During Chheri Chhera, a Chhattisgarhi festival during which young people go from house to house asking for grain, two lads, Mangloo and Jhangloo, meet two spirited girls; a flirtation follows, and they settle into a competition in love songs—a form of improvised singing known as Dadaria. Suddenly, the enraged father of one of the girls, Manti, bursts in and puts an end to the rendezvous. Jhangloo frivolously offers himself as a prospective groom; this desire turns earnest when she is later claimed in marriage by an elderly man who tricks her father into accepting him as a bridegroom. Jhangloo and his friends cannot stop the marriage since the old man is wealthy and they have no money. They come up with a plan. Disguised as Dewars, they set off to rescue the girl. Even the Gauri Gaura ritual is woven in—the actress, hearing the beautiful traditional songs, pretends to go into a trance and starts beating the old man. He thinks there's a *devi* or goddess in her who is beating him; she beats him so hard he runs away. The priest who is looking after the ceremony is one of the disguised friends of the young lover—he had already cooked up a false fight to drive off the original priest and take over to help her elope with the hero. But then the old man comes back in time. And the lover re-enters as a Dewar boy, providing the excuse for the 'Dewar Dewarin' comedy. In the end celebratory songs take place, the young lover gets the young girl, and there's a happy ending.[26] 'Thematically, the play sings of youth and its adventurousness. It is studded with rich satirical overtones touching a wide range of contemporary social values.'[27]

Here is a good example of a collaboration between the oral folk and the modernist sensibility of an urban director. The folk actors employ familiar material in their own characteristic style; the language, humour, acting style, pace, is theirs; the director gives it an overall structure and narrative flow, deftly adds connecting scenes and a few characters and brings in additional aesthetic elements in the form of rituals, dances and songs. Contemporary Nacha typically continues all night and has a maximum of 11 or 12 performers—all professionals with four or five actors and the rest singer-dancers, with men playing women's roles—and consists of short comic skits strung together with musical interludes in which film songs are sung and danced to, while the actors change their make-up for the next skit. Habib's production, on the other hand, used over 30 artists, a mixture of Nacha professionals and non-professional singers and dancers as well as women actors, and lasted for a structured two hours.

Special mention must be made of his use of song and dance, which went on to become a characteristic feature of his productions.

Habib had often talked of the rich heritage of songs that were once part of everyday life in Chhattisgarh—songs for every occasion, many of them accompanied by dances. These were part of a ritual life that was still alive in the culture, but practised in the field, the temple and the street; they would hardly ever feature in a Nacha performance. He wove in these 'un-institutionalised cultural expressions of the community'[28]—for example, the Gaura Gauri puja, Sua Karma and Rawat songs and dances. Apart from the desire to showcase fast vanishing oral culture, however, the director had a structural purpose:

> The songs between two scenes serve not only as a kind of 'dissolve' signifying change of sequence and locale but also as a comment upon events. The 'Sua' song at the end of the first scene, for instance, is relevant to the occasion both formally and thematically. The girl is pining for her husband's house—so goes the song. At the same time, the chanting of the song accompanied by the ritualistic 'Sua' dance fades out the previous image and serves as a natural drop curtain, closing one scene and ushering in another.
>
> Likewise, the Karma song danced by two men and an old woman at the end of the scene when the old bridgroom takes a young wife, serves both as a curtain and a comment. It closes the scene and induces the mind to dwell upon lost youth, which it laments in a hearty sarcastic vein. This is as Brecht would have it. Yet it is of the very essence of Indian dramatic tradition.[29]

Another innovation which he finds in keeping with the Indian folk aesthetic tradition is 'the freedom with which time and space are broken in Indian theatre in order to establish a peculiar inner harmony'.[30] This 'has served as an inspiration in the "Gaura Chaura" scene where, against a musical backdrop, three different locations are simultaneously projected'.[31] He

> montaged the Gauri Puja scene upstage with a wayside scene when some actors disguise themselves downstage in view of the audience and a domestic scene between the old man and his young bride centre stage ... the spatial dialectics of the stage experiment are aimed at emphasizing the ambivalence of a dramatic situation.[32]

Gaon Ka Naon Sasural was first staged at the Chhattisgarh Folk Arts Festival, Raipur, on 23 March, along with three traditional Nachas performed on other days. It appeared to get a positive response from the hundreds of villagers and folk artists who attended the festival. This was followed by two ticketed shows at the same venue on 28 and 29 March, which were also well attended. Word had spread, and at the next performance in Koora, a village near Raipur, thousands showed up to watch. At Bhilai and Rajnandgaon too there was a huge audience. The play was performed at the Bhopal Utsav 1973. In Delhi, it ran to packed houses, a big change from the earlier pattern of 50–70 people in the hall.

Habib saw this as a major breakthrough:

We had transcended the language barrier. People came again and again for the wonderful musical quality of the play and for the clarity of expression we had gained by this time, despite the fact that it is a specially difficult play in terms of dialogue, full of improvisation. In '*Devar Devarin*' they speak in words which are not easy to follow, for the Hindi belt. And yet they got a lot out of the slapstick and things became clear in a basic manner. In '*Burwa Biwa*' and '*Chher Chhera*' also, they have enigmatic and puzzling words, yet the *abhinaya* (acting) was clear, the jokes were followed in the main and the comedy came off. I realized that Delhi had accepted us.

This paved the way for *Charandas Chor* in 1974 and for all the other plays that followed. It was a turning point in my career, a breakthrough in introducing Chhattisgarhi as a language for a modern play. It gave me an all-Chhattisgarhi cast. Up to now I was combining them with urban actors. Now only folk actors.[33]

Notes

1. Habib Tanvir, *STQ*, pp. 16–18. The Memorandum of Association and Rules and Regulations for Naya Theatre (a registered society), dated 21 March 1964, mentions Habib Tanvir as director, Moneeka Misra Tanvir as manager, Mariam Bilgrami as secretary, and Kanwar Bahadur Singh, Santosh Chatterjee, Prem Prakash and Sahim-ud-din as members.
2. Habib Tanvir, '"Merey Baad"—Biographical drama about Ghalib', introductory note in play brochure, from the Natya Shodh Sansthan, file no. 208.
3. Ibid.
4. Ibid.
5. Tanvir, *STQ*, p. 19.
6. Ibid., p. 20.
7. Ibid., p. 22.
8. Habib Tanvir, interview with Bindu Batra, 'Folk Theatre—What Is Its Place in India Today?' *Youth Times*, 29 November 1974.

9. Ibid.

10. Ibid.

11. Tanvir, *STQ*, p. 22.

12. Habib Tanvir, 'Theatre Is in the Villages', *Social Scientist*, 2 (10), 1974.

13. Naya Theatre brochure for *Gaon Ka Naon Sasural, Mor Naon Damad*, Triveni Garden Theatre, 11–15 April 1973.

14. Tanvir, 'Theatre Is in the Villages'.

15. Ibid.

16. Ibid.

17. Tanvir, *STQ*, pp. 22–23.

18. The word *lathi* refers to a sturdy staff; here the reference is to the skill of twirling and 'duelling' with this staff.

19. Naya Theatre brochure for *Gaon Ka Naam Sasural, Mor Naon Damad*.

20. Tanvir, 'Theatre Is in the Villages'.

21. Ibid.

22. Ibid.

23. Ibid.

24. Ibid.

25. The Dewars are a nomadic tribe who make a living through singing and dancing, with a rich tradition of balladeers; the women are often kept by well-off men for a period, and each time there is a negotiated price or fee that benefits the girl's family.

26. Tanvir, *STQ*, p. 24.

27. Naya Theatre brochure for *Gaon Ka Naon Sasural, Mor Naon Damad*.

28. Ibid.

29. Ibid.

30. Ibid.

31. Ibid.

32. Ibid.

33. Tanvir, *STQ*, p. 25.

Habib Tanvir with his troupe in 1982.
Photo courtesy Avinash Pasricha

Agra Bazaar (1970). L–R: Brijlal, Thakur Ram, Majeed, Lakshmandas, children (Rajno Bhatt, Nageen), Madanlal, Bulwa Ram, Nazir Meenai. Photo courtesy: Naya Theatre

Habib always claimed that comedy came naturally to the talented Chhattisgarhi actors. A scene from the 1982 production of *Mitti Ki Gadi*. Photo courtesy: Avinash Pasricha

ABOVE: An economy of stage design, *Mitti Ki Gadi* (1982). Photo courtesy: Avinash Pasricha

LEFT: Habib plays Sansthanak in *Mitti Ki Gadi* (1985). Photo courtesy: Naya Theatre

Bulwa Ram and Habib in *Mitti Ki Gadi* (1990s). Photo courtesy: Naya Theatre

The precursor to *Charandas Chor—Gaon Ka Naam Sasural, Mor Naam Damad.*
A production from the 2000s. L–R: Bulwa Ram, Govind Ram. Orchestra in background.
Photo courtesy: Naya Theatre

Habib leads the way in *Gaon Ka Naon Sasural, Mor Naon Damad* (2000).
Photo courtesy: Naya Theatre

Habib in rehearsal for *Charandas Chor*. From the Natya Shodh Sansthan archive.
Photo courtesy: Naya Theatre

Charandas Chor in 1982–1983 with Govind Ram as Chor and Fida Bai as Queen.
Photo Avinash Pasricha, courtesy: Naya Theatre

A Mantri garlanded to the point of blindness. A scene from *Charandas Chor* (1982).
Photo courtesy: Avinash Pasricha

A comic moment—Deepak Tiwari and Habib Tanvir in *Charandas Chor* (n.d.). From the Natya Shodh Sansthan archive, courtesy Naya Theatre

Another production of *Charandas Chor* (n.d.). L–R: Habib, Poonam Bai, Nageen Tanvir, in chorus. Photo courtesy: Naya Theatre

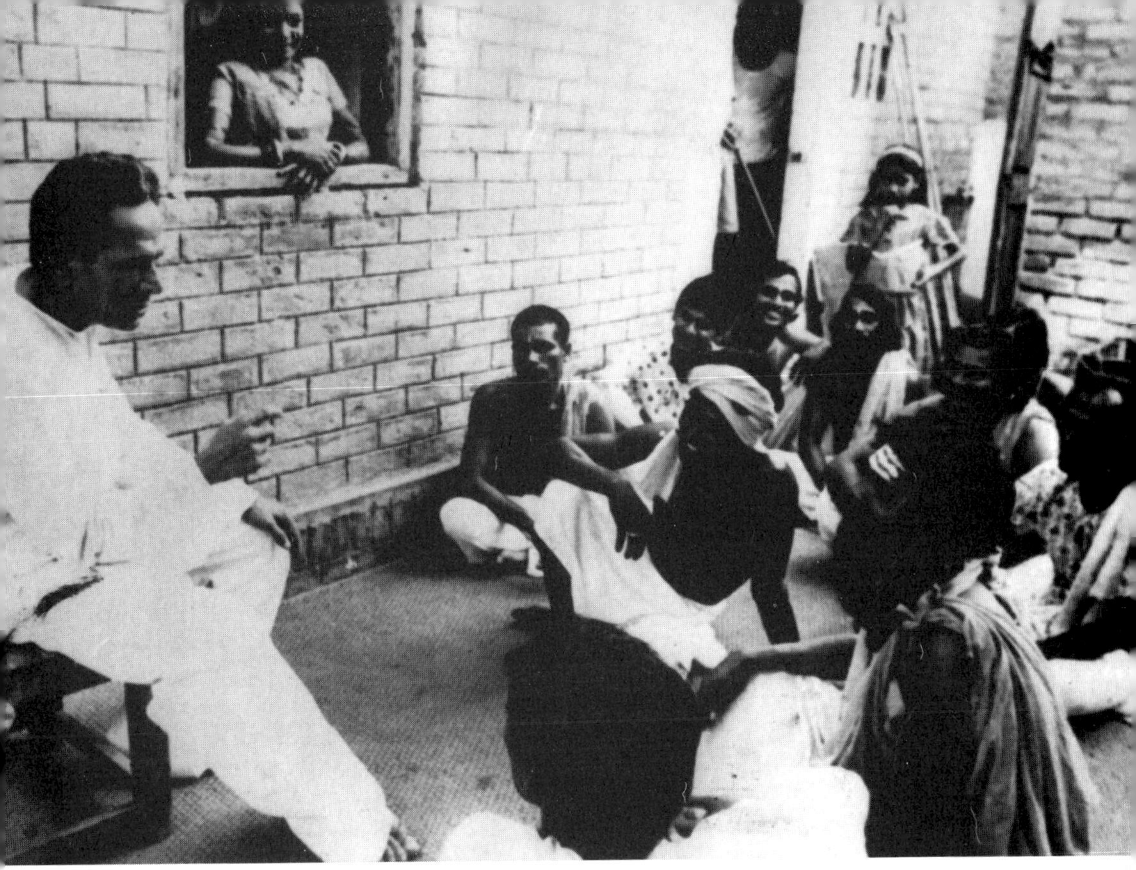

Interacting with the group. From the Natya Shodh Sansthan archive.
Photo Avinash Pasricha, courtesy Naya Theatre

Bahadur Kalarin (1983), a psychological drama. Photo courtesy: Avinash Pasricha

Another scene from the 1983 *Bahadur Kalarin*. Photo courtesy: Avinash Pasricha

Bahadur Kalarin (1983): a dance interlude. Photo courtesy: Avinash Pasricha

A tense moment from *Bahadur Kalarin* (1980s). L–R: Bulwa Ram, Chait Ram, Fida Bai, Govind Ram. Photo courtesy: Naya Theatre

Bahadur Kalarin at the London Lyric Theatre (1983), with Habib and Fida Bai.
Photo courtesy: Naya Theatre

Politics of the state and tribals—*Hirma Ki Amar Kahani* (n.d.). From the Natya Shodh Sansthan archive, courtesy Naya Theatre

A dynamic moment from *Hirma Ki Amar Kahani* (1985). L–R: Bulwa Ram, Fida Bai.
Policemen Anil Sharma, Yog Misra, Rajesh Gondwale, Pradeep Barua, with Bastar tribals.
Photo Avinash Pasricha, courtesy Naya Theatre

Hirma Ki Amar Kahani (1985). L–R: Deepak Tiwari, Fida Bai, Bulwa Ram, Poonam Bai.
Photo Avinash Pasricha, courtesy Naya Theatre

Simple visual design—a production of *Hirma Ki Amar Kahani* with Bulwa Ram, Fida Bai, tribal girls. Photo courtesy: Naya Theatre.

A troupe of tribal dancers in *Hirma Ki Amar Kahani* (1990). Photo Gurinder Osan, courtesy Naya Theatre

A scene from *Sajapur Ki Shantibai*, which has Habib Tanvir
alongside two of his best woman actors, Fidabai and Malabai.
From the Natya Shodh Sansthan archive, courtesy Naya Theatre

A scene from *Mudrarakshasa* (1997) with Udai Ram, Manoj Nair. Photo courtesy: Naya Theatre

Mudrarakshasa. L–R: Chait Ram, Rajiv Yadav, Deepak Tiwari, Sanjay Sarkar, Rahul Shankalya (Sainik). Photo courtesy: Naya Theatre

Dekh Rahe Hain Nain (1992) with Bulwa Ram, Ramcharan. Photo courtesy: Naya Theatre

Dekh Rahe Hain Nain with Deepak Tiwari, Habib. Photo courtesy: Naya Theatre

Post the Bhopal gas tragedy—or crime—*Zehreeli Hawa* (2003).
L–R: Manoj Nair, Chaiti Ghosh, Agesh Nag, Usman,
Chait Ram, Udai Ram, Rana, Abhisar Bose.
Photo courtesy: Naya Theatre

An emotional moment from *Jis Lahore Nahin Vekhya Voh Jammya Hi Nahin* (2004).
L–R: Agesh Nag, Anup Pande, Balendra Singh, Rana, Shyama. Photo courtesy: Naya Theatre

Another tense moment from *Jis Lahore Nahin Vekhya Voh Jammya Hi Nahin* (2004).
L–R: Ramchandra Singh, Hanvir Tanvir, Anup Pande, Balendra Singh (Dadi), Rajiv Yadav.
Photo courtesy: Naya Theatre

ABOVE: The folk satire that offended
the religious right—*Ponga Pandit
in Berlin* (2006) with
Manharan and Udai Ram.
Photo courtesy: Naya Theatre

LEFT: Ramchandra Singh with the child
Parul Singh in *Raj-Rakt* (2006).
Photo courtesy: Naya Theatre

A Community on stage—*Agra Bazaar*. From the Natya Shodh Sansthan archive. Photo courtesy: Naya Theatre

CHARANDAS CHOR

A 1975 production of *Charandas Chor* with Madan Lal as Chor
and Fida Bai as Queen. Photo courtesy Naya Theatre

The next major theatrical milestone in Habib's artistic trajectory is *Charandas Chor* (1974–1975). This is by far his most popular and well-known play, as well as the most critically acclaimed of his oeuvre. It bears all the characteristic features of his mature theatre form at its best.

The story of the play is based on a Rajasthani folk tale. Charandas is a cheeky thief (*chor*) and confident trickster with a kind heart—he can't bring himself to rob the helpless or the poor, but runs rings round policemen, greedy landlords and their strongmen and other such pillars of the establishment. When his guru demands that he give up his biggest vice, thieving, he

offers to make four other pledges instead—that he will never lead a procession on elephant back, that he will never eat off a golden platter, that he will
never marry a queen and that he will never accept the throne of a kingdom.
Unimpressed, his guru makes him swear a fourth vow—never to tell a lie.
Charandas does so, and manages to continue thieving successfully without
breaking his word. By a twist of fate, he finds himself in a situation where
he is confronted with everything he has forsworn, but still will not break his
word. Finally, his refusal to tell a lie in defiance of a royal command leads
to his being put to death.

Habib's *Charandas Chor* was the outcome of a workshop, just as *Gaon Ka
Naon Sasural* was. The production had a long gestation—it went through
several phases before finding its final form in 1975.

To begin with, Habib heard the story of the truthful thief from Vijaydan
Detha, the eminent writer and folklorist who recounted this Rajasthani folk
tale to him in 1973.[1] Later that year, he tried using it during the Khayal
workshop in Rajasthan, but, as he says, 'the story failed.... I realized they
were lacking in actors ... their whole strength lay in music. Wonderful
singers. And their form was opera—the little scenes that they enacted had
feeble acting. So I abandoned the thief-story'.[2] The story stayed with him,
however, and at the end of 1974, during a month-long workshop in Bhilai,
he decided to use it again, this time with greater success.

The Bhilai workshop was attended by several Chhattisgarhi groups.
During the course of the workshop, he worked on six skits of about 45
minutes or an hour in length: 'We got a very good response from the local
village audiences. They were their own plays—I just did some work on
them, injected some elements.'[3] In the last four days of the workshop, he
introduced the thief story—'I just tried it out ... with a very good actor
called Ram Lal who did the chor.'[4]

At the end of the workshop there was a show on the open-air stage of the
maidan (open ground) in Bhilai. As it happens, it was a Satnami occasion.
Habib explains about this sect:

> There are lakhs of Satnamis in this country and they've had quite a his-
> tory from Aurangzeb's time, quite militant. Every year they gather in Guru
> Ghasidas's place near Raipur, thousands, a great mela. They sing and dance.
> Like most untouchables they are given a separate *muhalla* or area, not in the
> village. In that *muhalla* they're given a *chauraha* (crossroads), a *chowk*. In that
> *chowk* they have a white flag, the Satnami flag, which is kept on a pedestal.
> There is some little ritual every day. Suddenly, when I was showing the skits
> on the open stage and the Satnamis were coming up on the stage again and

again, I was inspired by them. Towards six o' clock, I said, we have a play which is still…not quite ready and I'd normally never dream of showing it, but considering that this is a Satnami occasion and there're thousands of people sitting here and the play has something to do with Truth, which is the motto of Satnamis, I would like to dare to show it, knowing that you'll accept it with all its faults. And don't mind if I come in and change their positions etc.[5]

So he presented the improvisation, about 40 minutes long, which was at the time called *Chor Chor*. Encouraged by the positive response, he continued to evolve it as a production.

Habib wove the Satnamis into the piece. Referring to a Satnami book he had with him, he improvised by singing and asking them to repeat. Then he brought in the *panthi* dance party and choreographed them. '"Truth is god, god is truth" is their motto (*satya hi ishwar hai, ishwar satya*). And this is a play about truthfulness and truth. It blended well together.'[6]

At first the play was called *Amardas*, but Amardas happened to be one of the gurus of the Satnamis, and they protested at it being named after their guru. He tried another name but that also turned out to be a guru. Finally, *Charandas* was decided upon, and Charandas the *chor* remained.

At this stage, Shyam Benegal, the filmmaker, who was present with his crew, saw the improvisation and decided to film *Charandas* and turn it into a film for the Children's Film Society.[7] It is interesting to hear Habib talk of how he groped his way through various suggestions and inputs to his own instinctive realisation of what would best suit his play:

[Benegal] wanted a foil for the chor…. I trusted his good sense as a cinema man … and when he said children wouldn't take to a tragedy, I tried it on my daughter and she didn't like the story to end in the chor's death. So I produced a scene where Chitragupta, the *munshi* (bookkeeper) of Yama, Lord of Death, comes and Charandas steals his name from the register, and when he looks for his name he says it's not there. It's gone. He puts it in his mouth. He swallows it … there's great consternation because his name isn't there in the logbook, and the man is dead. Then Yama comes on his buffalo and gets down to examine it and Charandas rides the buffalo and runs away, stealing the buffalo, and what you see on the horizon in the evening is Charandas running and the havaldar chasing him. That's the end of the film. So he continues to steal even up there in heaven. Now this, plus a foil needed … Madan Lal became the foil. He was dishonest, would keep lying. This is the screenplay I had written. There was a court case and I played the judge. All this was in my own screenplay, my play ruined but I not knowing any better, loaded with these things, a foil, a donkey—I got four people to become a donkey—a court scene, all hilarious, enjoyed thoroughly by my wife Moneeka and some friends, and I then suddenly discovering that this is not my form. I don't need a foil, an actor can come on stage and simply declare that I'm a thief, my name is Charandas, that's good enough for the stage. So I cut the foil out. I made Madan Lal the actor; I cut out the judge scene, though I was acting in it and it was very funny and I enjoyed it. I cut out the posthumous scene, much to the dislike of Moneeka and others who said no, no, it's nice. I said, yes, but I will stick to the story.

Actually I didn't even stick to the story. Vijaydan Detha, who related the folktale, is also angry. His chor gets killed, but that's not the end. The queen takes the guru as her consort, because, in the story as written by Detha, in order to save face she proposes to the guru and the guru, who is very worldly, becomes her consort....Vijaydan's argument is valid enough, that if you're showing present-day conditions, evil continues, hypocrisy continues, the raj must continue with all its corruption, nepotism, everything; your story is romantic. He may be right there, but I wanted a cruel end. I wanted to say something different.[8]

So he trimmed his play of what he considered extraneous elements and ended with the unexpected twist of the *chor*'s death—the death of a comic trickster transformed into a tragic hero. Coming as it does on the heels of spirited slapstick comedy, the dramatic impact is powerful. 'People were stunned. Some didn't believe that he was dead, because I always used to get the actor to become very stiff. They thought it's a comedy and there'll be some trick and he'll come back.'[9] In fact, Habib recalls the audience reaction after the first auditorium show:

The very first night it was a stunning experience, in Kamani auditorium. He died. Total silence. Strange silence. People got up, thinking, when will the next line come? Disturbed. The restive, urban, Delhi audience was moved. And then, before going out, they stopped, turned and then stood for several minutes ... watching from the door, uncomfortably.[10]

Why did Habib insist on the *chor* sacrificing himself for Truth? He wanted to show how a common man can take the heroic stance of holding unswervingly to his word, his commitment to Truth—like Socrates, Jesus Christ, Gandhi—and in the end give up his life rather than betray his vow, although he may appear far from a heroic figure.

Here is a common man—and that's why he must remain a common man—an unheroic, simple man who gets caught up in his vows and though he fears death, can't help it and dies. And the establishment cannot brook this. So for me the tragedy in the classical sense was perfect because tragedy has to be inevitable. There is an inevitability to his death because he didn't go the convenient way of saying yes to the queen, which would be a way out. That way was barred, it was not an option. The queen is not simply a tyrant, but a politician. There is no way she can let him go free, because she entreats him not to tell anyone, and he says, but I must tell the truth; and as soon as she knows that the *praja*, the populace, will get to know, she fears for her position. As we have seen throughout history, such people are always eliminated. So the inevitability of it was perfect.[11]

This, then, was a political statement: the common man is inevitably crushed for daring to challenge, to confront, to refuse, the powers that be, the state. It was also good theatre:

[T]his is, in the classical sense, a perfect tragedy. It makes you laugh till the last moment and suddenly you're silent. You're in the presence of death.... Is it a tragedy? Yes. Is it a comedy? Yes. Is it a comedy? No. Is it a tragedy? No. I don't know what it is. It's difficult to put it in a category. And I think that's the secret of the success of the play. To this day I'm convinced that the death is the secret of its success.[12]

The play does not end with the death of Charandas, however. There is 'the whole ritual of the deification of the chor, the last song' which, Habib says, is a lesson learnt from Shakespeare, 'to always end with an anti-climax'.[13] It allows the audience to digest the unexpectedly violent ending—a shard of harsh reality piercing the feel-good aura that has engulfed them till that point, with the apparently invincible *chor* able to trick his way out of every dangerous situation. As the solemn ritual of deification takes place on stage, we see how a common man can become a legend, a saint or a folk hero, immortalised in song and myth; we see him take root in the hearts of the people.

Habib talks of how not just the narrative, but the formal elements also evolved till they achieved their final staged form:

I'd come to a very simple kind of stage set ... and learnt to have the stage set functional, very economical so that we remain mobile, for artistic as well as economical reasons. The architecture, set design, were also affected by the kind of awareness I gained in regard to the importance of the actor related to space and the relation of time to space and to actor and to action. All these things, I think, gave me very simple forms, like a rectangular platform with just one tree, to which I came after a few shows. In the beginning there was something like a curtain, with a temple or a queen's palace painted, on the platform—not the entire platform, just a little of it—and rolled up and down by an actor.... But I thought that was fussy, so I removed it during the shows and came to two bamboos and a little foliage piece, the branch of a tree connecting them, and through that people used to pass. Then I got rid of even that, keeping only one bamboo, one branch.[14]

Theatre scholar Javed Malick, in his introduction to the English translation of the play, says:

The design is austere in its simplicity but highly effective in functional terms. All that it requires is a stage and, mounted on that stage, a rectangular platform which is 9 inches high, 6 feet wide and 12 feet long, with just foliage or a leafy branch of a tree behind it.[15]

This spare stage design allows for tremendous flexibility; at times, the action takes place forestage; at others, groups of actors sit on the platform (as in the *guru dakshina*[16] scene or the landlord scene with the sacks of hoarded grain). The open space suits the folk actor, with his dexterity and physical agility, and allows for the introduction of choreographed group dances. Change of locale is indicated verbally or through the movement of the actors rather than through any re-ordering of the set or stage design. Props are kept to the bare minimum, just those items that are actually used as part of the action—sacks of grain, the thief's bundle, the idol in the temple.

This pared down, simple, flexible stage design is one of the features that makes this production such a perfect example of Habib's mature theatre and Naya Theatre's signature style. Let us study the other aspects one by one.[17]

First, the cast of Chhattisgarhi actors. By the time he mounted *Charandas Chor*, Habib had realised how to get the best out of his Chhattisgarhi cast. It was not an easy realisation and took him several years to work it out. After he invited the initial six actors to join his troupe in 1958, he found that all the acting power, skill and impact of which he knew them to be capable were missing from their work on stage in his plays.

I'd pull my hair and fret and fume, stamp, my foot and say, Thakur Ram, what the hell, I've seen you in the village and I know your strength as an actor; what is happening? Why can't you simply follow my instructions and give me that same strength? He'd also not know. He'd shout back and say, it's not your fault, it's my fault, my fault, my fault! So these kinds of scenes would be created without any one of us knowing what the fault was.[18]

Slowly Habib began to realise that the problem lay in the fact that he was trying to impose his Westernised training on the village actors:

[M]ove diagonally, stand, speak, take this position, take that position. I had to unlearn it all. I saw that they couldn't even tell right from left on the stage and had no line sense.[19]

As he observed the Nacha, he saw the basic difference between the way these actors were trained to perform and the demands he was making on them:

[W]hat do I see? A big platform and they're performing; thousands of people or hundreds of people on a small platform or no platform, at the same level—still performing; and nothing was lost. Or a stage, and some who didn't get a place … coming and sitting on the stage with the orchestra and the actors…. It didn't matter…. It didn't interfere … the audience was sometimes on three sides, sometimes on all four sides. Entry through the crowd, in the middle somewhere a performance, actors all around, invariably three sides, and wherever the response went, like a cow going through the audience, the actors would turn to that. Or a joke improvised, connected with some incident in the village which they'd come to know of, and a spoof or a line connected with it, and a response from a section, then they'd turn to that section. So I realized that those who were for years responding to an audience like this could never try to unlearn all this and rigidly follow the rules of movement and that was one reason why Thakur Ram, a great actor, wasn't able to be natural.[20]

Habib also realised that these actors were hamstrung by having to speak in a language not their own:

Another reason was the *matrubhasha*—he wasn't speaking in his mother tongue, so it jarred on my ears, because he was speaking bad Hindi and not Chhattisgarhi, in which he was fluent, which was so sweet. This realization took me years—naive of me, but still it took me years. Once I realized it I used Chhattisgarhi and I improvised, allowed them the freedom and then came pouncing down upon them to crystallize the movement—there you stay. And they began to learn. That quite simply was the method I learnt.[21]

Habib was working with actors who were skilled but not literate. They may not be able to read scripts or deliver lines by rote in an unfamiliar language, but when it came to improvising in their own tongue, they were past masters. Once he adapted to the oral performance culture to which they belonged and learnt how to work with it, he found his form—as in *Charandas Chor*. Asked about the actors' contribution to the evolution of the final production, Habib said:

> The actor's contribution in shaping the production was rich. It was mainly through improvisations. A scene like the 'Guru Dakshina', one of the temple scenes, is almost entirely based on improvisation. Improvisation has become quite my style of direction now. Not everything comes from the director, or from the actor, but a lot of it comes from this process of improvisation, interpretation of different imaginations and consciousnesses. In the process there is a lot of muck, a lot of repetitiveness, but also lots of gems. You clutch on to the gems and cut out the rest. Then I rush to my desk to write it all down. But some scenes are written down in bold outline from the start. For example, in *Charandas Chor* most of the scenes after the intermission, like the ones set in the queen's palace, are formally written. When there are more than two or three actors on stage, improvisation makes it easier to block. But I did not need improvation in these scenes, for by that time the play had taken root and I had an outline. I also had a structure worked out.[22]

In this play in particular, the slapstick comedy, with its deft timing and physical agility, its swift give-and-take of dialogue, works remarkably well. Habib explains that it took time and effort before he had a breakthrough:

> I was doing things in Chhattisgarhi during 1970–73. But I didn't have a breakthrough until this time because I suddenly got the language of the body through improvisations before *Charandas Chor* and through other means at my disposal—my vocabulary of the visual language of the Chhattisgarhi players had increased and so had my confidence in using it. It was simply that…. Suddenly we broke all barriers and people who'd never come to see Chhattisgarhi plays during those three years started pouring in.[23]

Another characteristic Habib Tanvir feature that this play employs with powerful effect is the insertion of ritual in the dramatic action. The play opens with a ritual dance by a traditional *panthi* troupe belonging to the Satnami sect; and it ends with the solemn deification ceremony at the end, complete with a lighted lamp, the breaking of a coconut and the showering of flower petals, as the Satnamis file past their white flag, singing their anthem of Truth. A third point for a ritual is the scene in the temple, halfway through the play, when a hymn is sung on stage, a traditional devotional song based on the *Ramayana*. About the use of ritual in his plays, Habib has this to say:

> I find in this drama in an embryonic form and I'm presenting it … as good theatre which fascinates you. Its magic is felt. I visualize the beginnings of drama in India like this, a semblance of the kind of hymns chanted around the fire in Vedic times; and this is dramatic because religion *is* dramatic.[24]

We will take this up in more detail later in Chapter 11, which looks at his use of ritual, music and dance.

Live music and the presence of songs and dances is another typical feature that Habib perfected the use of. His love affair with Chhattisgarhi music, begun in his childhood, grew stronger over the years. He found great value in the rich heritage of songs that were part of local culture and found ways of incorporating them into his plays. He also created fresh music for his plays. In *Charandas Chor*, the lyrics for the songs were written by Swaran Kumar Sahu and Ganga Ram Sakhet, folk poets, and most of them were set to traditional Chhattisgarhi melodies, except for the closing song, which was a tune composed by Habib. Some of the songs use choruses, chants or phrases which come from traditional folk material, juxtaposed with words written specially for this play.

As Javed Malick rightly points out, the songs, 'in a style reminiscent of Brecht' are used 'to comment on an action and to elucidate and underline its larger moral and social significance. In some cases they reflect a certain complexity of articulation and consciousness which is obviously Tanvir's contribution'.[25] Some songs have a tongue-in-cheek comment or ironic perspective to contribute, such as 'Nothing will work for you till you/Give the guru his due' on the subject of venial gurus or 'There are so many rogues about, who do not look like thieves/Impressive turbans on their heads, softly shod their feet,' referring to rich and powerful people whose ill-gotten gains come from robbing others. Songs also point to a conceptual development in the narrative—for example, 'Charandas is not a thief, not a thief, no way' is sung at the point in the plot when he transforms from simple thief to people's hero by distributing the grain he has stolen from the corrupt landlord to the starving villagers. In Act Two, the *panthi* singers sing, 'Oh Charandas don't try to rob Death of its due', thereby planting the thought of death in the audience's mind and subliminally preparing them for his assassination at the end of the play.

Apart from this, the live music and singing add an aural texture to the performance just as the rituals add a visual richness, enhancing the overall dramatic and theatrical experience; they underline the inclusion of an oral tradition that is increasingly marginalised in contemporary performance. These features are to continue to remain unique to the productions of Habib and Naya Theatre.

For all its hilarity and slapstick tomfoolery, *Charandas Chor* makes some sharp political comments.[26] The figure of the honest thief who makes no bones about his profession is held up in pointed contrast to the hypocrisy of those who profess to serve the people but who are slyly exploitative—the policeman, the guru, the priest, the government official (*munim*). Charandas is shown systematically exposing the greed and corruption of all the pillars of conventional society—the forces of law and order, the landlord-moneylender, organised religion, the ruler and her henchmen. He expresses his solidarity with the poor and a strong sense of social justice through his actions, such as sharing *sattu* (gram flour) with the peasant and redistributing the sacks of grain amongst the villagers. He is never subservient and refuses to be cowed by threats from bullying landlords or irate queens. He is clever and quick-witted, a true folk hero in the tradition of the subaltern trickster figure who outwits his social superiors.

Another strong political comment that runs through the play is the undermining of religious figures and practices. The guru's *ashram* is a den of gamblers, drunkards and addicts; the guru himself is more interested in his *dakshina* than in the well-being of his disciples. In the temple scene, even as devotees intone a hymn, Charandas and the policeman play an elaborate game of cat-and-mouse, undercutting the solemnity of the atmosphere with their antics. The priest is quite content to receive stolen loot as long as it enriches his temple. Even the deification process with which the play ends 'shows us the actual process through which a very ordinary man attains sainthood in the eyes of the common people and we recognize that the process is entirely this-worldly. In other words, we see the secular and historical stuff that saints are made of'.[27]

In a final political statement, the play celebrates the folk hero with his utopian ideals of an equitable social system and the people's 'desire for truth and justice'.[28] This, to my mind, is what lifts the play from being just another enjoyable comedy to the status of a modern classic.

Notes

1. Vijaydan Detha (b.1926) is a writer and expert on Rajasthani folklore.
2. Habib Tanvir, *STQ*, p. 25.

3. Ibid.
4. Ibid.
5. Ibid., p. 26.
6. Ibid.
7. *Charandas Chor* (1975/156 mins/Hindi), directed by Shyam Benegal, produced by Children's Film Society of India, starring Smita Patil, Lalu Ram, Madan Lal, Sadhu Meher, Habib Tanvir, Sunder and others.
8. Tanvir, *STQ*, p. 27.
9. Ibid.
10. Ibid., p. 28.
11. Ibid., pp. 27–28.
12. Ibid., p. 28.
13. Ibid.
14. Ibid., p. 29.
15. Javed Malick's 'Introduction' to Habib Tanvir, *Charandas Chor* (Kolkata: Seagull Books, 2004), p. 10.
16. According to the Indian tradition, this is an obligatory gift or a fee due to the teacher.
17. For an extended discussion on *Charandas Chor* and other aspects of his theatre, see Habib Tanvir, 'In Conversation with Javed Malick' in Neeraj Malik and Javed Malick (eds), *Habib Tanvir: Reflections and Reminiscences* (Delhi: SAHMAT, 2010), pp. 103–122.
18. Tanvir, *STQ*, p. 21.
19. Ibid.
20. Ibid.
21. Ibid., pp. 21–22.
22. Habib Tanvir, 'In Conversation with Javed Malick', p. 114.
23. Tanvir, *STQ*, pp. 28–29.
24. Ibid., p. 22.
25. Javed Malick's 'Introduction' to Habib Tanvir, *Charandas Chor* p. 11.
26. For an insightful political analysis of the play, see Javed Malick's 'Introduction' to Habib Tanvir, *Charandas Chor* pp. 1–17.
27. Javed Malick's 'Introduction' to Habib Tanvir, *Charandas Chor* p. 15.
28. Ibid.

CHAPTER EIGHT

WORKING WITH THE CHHATTISGARHIS

Bastar tribals dance in *Hirma Ki Amar Kahani* (1985).
Photo Avinash Pasricha, courtesy Naya Theatre

With *Charandas Chor*, as Habib has said often, he achieved his mature form.

> My yatra is from *Agra Bazaar* to *Mitti ki Gadi* to *Gaon ka Naam Sasural*, which paved the way for *Charandas Chor*, which was such a big hit and turned into a classic, almost. And then followed many other plays, but there was no new ground broken, except, you might say, in terms of content.[1]

Hereafter, we see him presenting a wide range of material (from Indian and international classics to social and political message plays), but the basic principles of his theatre remain in place: Naya Theatre productions would typically feature Chhattisgarhi actors performing in their mother tongue, live music and songs, dances and rituals, and minimal stage and lighting design and props.

What remains central to his work from now on is the presence of Chhattisgarhi actors. Since this is a defining factor of Habib's theatre, let us pause to take a closer look at the relationship between the Chhattisgarh actors, and Habib Tanvir and Naya Theatre.

Habib's attitude towards his troupe has been described as 'paternalistic' by some, including theatre scholar Erin Mee in her study of the 'theatre of roots' in India. She finds in his conversation about the actors in his company a 'definite paternalism'. 'He speaks of them as badly behaved, badly educated children, of whom he is nonetheless fond,' she states.[2] Let us see how justified such a charge is.

We have already read about his first meeting with the actors who were to form his core troupe—Bulwa Ram, Babu Das, Thakur Ram, Madan Lal, Lalu Ram and Jagmohan.[3] Fida Bai, who was to be his mainstay as leading lady for many years, was invited to join the troupe after the Nacha workshop in Raipur.

> I saw her just before the workshop in a Nacha, in the village, singing and dancing. A boy in the audience whistled and accosted her, making a pass. And from the stage, on the microphone, she abused him and stamped her foot, saying that I'll crush you like this, and he subsided. And I decided then, that's the girl who can act.[4]

His instinct was correct, although the others told him that she was just a singer-dancer with no previous acting experience. Under his direction, she evolved into a powerful actress.

Other actors who joined his troupe included Brij Lal whom he had known as a child. Of his troupe he says:

> Most of them were female impersonators. Thakur Ram and Madan Lal were the only male actors. Otherwise Bhulwa Ram had never acted in a male role except in my theatre, Brij Lal always in women's roles, Devi Lal, who played the harmonium, all played female roles. So it became a professional theatre by 1973 and we haven't looked back.[5]

These actors were mostly associated with Nacha, as musicians, singers, dancers, female impersonators, 'jokers' or comic actors. Most of them could not read or write though they had the efficient memorisation skills developed by an oral culture. They were rural people: 'Quite a few of the actors are connected with the land. Others have other work—cycle repair shop, pan shop, dhobi shop.'[6]

The life experiences and socialisation of an urbane, intellectual, liberal poet-artist and the underprivileged, struggling, hard-bitten village performer who finds it difficult to trust an outsider could not have been more different, nor did they make for easy collaboration. Value systems were very different, and clashes typically arose over issues of discipline, keeping one's word and what Habib saw as betrayal and lies. Yet there was a recognition on both sides that this relationship was worth working at, and over the years, each grew to understand the other better.

Habib grappled with this cultural and social difference during the group's interaction with the outside world as well:

> The Naya Theatre artists generally belong to a very low social level. They come from scheduled castes and tribes. The girls are drawn from the nomadic Dewar tribe, who traditionally must live in improvised tents outside the village. There is a fire in them which comes from their class basis. And due to this we have suffered. They are never treated as equals in [an] urban milieu, except in the enlightened circles of artists.[7]

However, travelling abroad was an eye-opener: the group was treated with a courtesy and respect that led to its becoming

> very conscious of its rights as it was exposed to a very different way of thinking.... They come back and face their reality here in India and feel the need for change.... I think it will mean that stronger ideas and views will be expressed when we work out the contents of our productions.[8]

Habib would often repeat that he never ran after folk forms, only after folk actors. It may have been said humorously, but it was nothing less than the truth—he did have to keep running after the folk actors. In fact, the relationship was quite a volatile, and often stormy, one. He himself calls it his 'long courtship of the Chhattisgarhi folk player'.[9]

> Of course they let me down too, these actors, saying that we want to go off for a short while, and producing some false telegram or something—they never came back ... making me very angry ... and I went pursuing them, again and again, and brought them back, till I came to the conclusion that

it must be an open door policy, that if they wanted to go, I'd allow them. They always wanted to come back sooner or later and I always took them back, without acrimony.[10]

For the actors, there were the compulsions of the agricultural seasonal cycle—hands were needed in the fields, to plough, seed and harvest; major festivals like Holi and Diwali demanded their presence in the family, as did births, weddings and deaths. Nor did theatre generate enough of an income to become the sole source of subsistence—the ties with traditional livelihood and the rural economy had to be kept up. At times, there was the ambition to try something of one's own, to start a performing troupe or join one, but these impulses seldom lasted long. Most found themselves returning to Naya Theatre.

Naya Theatre actors were 'on a regular salary,'[11] small amounts which grew over the years as government subsidies were raised, although they always remained woefully inadequate in terms of livelihood.[12] However, there was 'no written agreement, nothing'[13]. It was all a question of relationships. Ramcharan analyses the bond between the actors and Habib:

> Habib Saab ... scares me. Though of course, he does joke around a lot.... No matter how much I'm scolded or berated.... I spring back, like a tree in a gale. It doesn't bother me. Staying on with him has allowed me to see the world—if I hadn't been able to take the scolding and had left, I wouldn't have travelled the world.... I have benefited, as a family man, even in times of famine I have managed to raise my children on my earnings from here ... and I have thought to myself that a man works to support his own family, but Habib Saab, through the power of his intellect and his learning, is helping support the families of his entire troupe.... And it's only right that a man like that should be hard, stand firm, to keep things going.... So yes, he scares me even today, I shake at the sight of him, but it's good. The only reason he gets angry with us is over work. The rest of the time he speaks affectionately, jokes with us ... in all these years I've been with him, 28–29 years, he's liked our art, our skill, and we've liked him, we've been good for him, that's why we've managed to stay together so long.... If he hadn't liked us, we'd have been off home in five days, and if we hadn't liked him we'd have left in two. So if we've been together 28 years, we must be good for him and he must be good for us.[14]

Amardas, who joined Naya Theatre in 1971, explains why, in his opinion, the troupe has stayed together: 'I think the reason is that we get on very well, we have a good interaction ... he scolds us, but it doesn't bother us a bit. We know the bonds of affection are strong. That's why, in my opinion, the group is still going strong.'[15]

Habib recalls:

> As a matter of fact when Peter Brook came, he wondered how I have had them for so long, with no trace of staleness or being tired…there's one credit that I accept unabashedly, that I have held a group for so long…because it is a credit…You've no idea how difficult it is to live with them and work with them. The tantrums, the scenes, the *gaalis* (abuses), I can't even go on record saying what else.[16]

Fida Bai, for one, Dewar by birth, has a storm of stories around her worthy of any diva. Habib had been forewarned: 'I had been warned by the others that she was a difficult person, trouble of all kinds.'[17] It is worth getting the Fida Bai tales in Habib's inimitable storytelling style:

> Now … we had invited trouble when we asked Fida bai to join us. She came to live with us and after a day or two came her husband, Rohit, and her mother-in-law, and they brought a lot of trouble. The mother-in-law was a very energetic old woman, very quarrelsome with a big voice, noisy, making a racket all the time. So was the husband, and they began to make trouble by fighting over every scene. And Fida herself objected to being betrothed to Thakuram as an actress in a scene, because of the authenticity of the ritual. That was, for her, as good as getting married to Thakuram and Thakuram himself claimed that now he was as good as married to her. She was a very attractive girl. And he found an excuse to declare that he had a right over her. I tried to explain that this is make believe, this is drama and it has nothing to do with life and reality, that they should rehearse and do the play. But the mother-in-law wouldn't have it, Fida herself wouldn't have it, and Thakuram loved it, for his own reasons! This was not the end of the trouble.[18]

They set off for a festival in Raipur. Habib was in the Rajya Sabha at the time. The next show was in Bhopal, but Fida didn't arrive in time to take the train with the rest of the troupe. Habib now had a crisis on his hands—an absconding leading lady. A minister associated with the tour who was from Rajnandgaon and wise in the ways of the Dewars, phoned the deputy general of police of the area and ordered him to go to Fida's house and investigate. There, the mother-in-law denied all knowledge of the missing Fida and sent them off on a wild goose chase. Realising they had been duped, they returned, demanding that Fida be handed over. They insisted that she was being kept locked up there, that they could hear a woman weeping. And sure enough, they found her locked into a small room and forcibly set her free. She was sent, accompanied by her uncle and a young boy from the troupe, to Bhopal, and reached just an hour before the show.[19]

Later, she decided that she wanted a divorce.

It's a very long-drawn-out process in their tradition … but she was determined, and … nothing can be more determined than a Devarin determined. She collected the whole village and she had to pay back the bride price or something; she arranged all that from the money-lender, and she did it. And then rejoined Naya Theatre, as a free woman. She lived on with us and there were many moments of trouble.[20]

However, everything was worth it when she took the stage:

[W]hat an actress!…. She really enjoyed it. The roles come to her so naturally—you explain just a little, and she'd do it softly, subtly, dynamically, loudly and also lyrically. In *Good Woman*, the impersonation of the man came so naturally, and so gracefully, it was amazing, and in *Kalarin* her maturity was really immaculate as an actress. I think that's the best role she's ever done in her life, a tragedy in which she plays the role from a teenager up to a mature woman.[21]

Bulwa Ram, interviewed after 25 years with Naya Theatre, reiterated the often stormy relationship between Habib and the actors: 'If Sahib gets excited and curses us, we also curse him back, and then he starts laughing.'[22] Govindram said:

I've been close to him, and he has seen us from close. We're together about 300 days a year—like a family—there are bound to be disagreements, distances, people leave, rejoin—but like a son or daughter would. It's not enmity. Even I've left in a huff, thinking I'll never come back, but somehow I can't manage to stay away.[23]

Habib was 'Babaji' or 'Saab' to his actors; Moneeka was simply 'Ma ji'. Habib, talking of losing his temper with the actors, said, 'I feel angered like a father, she feels angered like a mother.'[24] Moneeka was the one they went to with their domestic and emotional problems; she was the mediator between them and Habib, who they considered their guru.

Habib's towering temper, the scoldings the actors faced in the course of their work, the relentless, exhausting repetition of rehearsal until the perfectionist in him was satisfied, the long hours—often without a meal—as he went over and over a movement or sequence, are testified to by several of the actors in their interviews.[25] Habituated to the easy-going Nacha, where there was no director and the actors themselves improvised at will and pretty much did as they pleased, this tough, demanding discipline took some getting used to. The old-timers say that many newcomers, unable to take the pace, left the group.[26] However, if they were being worked hard, Habib was working himself equally hard. If they hadn't eaten in hours, neither had he. His daughter Nageen, who is part of the troupe, a trained singer who performs regularly in Naya Theatre productions and whose earliest memories include playing and singing with the Chhattisgarhis, recalls her father's fits of rage, especially when he felt betrayed or lied to by his actors, which happened frequently; at times, Moneeka had to intervene to calm him down. Nageen says that his hot temper led them to nickname him *baghwa*, which means 'lion' in their language; and yet 'there were times when they joked together and drank together' too.[27] Bhulwa comments, 'Tanvir Sahib has become stricter over the years. It seems as if he is becoming more angry because the *samasyas* (problems) ... are so much more today than they were when we started off.'[28] Govindram says:

> He is tough and hard on us. We are used to him now, we know that if he scolds us, it's to do with our work, so we don't let it affect us. We try and understand what we're being scolded for, what we've done wrong. Only those actors who figure this out are able to succeed with him.... And it's not that he only scolds us to get us to work—it's done to get us to work better. This is his way.[29]

In their interviews they express awe and respect for Habib 'Saab'. Govindram said, 'In my eyes he's a great man.'[30] And for Bulwa, 'He is our great guru. We ... have learnt so much.'[31] In addition to respect, what runs through their accounts of their relationship is a sense of mutuality. Not only do they 'curse him back', Bulwa says, 'It is not as if this respect is one-sided. If he sees any person who has great artistic powers, he respects him and seeks him out.'[32] Continuing, he talks of their working process: 'We work together, exchanging ideas all the time.... But he is the only one who can spot the *bareek* (finer) details and that is why he is so important to us.'[33] Thus, speaks an accomplished actor appreciating what a good director can bring to the joint process; this is far from blind flattery.

It is important to make a point here about Habib's freedom from common middle-class attitudes towards sexual mores, an approach in which it seems that he was solidly supported by Moneeka. There is never a hint of moral judgement or disapproval when he recounts, with his usual relish for storytelling, tales of how his actors—including the women—got drunk and disorderly, switched partners or walked out of marriages. He was comfortable with the knowledge that tribal mores of man–woman interaction, sexual behaviour, marriage and so on are very different from mainstream ones, and celebrated rather than deplored the gutsy, colourful, headstrong, vivacious women in his troupe. This cosmopolitan openness played a significant part in shaping the relationship between him and the Chhattisgarhis—they would have immediately sensed the first hint of moral censure over such issues.

Another factor of their relationship was closeness and caring. Govindram said, 'There is no shortage of love—he loves his actors a lot.'[34] Bulwa felt, 'Acting and working with Naya Theatre has been like working with a family. Even in Raipur we meet at Sahib's house and eat together. The best part is that if he needs anything or has any problems we are the first persons he contacts.'[35] Dhanno, who joined the troupe as late as 2000, values the sense of belonging:

> In Naya Theatre we have big names, lowly performers, people from different class, caste and religious backgrounds, and I like the fact that we get to know about Bihar, Uttar Pradesh, we get to know about all of Hindustan as part of Naya Theatre. It's not just the touring, Habib Saab makes it a point to talk to us about world news. Naya Theatre offers us a family atmosphere. We share each other's joys and sorrows, if someone is unwell we all help out, if not monetarily, certainly in other ways, emotionally, physically.[36]

On Habib's side, there are several instances of caring for them, of looking after and out for them, that speak of his emotional connection with his actors. Just two such examples will support this. One was when Fida Bai had a medical crisis:

> Fida Bai is with us still, but not as an actress, because she got herself burnt in 1987. It was providential that I was travelling by train to Raipur. A man boarding the train, an old friend of mine, said, d'you know what happened? Fida Bai burnt herself, two days ago. She's in the hospital, dying. So I didn't go to Raipur, I got off at Rajnandgaon and went straight to the hospital and saw that she was hardly likely to survive because she was all bloated, and she was in the general ward under very unhygienic conditions. I thought she was unconscious but when she heard that I'd come she folded both her injured hands and tried to do a pranam to me. I shifted her to Bhilai where there was a burn unit—with great difficulty because that's only for the steel plants and

anyone coming from outside had to pay through his nose. Then I shifted my
headquarters to Bhilai to look after her, she was in the hospital for one month
and we did a play with the IPTA and my group there and looked after her,
taking her soup and this, that and the other and then brought her to Delhi
and the treatment continued; she's had no end of operations … she speaks
in a hoarse kind of voice, she can't sing and the doctor says she cannot act.
But they're trying still, maybe they can repair the glands.[37]

Another time he talks of protecting the interests of his older actors,
though they are no longer with his troupe full time:

Only last year Bulwa and Ramcharan said, we're too old now and we've got
some domestic problems and we want to go…. I called them to Raipur to
meet and talk about a pension scheme which I'd discovered … and I said,
'Going like this isn't going to help. Fill up the form…. Then you have to sign
it and I'll submit it. You must, because you've worked in the theatre for so
long. But tell me,' I said, 'Many of my old plays are constantly in demand.
I wouldn't like to close them. In new plays I'll have the new cast. But in the
old plays I cannot do without you. So for the shows of old plays will you
come?' They said, 'Whenever there's an old play, we'll come.' What I'm
trying to say is that this has been my handling in my maturer years. And it
has worked very well.[38]

In terms of training, Habib has spoken of his gradually growing
understanding of how best to work with these actors steeped in the oral
tradition—of how he would ask them to improvise and, then, at one point,
'pounce' and freeze it.[39] Habib says, of his actors:

To be a good actor one either needs training and stage experience or the
experience of life and some skill. In the Naya Theatre, there have been actors
who did not have any formal training or acting experience. What they had
was the experience of life and natural talent.[40]

Nageen, recalls the rehearsal process, 'the making of a scene … in a new
production':

Baba used to first explain to the actors the theme of that particular scene.
What happens in the scene, what does the scene say? A scene is made up of
units, the units have sub-units and these are further subdivided…. Each of
these has a focal point. After explaining the scene to the actors he would ask
them to improvise the dialogues and the movements and hand gestures freely.
Then he would ask them, what does the scene say, to test whether the actors
had quite understood…. What he found irrelevant in the improvisation he

put to them, and would ask them whether it helped the focus of the scene or not, or rather what they found irrelevant in their improvisation. So, putting the ball in their court, he would provoke them to think and think and feel deeper. If they did not understand a point, he would go into lengthy discussions explaining with the help of examples from their own lives and the actors would become articulate. This process would help Baba in script writing. It was then that he would write the scene, after two to four days.... He said, 'Not a movement or a hand gesture in theatre takes place without a motive.' He explained what an actor's psychology should be while speaking certain lines.... He worked in great detail, meticulously, untiring, with a strange, extraordinary energy. He lost track of time.[41]

More often than not in our country, when a director from an urban, educated or higher class background is working with actors who are either not literate or come from a lower social class, the director tends to tell them exactly what to do; almost no intellectual engagement is expected of them; they merely carry out the bidding of a 'superior' visionary, the director. This was clearly not the case with Habib Tanvir and Naya Theatre. Here the actor is expected to participate physically, emotionally and intellectually.

Importantly, Habib brought a deep understanding of the actors to his directorial process. According to Govindram, 'He has understood our roots, our ways, how we can speak, how we can act.'[42] Deepak Tiwari, who made a charismatic Charandas, testifies that Habib Saab's way with his actors was unique:

> Habib Saab's way of working is different from other directors I have known—that is to say, he manages to get something of the Nacha quality out of one. He explains the story, and says, now prepare something and show me, cut out what you don't like, or keep just this much, add something here—this helps the actor gain confidence, feel that his ideas are being accepted. Habib Saab interferes only as far as to bring out the theme or subject matter—beyond that he leaves one free ... that's why Habib Saab's actors are so uninhibited, so unfettered, free.[43]

And yet, Habib also pushed them to develop as actors, to acquire new skills. Deepak talks of how he would 'work on one tiny portion or movement for hours at a time'.[44] Govindram recalls how Habib encouraged him to try something outside his comfort zone:

> I remember once he wanted me to play Bottom[45] and I had a long speech in it (*rattles off the soliloquoy*). I was nervous, I wasn't used to learning dialogue. I went and told him I won't be able to handle it. But Ma ji persuaded me,

saying it will suit you—you'll just have some trouble learning the dialogue, but you'll do well. I was nervous, till I learnt the speech by heart. After that I began to enjoy the role. So he does take this trouble with his actors.[46]

Habib himself, when asked what his actors had got from him in return for all he had learnt from them, replied: 'I gave them a sense of choreography, a thematic sense, and participation of many actors. The nacha form is very simple, it does not go beyond two actors in the main.'[47]

Not all Habib's efforts were successful. We already know that he failed in conveying conventional blocking, entries and exits. Habib also remembers trying to train them in breathing: 'I keep telling my actors that some sentences are to be spoken in one sentence, not to be broken into bits; train yourself like a musician breathes, this is very important in an actor. But it wasn't possible for them, so I stopped.'[48]

Given that he ventured into texts by Brecht and Shakespeare, it is interesting to hear how he grappled with the psychological dimension of actor training. He says, 'I use all the methods that I've learnt from them, and then what I've learnt from myself and my studies.'[49] Most of the time, it worked:

As for ... psychological nuances, I'm all the time talking about it and they are capable of imbibing it. In *Good Woman of Schezuan*, I only tried out one scene as an improvisation and that was in the tobacco shop—one after the other a family of nine or perhaps eleven, including the little child and the grandfather, just comes and starts sponging off them, a cup of tea, no harm in one cup of tea, oh, one cigarette wouldn't make a difference, and helping themselves. They did it so effortlessly, so naturally—they are used to so much poverty and to sponging, they understand all about greed. The instinct to survive makes them sly and clever. They don't have to be taught how to behave like greedy people who are parasites on the family.... But when I came to the aviation man, the pilot with the dream, talking about the aircraft with so much love and poetry, that they couldn't get. That was a problem. I had to tell them to forget the aeroplane, but to think of the moon, of a bird, a flower, whatever they love, in their own village, whatever pleases them, and think in terms of love for those things and just use the word 'aircraft'. And then Amarsingh, who was doing the role, brought beauty and poetry to the aircraft, by imagining all this. So I do feed them with these psychological methods.[50]

Eloquent testimony to the success of Habib's approach is Govindram's statement: 'I prefer drama to Nacha. In Nacha, it's all improvisation—you say and do as you like—but in drama you have to think, use your head, there's a story.'[51]

Adapting to the oral tradition to which the actors belonged also demanded a fundamental re-orientation for Habib when it came to issues of plagiarism and copy-cat productions. Never one to resist telling a tale against himself, he recounts:

> There was a fellow from one of the local villages, who did some kind of travesty of *Charandas Chor*, and presented it as his own play and direction etc. And this used to make me very angry.... I went to Haider Ali Vakil, he was a neighbour ... a social activist and writer, a leftist and a pleader with a difference. Not out to make money. So I ... asked him what to do. Haider bhaiyya ... said, 'Habib, you're working with folk actors. You know them by now ... *why do you want to sue them*? You are a social worker also, you care for them. Forget it. Do a panchayat—go to them, call fifty people, talk to them plainly *ki* why do you cheat me? Why don't you announce it is my play? Give them the liberty to do it if they like. But ask them why they're telling lies.' It was very good advice.[52]

Habib did just that. He went to Rajnandgaon and addressed a gathering in Lalu Ram's house, which included the culprits. He told them that he was not asking for any money or royalty, that he was okay with their not crediting anyone for the play, but why were they lying and passing it off as their direction, their play? 'They all agreed before everyone and they went back and merrily continued to this day; and not one, several groups are doing it. Now it doesn't touch me. But my understanding has changed now.'[53]

On the whole, it seems that the Chhattisgarhi actors and Habib understood each other, warts and all, and shared a close relationship with all the ups and downs that such closeness inevitably entails. There is ample evidence that the path was not a smooth one; there were clearly plenty of battles over a whole range of issues, and both Habib and the actors admit as much; but equally clearly there was engagement, affection, caring and mutual respect. Govindram says:

> I even left for a year. But my mind wouldn't switch off—I'd feel low at home, and then my family would find a way of telling me, you're not feeling happy, why not go back. And I thought I'd end my days here, even though the Company has changed, people have died, left, new people have joined.[54]

This connection was the backbone of Naya Theatre. A simple tag like 'paternalism' fails to capture the complexity, depth and nuances of a committed relationship like the one between Habib and the actors, with all its contradictions and difficulties. It also smacks of a certain condescension, which was not present in the relationship; if it had been, as Ramcharan says, they would have been 'off home in five days'.

Habib, the demanding and perfectionist director, talking of his company, had the ultimate praise to bestow:

> I have occasion to complain a hundred times about a hundred things, but never on stage. They're absolutely punctual, they get ready on time and long before the opening time, whatever the time of opening, they are there, absolutely professional in their attitude to the shows. Being groomed in Naya Theatre this quality got further sharpened. If 'professional' means virtuosity, an unselfconscious attitude and sheer excellence and deep involvement, they have it.[55]

Notes

1. Habib Tanvir, 'My Milestones in Theatre' in Habib Tanvir, *Charandas Chor*, translated by Anjum Katyal (Kolkata: Seagull Books, 1996/2004), p. 18.
2. Erin Mee, *Theatre of Roots: Redirecting the Modern Indian Stage* (Kolkata: Seagull, 2008), p. 89.
3. See Chapter 5 ('Coming Home to *Mitti Ki Gadi*')
4. Habib Tanvir, *STQ*, p. 23.
5. Ibid., p. 20.
6. Sameera Iyengar (ed.), *On the Road with Naya Theatre* (Mumbai: Prithvi Theatre Year-book, 2006, entry for 29 July).
7. Habib Tanvir, 'Subversive Processes in Third World Culture: The Question of Liberation in Theatre.' Second Pablo Neruda Lecture, reproduced in in *Nukkad*, p. 30.
8. Iyengar, ed., *On the Road with Naya Theatre*, entry for 24 July.
9. Tanvir, *STQ*, p. 29.
10. Ibid., pp. 20–21.
11. Ibid., p. 21.
12. By way of indication of how small the amounts were: In 1970, Naya Theatre starts paying each actor about ₹150 per month; in 1973, Naya Theatre gets a Department of Culture subsidy for 10 actors of ₹300 per month per actor. By 2004, inclusive of salary, per show payments and perks, actors are getting a total of ₹5,000–6,000 per month while Habib himself gets ₹10,000, very modest sums by any standard. Information from Iyengar, *On the Road with Naya Theatre*, entry for 28 July.
13. Tanvir, *STQ*, p. 21.
14. Ramcharan Nirmalkar, 'Naya Theatre ke Abhinetaon se Bath Cheet' (Talking to the Actors of Naya Theatre) in *Nukkad*, p. 168. Translation from Hindi by Anjum Katyal.
15. Amardas, 'Naya Theatre ke Abhinetaon se Bath Cheet', p. 159. Translation from Hindi by Anjum Katyal.
16. Tanvir, *STQ*, p. 21.

17. Ibid., p. 23.

18. Ibid., p. 18.

19. Ibid., pp. 29–30.

20. Ibid., p. 30.

21. Ibid.

22. Bulwa Ram, '25 Years with "Babaji"', *The Telegraph* Colour Magazine, Kolkata, 17 April 1983, p. 6.

23. Govindram Nirmalkar, 'Naya Theatre ke Abhinetaon se Bath Cheet', pp. 139–140.

24. Habib Tanvir, 'Naya Theatre ke Abhinetaon se Bath Cheet', p. 126.

25. See 'Naya Theatre ke Abhinetaon se Bath Cheet', pp. 136–191.

26. Ibid.

27. Nageen Tanvir, personal correspondence, 31 March 2011, unpublished.

28. Ram, '25 Years with "Babaji"'.

29. Nirmalkar, 'Naya Theatre ke Abhinetaon se Bath Cheet'.

30. Ibid.

31. Ram, '25 Years with "Babaji"'.

32. Ibid.

33. Ibid.

34. Nirmalkar, 'Naya Theatre ke Abhinetaon se Bath Cheet', p. 138.

35. Ram, '25 Years with "Babaji"'.

36. Dhanno, 'Naya Theatre ke Abhinetaon se Bath Cheet', p. 185.

37. Tanvir, *STQ*, p. 30.

38. Ibid., p. 21.

39. See Chapter 7 ('*Charandas Chor*').

40. Habib Tanvir, Preface to the Revised Edition, *Agra Bazaar*, translated by Javed Malick (Kolkata: Seagull Books, 2006), p. 11.

41. Nageen Tanvir, personal correspondence 31 March 2011, unpublished.

42. Nirmalkar, 'Naya Theatre ke Abhinetaon se Bath Cheet', p. 138.

43. Deepak Tiwari, 'Naya Theatre ke Abhinetaon se Bath Cheet'.

44. Ibid.

45. In Naya Theatre's adaptation of *Midsummer Night's Dream—Kamdev ka Apna Basant Ritu ka Sapna*.

46. Nirmalkar, 'Naya Theatre ke Abhinetaon se Bath Cheet', p. 138.

47. Habib Tanvir, 'In Conversation with Javed Malick' in Neeraj Malik and Javed Malick (eds), *Habib Tanvir: Reflections and Reminiscences* (Delhi: SAHMAT, 2010), p. 120.

48. Tanvir, 'Naya Theatre ke Abhinetaon se Bath Cheet', p. 126.

49. Tanvir, *STQ*, p. 35.

50. Ibid.

51. Govindram Nirmalkar, 'Naya Theatre ke Abhinetaon se Bath Cheet', p. 140.

52. Tanvir, *STQ*, p. 20.

53. Ibid., pp. 20–21.

54. Nirmalkar, 'Naya Theatre ke Abhinetaon se Bath Cheet', p. 138.

55. Tanvir, *STQ*, p. 31.

CHAPTER NINE

THE CLASSICS AND LITERATURE

Habib (front stage) in *Mitti Ki Gadi* (1982).
Photo courtesy Avinash Pasricha

Considering that Habib Tanvir is famed for the folk flavour of his productions, it can come as a surprise to realise that in the course of his career he
produced a large number of classical texts, both national and international,
as well as plays based on literary works. A surprise because one does not
usually connect the improvisatory, oral nature of his signature style with
scripted drama heavy in prescribed dialogue. It is, therefore, all the more
interesting to take a look at how his theatre related to uch play texts.

A quick survey of the broad range of classic texts c)vered by him shows
the wide variety he covered. Sanskrit material includes Sudraka's *Mrichhakatikam* (*Mitti Ki Gadi*), Visakhadatta's *Mudrarakshasa* (as *The Signet Ring*

in P. Lal's English translation, and also in Hindi in Habib's own version), Bhavabhuti's *Uttaramacharit*, Mahendra Vikram Varman's *Bhagavaddajuk-kam* (in Hindi, listed as 'translation of Sanskrit drama' by Naya Theatre, first presented at Ravi Shankar University, Raipur),[1] Bhasa's *Urubhangam* as *Duryodhan* (listed as 'Bhasa trilogy' and first presented by Naya Theatre in Chhattisgarhi at Mavalankar Hall, Delhi, in 1978)[2] and Balkrishna Bhatta's *Veni Sanhaar* (presented at the Kalidas Samaroh in Ujjain, 2001).[3]

He often turned to Indian literature for material for his plays: *Shatranj Ke Mohre* and *Moteram Ka Satyagraha* from Premchand, *Rustom-o-Sohrab* by Aga Hashr Kashmiri, *Jis Lahore Nahi Vekhya Voh Janmya Hi Nahi* by Asghar Wajahat, *Bagh* from Sisir Das and Manoj Mitra's *Rajdarshan* as *Nand Raja Mast Hain*. Late in his career, Habib turned to Rabindranath Tagore. He presented *Visarjan* first as a collaborative production with Rangakarmee, Usha Ganguli's Kolkata-based company and, later, reworked it as *Raj-Rakt*, drawn from Tagore's drama *Visarjan* and his novel *Rajarshi*.

Habib worked quite extensively with international literature as well. *Jaalidar Parde*, adapted from the Soviet play *The Feminine Touch*, was done with the J. J. School of Arts, Bombay as far back as 1952–1953. Over the years he did *Saat Paisey*, a dramatised Czech short story; *Khudkhushi*, from a story by Dostoevsky; *Phaansi*, an adaptation of an English play; Goldoni's *Servant of Two Masters*; Lorca's *The Shoemaker's Prodigious Wife*; *Lady Windermere's Fan* and *The Importance of Being Earnest* by Oscar Wilde; Gogol's *The Government Inspector* as *Shah Badshah*; Gorky's *Enemies* as *Dushman* (adapted by Safdar Hashmi); and Canadian playwright Rahul Verma's *Bhopal*, translated as *Zehreeli Hawa*. He also did a story by Stefan Zweig, 'The Eyes of My Undying Brother', as *Dekh Rahe Hain Nain*; and Moliere's *The Bourgeois Gentleman*, first as *Mirza Shohrat Beg* and later as *Lala Shohrat Rai*.

William Shakespeare's *The Taming of the Shrew* and *A Midsummer Night's Dream* (as *Kamdev Ka Apna Basant Ritu Ka Sapna*), about as far from oral folk material as one can get, were both done by Habib—the former at the start of his career, around 1961, with Unity Theatre, Delhi, and the latter as a Naya Theatre production in circa 1993.

One playwright-director and theatre theorist who influenced him strongly was Bertolt Brecht (1898–1956). Habib did the *Good Woman of Schezuan* twice—once in 1961, as part of a College Drama Teachers' Workshop in Pachmarhi and, then, with his Chhattisgarhi troupe as *Sajapur Ki Shanti Bai*.

ॐ

Habib's approach to the Sanskrit scripts was that of a theatre man. You could say that he liberated Sanskrit drama from its confinement to the pages of literature and freed it for the stage; one can make a comparison with Shakespeare here.[4] Following the flow of the action in the text, his director's eye could see clearly that elaborate sets and technology were counter-productive: they hampered the fluidity with which the action moved from locale to locale. The language itself was enough to suggest different settings; the rest was conveyed through the movements of the actors.

> [G]oing by the internal evidence and the reading, I arrived at the conclusion that there were neither curtains, nor machinery, nor a revolving theatre in the classical theatre days. There was utter simplicity—it was an actor's theatre. Whether the actor danced it out or acted it out.[5]

I have already quoted him extensively on how he applied these discoveries to *Mitti Ki Gadi*;[6] indeed, they became basic to his dramaturgy, and future productions followed his minimalist approach to stage design.

> It's a very simple drama, the Sanskrit drama.... That is why I go about it in an utterly simple way ... in *Mudrarakshasa* (*The Signet Ring*) I just used nothing—no set, not a platform—nothing but a cyclorama. And the actors moved in and out quite simply. Only their lines of movement, each time they described a different scene, differed one from another. The entry and exit points were different. So that you can visualize lanes and entrances etc.[7]

As he began to produce Sanskrit plays with the simplicity, directness and energy of his Chhattisgarhi-inflected style, he also propounded his theory that the classical Sanskrit drama and folk drama were intrinsically connected: 'Now, in our country, the folk theatre and the classical theatre ... are but two sides of the same coin.... The Sanskrit drama ... is but one terse crystallization of what has gone before it by way of folk traditions.'[8] In fact, it is the ubiquitous and living folk theatre that rescues the moribund Sanskrit drama tradition from obscurity—'In this country, the classical Sanskrit drama has ceased to be written or produced, for all we know for the last 1000 years. But the one thing that has not ceased to be continued or to grow has been the folk theatre tradition.'[9] As Sudhanva Deshpande elaborates:

> In other words, there was a line that connected the classical drama of ancient India with the rural theatre forms of modern India. The line was circuitous, it was broken, and the links were not always clear, but there was a connection.

And if there was such a connection, then clearly there could not be a radical chasm between 'classical' and 'folk', between high and low, between margi and desi. This was a phenomenal insight, but not one easy to arrive at. The invention of the 'classical' tradition in dance and in music had emphasised the very opposite—the dissociation between the desi and margi. Habib Tanvir was one of the first to see through this obfuscation.[10]

Habib offers several sound reasons for his belief in the interconnected-ness of what scholars at the time insisted on polarising as the 'high' and 'low' forms of theatre, the 'great' and 'little' traditions: 'classic' and 'folk'. He feels that there is a 'mutual inter-flow of influences between the two categories of arts'.[11]

Classical scholars and theorists, he feels, are unable to see the connection between the folk and classical forms because Sanskrit drama has ceased to exist in India for thousands of years as a living art form while vernacular folk forms continue to thrive and evolve.

> They forget that the various musical theatre forms, practised through the ages by rural artists all over India and enjoyed so enormously today by millions of country people everywhere, must carry a strong dose of the aesthetic values contained in the Sanskrit drama, which in a sense represents the quintes-sence of Indian culture.[12]

According to him, the pedants focus on the lofty poetry, complex plot struc-ture and fine characterisation in Sanskrit drama, but are unable to visualise the production design or the actor's craft it necessitates. They feel that the language and thought of classical drama being 'so rich, sophisticated and ornate', and the speech and expression of folk drama, improvised in often unwritten dialects by illiterate actors being 'coarse, primitive and prosaic' there can be no artistic link between the classical and folk theatres.[13] They are unable to appreciate the 'verbal sophistication and the imaginative use of the spoken word in the rich dialects of the people' or 'other dramatic elements in folk theatre improvisations'.[14]

The danger of this attitude is not just aesthetic and scholarly blindness; it has a deeper impact, fostering a class divide between popular culture and so-called 'high art':

> These other aspects of acting and stage-craft in folk theatre also share a con-siderable common area with the Indian classical drama. In fact they are but two sides of the same coin, two facets of the same culture. To compartmentalise them is like depriving the people of one half of their rightful cultural heritage

and dividing culture in terms of classes, superficially and quite arbitrarily. It is like saying that the Commedia de'l arte was coarse art, which had nothing to do with the art of Goldonni. And it is this attitude which tends to push the arts into ivory towers and keeps them from establishing a rapport with the masses of people. Bertolt Brecht's dramas would never have been written if he had shunned the German folk idioms and all the other folk theatre techniques of other countries from which he drew such rich inspiration.[15]

Habib states that the classic and the folk have 'common structural elements' and it is through these elements that 'oneness of feeling is created and an epic dimension opened up, reconciling all apparent discrepancies of time and space and casting a spell that only total theatre of this kind can cast over its audience'.[16] There are certain features common to regional folk theatre forms:

> The numerous forms of Indian folk theatre all share some common fundamental values. They all have an epic approach to story-telling in the theatre. Nearly all of them abound in songs, dances, pantomime, improvised repartees, imaginative movement, slapstick comedy, stylised acting, even acrobatics. Almost all of them usually cover a large canvas in their stories and denote change of location by movement and word of mouth rather than by a change of sets and decor. They often have a sort of stage manager, a comic character, who opens and establishes the play and provides the link scenes.[17]

As he points out:

> [T]hese are the very elements upon which the classical Sanskrit drama is also based, in a broad sense. The difference actually lies in the improvised dialogue of the folk theatre and its stock situations and plots, which remain nonetheless flexible, incorporating the latest local events and the changing social temper of the people, and satirising topical happenings as they go along.[18]

Another common feature between the folk and classic theatre of India concerns the question of unities. Aristotle's unities of time, space and action, the basis of classical western theatre, is irrelevant to our plays, which 'demolish these unities systematically, everywhere, acknowledge only one unity, the unity of rasa. Rasa can be … explained as taste or flavour or feeling or mood or atmosphere.'[19] Bharat Muni's *Natyashastra* lays down the principle of *rasa*, which is the 'mood created by the performer in conjunction with the audience'.[20]

In terms of the relationship with the audience, Habib reminds us that the rural audience normally sits on the ground on three or all four sides of the acting area, which is usually just a rectangular platform or a circular clearing, a form of staging that does not seem to be significantly different from the classical theatre.

As for acting styles, here he does see a divergence:

> We do not know exactly what points of contrasts there might be between the acting methods prevalent in the contemporary folk theatres and those of the actors of classical drama in ancient times. But this is immaterial. It is perhaps enough to suggest that the folk actors are usually terrific performers with highly stylised acting techniques of their own. As for the classical codes of acting, enumerated elaborately in *Bharata's* ancient treatise on drama, the *Natya Shastra*, and illustrated in the mediaeval sculptures and paintings in temples and caves all over the country, many of these are to be witnessed to this day in the mudras, gestures and postures of the living masters of Indian classical dances. To an extent, they may also be witnessed, though in a diluted and apparently corrupted form, in the actor's craft in some traditional dramas, as distinct from folk dramas, particularly in the South.[21]

Bharata's theory of the *rasas*, borne out in classical music and dance practice, is another aspect of classical performance that finds no echo in the folk forms. 'The folk artist normally does not believe in the purity of an art form. Hence, he does not follow a rigid code of discipline but is often apt to mix up several moods.'[22] For Habib, the result is positive, 'a happy abandon, an exhilarating freedom of expression, an extraordinary aesthetic harmony, original and almost contagious in its appeal'.[23] But, he stresses, even classical drama exhibits this variability—'Sudraka did precisely this in his prakarana "*Mrichcha-katika*."'[24]

There are other areas of similarity too:

> Make-up in the folk theatre in some cases, especially in the South, is extremely elaborate and close to classical patterns. Sometimes, stylised masks are also used.... Austere economy used to great dramatic effect is applied to the actor's props, which again perhaps smacks of a classical flavour.[25]

He concludes:

> Lastly, the Indian folk theatre is total theatre in much the same sense as the classical Indian theatre is. It is at the same time very often a ritualistic theatre, which at once brings it close to both the classical and the modern

theatre in the best sense of those words. It is these fundamental links and, above all, the fact that its numerous beautiful forms all represent a people's living theatre that compel us to view it as invaluable source material on which to strive to build the edifice of contemporary Indian drama. Even for thematic considerations of our times, some of the folk theatre techniques would appear to provide the aptest instrument of communication, if only for reasons of extreme flexibility of form, which has so far apparently absorbed and reflected the changing social patterns of Indian rural society with a remarkable degree of success.[26]

Habib claimed that a major motivation for him to take up Sanskrit classics was to 'break the barrier between the so-called great and little tradition.'[27]

I don't see any compartments, I feel there is an interplay and a flow between the two. I feel that the first drama in embryonic form is a people's ritual, a people's creation in terms of songs, tunes, words, all created by the people in the dramatic form of the ritual. So these forms become the people's and they're beautiful and a giant comes along, an intellectual or poetic giant, who drinks in that tradition. After assimilating it, he reproduces it in a form which is not just a reflection of it, but much more, very ornate, injecting a lot of his personality and imagination into it, and that gets crystallized and that's what we understand by the classical, which influences the people in its turn and so their forms get equally affected and this process keeps going on.[28]

Far from treating the Sanskrit plays as quaint old-fashioned museum pieces, Habib sees much of contemporary interest in them, which infuses them with a fresh energy. To him, *Mrichhakatikam* has 'two parallel stories— one of love and the other of political tyranny. Political tyranny does not allow love to flourish ... love as opposed to tyranny is not something which is unknown to us. We all know about that'.[29] He also finds the number of 'plebeian' characters interesting, as well as the fact that the villain, who symbolises tyranny, is a clown—an unusual combination. According to him, 'love and politics' is also the theme of *Uttaramacharit*, with Ram being 'not a demi-god but a human being'; while *Mudrarakshasa* is 'a unique political play ... all about statecraft and about spies, espionage and different devices used as political stratagems and strategies and tactics ... a masterful play, a wonderful plot'.[30]

Habib's approach to staging the Sanskrit classics in Chhattisgarhi, with folk actors, initially came in for severe criticism from scholars and purists, on the grounds that he was debasing a classical form.[31] His theory that folk theatre was the basis for classical Sanskrit theatre was challenged by several authorities, but he was insistent that he was right:

> I don't believe for a moment that Sanskrit drama, when it was being prac-
> tised, was confined to the courts. After all, you have got the Sanskrit language
> confined apparently to the Brahmins and dramas were being written in that
> language, but not without the use of Prakrit…. It is a great misunderstanding,
> as some of the misguided scholars of Sanskrit have been telling us, that this
> was court theatre only … by and large, Sanskrit drama was a living theatre,
> which had a relationship with the people, took from the people's forms.
> When the people practised their own forms they could not but be influenced
> by what was around them.[32]

Convinced that he was correct, and driven also by his strong inclination towards people's cultural forms, he decided that the best way to revive
Sanskrit drama was to incorporate the living folk tradition into it:

> I have come to this conclusion that if you want to interpret your Sanskrit
> drama you must go back to your folk theatre traditions and draw from them,
> even take folk actors to introduce these techniques…. The two together, the
> folk and the classical, are going to give to our modern type of Indian produc-
> ers lots of ideas, lots of inspiration. Everything new and yet Indian can, in
> my belief flow from this kind of a background.[33]

ॐ

Looking at the body of plays done by Habib which were based on Indian
literature what comes through as a common feature is a certain political
approach. Not in any narrow dogmatic sense, but rather in the awareness
of the political importance of a particular stance or social message. For
example, in the director's note in the brochure for *Shatranj Ke Mohre* (a
dramatisation of Premchand's famous short story 'Shatranj Ke Khilari') in
August 1969, he talks about Naya Theatre deciding to 'concentrate on Urdu
drama' that year, by also reviving *Agra Bazaar* and *Merey Baad*.[34] He explains
that he has expanded on Premchand's text, 'building up the atmosphere
of decadent Lucknow of the mid-19th century [with] phrases stocked in
the encyclopaedic "Fasana-i-Azad" by Pandit Ratan Nath dar Sarshar' not
just because he needed to expand the short story into a full-length play, but
because he 'could not think, in the days of dwindling Urdu readership, of a
better use than to incorporate some of its gems into the fabric of the drama'.[35]

Later, at a talk he delivered in June 2004, he was to wax eloquent about the neglect of Urdu in India, a language he insisted was not just a language of the Muslims, but of a culture that extended across religions:

> I resent the emasculating of one of the rich languages of the country by politicians, who did not give a home to Urdu, not one state, not one city, not even one mohalla, though Urdu was the spoken language of a vast region, extending from north to south. Urdu was not the language of Muslims alone but of the people comprising both Hindus and Muslims. Among those who nurtured Urdu prose and poetry were not just Muslims but also eminent Hindu writers such as Pandit Ratan Nath Dar Sarshar, Munshi Prem Chand, Chakbast, Raghupati, Firaq, Krishen Chandra, Rajendra Singh Bedi—to name only a few.[36]

We already know that Habib had an abiding interest in Urdu poetry and literature, that he himself wrote poetry in that language and that he had put considerable research into constructing two plays on the lives and works of major Urdu poets: *Agra Bazaar* (on Nazir Akbarabadi) and *Merey Baad* (on Mirza Ghalib). He had also presented *Rustom* way back in 1961, and in 1990, *Jis Lahore Nahi Vekhya Voh Janmya Hi Nahi*, in which he dealt with 'the aftermath of Partition' and attempted to 'show how a handful of dogmatic people can hold a whole people to ransom'.[37] Doing *Shatranj Ke Mohre* could be seen as part of a larger concern with the marginalisation of Urdu as an Indian language.

Another Premchand story that he produced, along with political street theatre group Jana Natya Manch and Safdar Hashmi, was *Moteram ke Satyagraha* in 1988. This tale about an 'ironic inversion of the political–ethical concept, developed by Gandhi as a tool of resistance', in the words of theatre scholar Vasudha Dalmia-Luderitz,

> though hilarious ... lingers on the verge of the violence so familiar to the contemporary political landscape of the country. Linked by narrative verse recited by a lively chorus, the play improvises freely on Premchand's story....
> In the present political climate, such political alignments with religious forces, which easily erupt into communal violence, are the order of the day.[38]

Here is another political stance—against the forces of religious fundamentalism and inter-faith violence that continue to haunt the country even today.

In the last few years of his life, Habib turned his attention to Rabindranath Tagore. He first took up *Visarjan*, a play written in 1897 based on the novel *Rajarshi* which Tagore had written in 1890. This production was a collaborative work with Usha Ganguli of Rangakarmee, and it was premiered in early 2006. Habib, however, felt that the text was weak and uneven:

> Its dramatic structure was faulty ... some characters were overwritten, while some other very important characters like Raja Govind Manikya's younger brother Nakshatra Rai and Rani Gunwati, even the adopted child Dhruv, were extremely ... underwritten.[39]

He felt that the reason for this was that *Visarjan* belonged to an 'immature' period in Tagore's development, before he found his mature form in 'his newly invented dramaturgy from 1920 onwards, when he appears in masterful control of his form in plays like Raktakarabi, Raja, Chitrangada'.[40] This 19th century play was staged twice by Tagore himself and later by many producers, including Sombhu Mitra. However, each time it proved a flop, despite excellent acting and other inputs.

Habib decided to combine elements from the original story and the play to create a fresh work, *Raj-Rakt*, which premiered in Kolkata in August 2006. Habib stated, 'In my new Chhattisgarhi avatar of the play, I have slashed much, added much and drastically restructured the form. *Raj-Rakt* is a new play.'[41]

The story is about a power struggle between religious and secular authority. The king, Govinda Manikya, orders a ban on all sacrifice, after a young child is traumatised at the sight of a sacrificial goat's blood. Raghupati, the head priest, fights tooth and nail to overthrow this decree. Jai Singh, the beloved adopted son of the priest, is caught in a three-way conflict between his loyalty to his guru and the goddess, his respect for the king and his love for the guileless beggar girl, Aparna, who wants him to walk away from it all. 'Raj-Rakt is the story of a kingdom and its individuals playing out the conflict between church and state' says the director's note in the brochure.[42] Like much of Tagore's work, it is a deeply philosophical argument worked out through symbolic characters; in Habib's hands it is played out as a political battle between dual power blocks.

෴

As we have seen, Habib worked with a wide range of international material as well. His nose for a story that made a political or social point led him to most of the texts he chose to produce in his early career. With Naya Theatre and his Chhattisgarhi actors, the major productions of non-Indian writers he did were by Zweig, Moliere, Brecht and Shakespeare. These remained in his repertoire and were re-presented over the years. It is worthwhile to see what he did with them and how they were adapted to the abilities of his troupe.

Interestingly, the Stefan Zweig story ('The Eyes of the Undying Brother', published in German in 1922) had been with him for a long time.[43] It was first narrated to him by his friend Elizabeth Gauba as far back as 1954. What intrigued him was the character of Virat in the story and the universal nature of his dilemmas. He decided to write a play about it at once, but one thing or the other intervened, and it was only in 1988 that he finally wrote the script. It was the death of his old friend Elizabeth that reminded him of his promise to her to do so. He was unable to find an English translation to work from, but, he says,

> by this time … I was so full of it that I wrote the play without recourse to the book. Soon after my efforts had borne fruit, I got the book in English from two different sources at once. Just as well. Had I read the story before writing the play, I might not have been able to create the new characters that had already crept into the body of the play. Yet, after reading the 'Eyes of the Undying Brother' I did revise the text. And it took me another four years to produce it.[44]

What was the 'universal dilemma' that haunted Habib enough to drive him to write a play more than 30 years after he first heard the story? In the play, the loyal Virat, under cover of darkness, undertakes a wholesale massacre of the enemies of his king. In the morning he sees that his own brother was one of those he had killed. When his king makes him commander, how can he be ruthless while he feels the eyes of his dead brother upon him? When he is appointed judge, how can he, with a clear conscience, convict a killer? In Habib's words:

> There are moments in our life when we are assailed by doubt.… The humblest man wonders. The man at the highest station has restless moments. The social worker doubts. The bureaucrat does not know the object of his life and career. Even the worst politician must on occasion question which way he is going. And artistes universally are so prone to these nagging[s] of self-abnegation.[45]

Reviewing the play for the *Times of India*, Nikhat Kazmi writes:

> The time was just right for introspection. The Wall had been mowed down, the Soviet Union no longer remained the same, Eastern Europe had a

different story to tell … it was obviously time to seek out answers, explanations, rationalizations…. Disillusion coupled with a desperate search for a
new millennium: Habib Tanvir's new play, *Dekh Rahen Hai Nain* almost
had to happen.[46]

Once again, we see a political motivation for what may appear to be a purely
philosophical play.

Javed Malick considers this play 'one of the most outstanding examples'
of Habib's style of working. He writes that Habib

has successfully represented a complex theme without compromising the
vitality and creativity of his folk actors. It was the moral dilemma embodied
in the protagonist … which had attracted Tanvir to Zweig's story. However,
in writing the play, he went beyond the story and invented new events, situations, characters and added dimensions and nuances which significantly
enriched the story and made it more poignantly relevant for us today. The
result is a play that traverses a complex gamut of motifs from the abstract,
almost metaphysical, quest for inner peace to the concrete, material problems
of the ordinary people in wake of a war, economic inflation and political
corruption…. Tanvir's contribution to Zweig's simple moralistic tale is
precisely this complex and dialectical way of seeing, which foregrounds the
contradiction between the philosophical and the political, the individual
and the collective.[47]

By the time Habib wrote the script, his Chhattisgarhi troupe was firmly
entrenched in Naya Theatre. Clearly he intended this text to be performed
by them. This was a soul searching text on the theme of war as fratricide,
with overtones of the Cain and Abel story from the Bible and the theory of
Karma from the Bhagavad Gita and, according to Habib, 'another dimension
… an admixture of the theory of cause and effect as elucidated in Marx's
dialectical materialism to obtain new results and a different end'.[48] Not an
obvious choice, one might have thought, for his group of unlettered actors,
bred on comedy Nacha style. But by now Habib had enough confidence in
his working method with these actors to know that he could get them to
relate to the human situation at the heart of the story.[49]

Like all his productions, this one had songs as well, using the tunes and
metres of lively Chhattisgarh fertility rites such as 'Jawara'.[50] Javed Malick
has this to say about the songs in the play:

Tanvir wanted the play to be a gripping experience not only in terms of its
politics but also of its poetics. Since the language of poetry seemed far more

effective in 'fabricating the mystique so essential to the meaning of the play', one of the things that Tanvir did was to change all pieces of narration from prose to choric songs. The play's music is simply enchanting. Composed by him and Devi Lal, a veteran Naya Theatre artiste, it is not only dramatically effective in its choric function but also rich in poetry, rhythm and timbre. It encompasses vigorous, swinging rhythms of the tribal percussion, the liveliness and sweet melodiousness of folk tunes, and the frenzied energies of devotional music.[51]

And it clearly worked, because the play remained in repertory and saw repeat shows.

Moliere's *Le Borgeois Gentilhomme* was presented by the Chhattisgarhi troupe as *Lala Shohrat Rai,* 'a hilarious and delightful adaptation'.[52] This satire on class relations and the pretensions of the bourgeoisie can be seen as a more obvious choice of material for Naya Theatre, with a theme of social and class conflict that the actors could relate to in daily life and plenty of scope for comedy. The brochure says:

> Shohrat Rai is an upstart. Originally a cloth merchant with a rural back-ground, he aspires to be considered a member of the urban elite. He adopts several measures to achieve this end. He starts learning English, the fine arts and the martial arts, for which he employs a dance master, a music master, a body-builder and a philosopher. He begins to dress up like an urban gentleman and gives up his traditional clothes. He adopts Hindi, in lieu of his dialect which is his mother-tongue.[53]

There are many resonances here with real life, particularly the aspect of Hindi versus the mother tongue: it is clear that the Chhattisgarhi actors would have no trouble personalising—or enacting—this tale.

Bertolt Brecht was a major influence on Habib. He says that he first 'encountered' Brecht in England; we know that he travelled to Berlin in the hope of meeting him and that he reached too late for that, but spent a lot of time with Brecht's theatre company and saw several of their productions.[54] According to Javed Malick, 'He was more profoundly influenced by [Brecht] than by anything that RADA could teach him.'[55]

The encounter with Brecht's theories of theatre came at a time in Habib's trajectory when he had already realised that the only meaningful theatre for him was one that was not an imitation of the west. Habib saw that Brecht too had turned his eyes away from the mainstream western idiom:

> Brecht looked at the medieval times and commedia dell'arte, the American jazz, the African blues, Indian, Chinese and Burmese theatre and also the

German musical tradition and went against that tradition when necessary. He did all this and produced something totally new in his time.[56]

So the example of Brecht, says Habib, led him straight back to India.

[I] came to realise that imitation doesn't take us anywhere and what the villagers do by way of simplicity of staging, the imaginative use of space, in regard to make-believe and the manner in which they deal with time, haunted me. I saw that simplicity in Brecht also. So I came right back to Indian-ness in the sense of realising that you cannot possibly excel in imitating western dramaturgy and western methods, you must come back to our Sanskrit tradition and folk traditions.[57]

In other words, for 'us to be Brechtian would mean that we have to be more Indian!'[58]

How Brechtian *is* Habib's theatre? Undoubtedly, there are elements that one can recognise as 'Brechtian' in both intention and aesthetics. However, as Vasudha Dalmia-Luderitz states in her essay on Brecht and Habib:

The absence of illusion, the use of 'distancing devices' such as masks, the social typification of character and the consequent disregard for psychological interpretation, and finally, the episodic narrative structure, held together by the narrator, are all categories large enough to be amenable to comparison, if not total identification with the practice of the most diverse forms of theatre variously classified as 'traditional' and 'folk' forms, which in their turn have repeatedly been proclaimed to have been encompassed by the classical Sanskrit aesthetic theory, organised around the concept of *rasa*.[59]

If one looks just at the aesthetics and the formal features she has identified, there seems to be a strong case for attributing them to tradition, as she points out.[60] However, in Habib's case there is the added political dimension—from challenging entrenched prejudices to questioning the inequitable basis of society to exposing the corruption of the established authorities. This echoes Brecht in a much more fundamental way—like Brecht, Habib intends to make his audience question and think rather than be absorbed and identify: he is looking, like Brecht, for an intellectual connect rather than emotional impact. 'My plays ... raise questions but do not hand out answers on a platter',[61] he says. 'What's the point of giving you the problem and the solution? You must be given some room to sort out matters for yourself.'[62] Thus, when evaluating how much of Brecht actually made its way into Habib's dramatic output, I would be tempted to go with Habib's own assessment of the dynamics between him and, in some senses, a mentor:

In 1954, when I did *Agra Bazar*, I had no knowledge of Brecht. I become
acquainted with Brechtian technique and his Epic Theatre only in 1955. Even
then one moved as a companion, a sympathizer not a self-conscious imitator of
Brecht. One must do it naturally … Brecht … inspired me more … propelled
me along the same line. One acquired a greater sense of design maturity.[63]

Perhaps the single largest Brechtian influence on Habib's theatre *form* is
his manner of using music and song, which he insists is as much Brechtian
as it is typical of traditional folk and Sanskrit theatre. We will be looking at
music and song in a later chapter; so I will refrain from any further elabo-
ration here.

In *Sajapur Ki Shantibai*, three gods come to earth to locate a single good
human being. If they find one, it will allow the world to remain unchanged.
In Sajapur, they meet Shanti the prostitute, the only one who shows them
kindness and compassion, inviting them to stay in her home. As a reward
for her goodness, they give her some money, hoping it will help her stay
good. Shanti uses the money as capital to lease and run a small tobacco
shop. Soon her good nature is being tried to the limit as her acquaintances
among the poor exploit her to the point of ruin. She decides to change her
identity and appears as a man, Shanta Prasad, her own brother, who is a
hard-headed businessman. The dichotomy between the two personalities,
between her 'good' self and her 'bad' self, leads eventually to a scene in court,
where the three gods, who are the judges, find that Shanti Bai and Shanta
Prashad are the same person.

> But they are unable to resolve whether the world should be allowed to con-
> tinue as it is or it ought to be altered. They finally decide against changing
> the world. The Chorus invites the audience to think out the problem for
> themselves and find a solution.[64]

And so the play ends in a Brechtian mode—inviting the audience to participate by thinking through the central question of the play.

We have already, in an earlier chapter, read how Habib worked with his
actors on the context and approach to the text.[65] He also praises Fida Bai's
'dialectical' treatment of her character:

> She used to underplay with confidence—the transformation into the man's
> role, the lyricism of the girl, the dichotomy, the dilemma when she was
> caught in pregnancy. She was marvelous … she played the two extremes.
> She was very, very feminine. On the other hand, she was harsh also, in her
> own personality. That came across beautifully.[66]

Vasudha Dalmia-Luderitz finds this Brecht play remarkably at home in its Chhattisgarhi incarnation :

Tanvir found the theme, the poverty and the hypocritical preaching of the trinity of the gods, to be specially applicable to the Indian situation, and the characters—prostitute, the waterseller, the barber, the destitute Family of Eight—familiar figures in Indian village life. The industrial suburban misery of Brecht's play was transferred to a Chattisgarh village and remained bound by its horizon and the Chattisgarh dialect into which Tanvir adapted the play. If the desire to become a pilot seemed anomalous in this setting, the lexical poverty of the English translation was more than compensated for by the social vivacity and the forceful use of a dialect which preserved the rhythms of spoken language. The songs were recast in the idiom and metaphor of life in the village, melancholy alternating with mocking gaiety, riddles with harsh comment.[67]

It was a British theatre group—The English Theatre Company—that approached Habib with the idea of doing a Shakespearean play as a joint production, with both English and Chhattisgarhi actors. Habib was intrigued by the idea, but his actors were unlettered and had never heard of Shakespeare. How to go about it? He began re-reading Shakespeare's plays and finally came to *A Midsummer Night's Dream*, which he felt was a possibility:

My reading of it, my understanding of it was that this is a most fragile comedy, this has got a scheme in terms of metre, variety of metre and verses, which is intricate. Seemingly, it looks very light and nice, but it is intimidating.... Now my scheme was that the general people, the forest people, will speak the Indian dialect, including Puck, Oberon, Titania, the fairies, the mechanicals and Bottomkins but Theseus, Hippolyta, Lysander, Demetrius, Helena will stick to English. And when they move into the forest Puck would crack a few practical jokes and play with them and echo their voice and words. He would speak Hindi and they would be doubly confounded because they don't know the language. [68]

However, by the time Habib was ready (on schedule, he claims), the Arts Council of Britain had stopped giving money to the The English Theatre Company. 'So they had folded, had become defunct.'[69] Habib decided to go ahead with the production anyway. He took out a large segment of the original, presenting 'only one of the two strands in the plot. The story that remains has been left more or less intact'.[70]

The subplot became the focus; the main protagonists being Oberon, Titania, Puck and the amateur actors who set out to rehearse a play in the forest. Habib insists that this was not an adaptation because 'Bottom remains Bottom, Theseus remains Theseus and all the rest'.[71] The reception, he says, was good. In the rural areas 'it was received as an Indian play; many villagers don't know Shakespeare'.[72] In cities, the play met with appreciative reviews. The *Times of India* said,

> Here was a gripping rendition of Shakespeare with no ornate sets, no pen-
> dulous costumes. Just a bare stage where two white muslin sheets celebrated
> the mysterious folds of a charmed wood; a posy of gossamer flowers defined
> the irrepressible magic of Puck, the elfin devil, and a nautanki style of dia-
> logue rendition created a native flavour…. It was the engrossing simplicity
> of Habib Tanvir's direction that shone through.[73]

For Habib, his production was about 'different kinds of speech, different kinds of poetry, and different kinds of people within the same milieu.'[74] This was an inclusive society, in other words, with space in it for everyone.

There is a tendency to assume that Chhattisgarhi actors speaking in their own language will handle folk material well, but that they will not be as successful with more sophisticated—or cosmopolitan or universal—textual matter. Habib proved that this was untrue. With the will to find solutions, and working with the confidence that the actors were more than capable of absorbing complex ideas and depicting nuanced emotions, Habib presented successful plays by the world's most famous playwrights and adapted from the world's best literature, to critical and popular acclaim. By doing so he quite simply proved that it could be done.

Notes

1. Chronology of plays directed by Habib Tanvir, *Nukkad*, p. 197.
2. Ibid.
3. Ibid.
4. Shakespeare's plays too are studied more widely as literature than as scripts to be staged.
5. Habib Tanvir, *STQ*, p. 17.
6. See Chapter 5 ('Coming Home to *Mitti Ki Gadi*')
7. 'Habib Tanvir Interviewed' by Rajinder Paul in *Nukkad*, p. 85.
8. Ibid.
9. Ibid.
10. Sudhanva Deshpande, 'Habib Tanvir and his Red-hot Life' in *Pragoti*, 2012, http://www.pragoti.org/hi/node/3456, accessed on 27 May 2012.
11. Habib Tanvir, 'Theatre Is in the Villages' in *Social Scientist*, 2 (10), 1974.

12. Ibid.
13. Ibid.
14. Ibid.
15. Ibid.
16. Habib Tanvir, 'Journey into Theatre' in *Nukkad*, p. 102.
17. Tanvir, 'Theatre Is in the Villages'.
18. Ibid.
19. Habib Tanvir, 'Indian Theatre' in *Nukkad*, p. 67.
20. Ibid.
21. Tanvir, 'Theatre Is in the Villages'.
22. Ibid.
23. Ibid.
24. Ibid.
25. Ibid.
26. Ibid.
27. Tanvir, *STQ*, p. 36.
28. Ibid.
29. Habib Tanvir, 'Indian Theatre' in *Nukkad*, p. 66.
30. Ibid.
31. See Chapter 5 ('Coming Home to *Mitti Ki Gadi*').
32. 'Habib Tanvir Interviewed' by Rajinder Paul in *Nukkad*, p. 86.
33. Ibid.
34. Fine Arts Theatre, 'Brochure for *Shatranj ke Mohre*' (Delhi: 19–20 August 1969).
35. Ibid.
36. Habib Tanvir, 'Sustaining Vitality' in *Nukkad*, p. 58. Lecture delivered at the International Conference on the Vitality of India in the Regional and International Perspective, Shimla, June 2004.
37. Brochure for *Jis Lahore Nahi Vekhya Voh Janmya Hi Nahi* at Bharat Mahotsav, 3 March–11 April 2000, National School of Drama's second National Theatre Festival. Special feature, Naya Theatre, Bhopal, 6 April 2000.
38. Vasudha Dalmia-Luderitz, 'To Be More Brechtian is to Be More Indian: On the Theatre of Habib Tanvir' in Erika Fischer-Lichte, Josephine Riley and Michael Gissenwehrer (ed.), *The Dramatic Touch of Difference: Theatre, Own and Foreign*, Forum Modernes Theater, Schriftenreihe Band 2 (Tubingen: GNV Gunter Narr Verlag, 1990), p. 228.
39. Brochure for *Raj-Rakt*, Naya Theatre, August 2006.
40. Ibid.
41. Ibid.
42. Ibid.
43. Brochure for Bharat Mahotsav 2000, 3 March–11 April. 4 April 2000.
44. Ibid.
45. Ibid.
46. Nikhat Kazmi, 'In Search of the Utopia', *The Times of India*, 17 August 1992.
47. Javed Malick, 'Habib Tanvir: The Making of a Legend', in *Nukkad*, p. 11.
48. Brochure for Bharat Mahotsav 2000.
49. For a discussion of Habib's working method with his actors, see Chapter 8 ('Working with the Chhattisgarhis').
50. Brochure for Natyotsava 93, Kadambari, 17–19 December 93. 17 December.
51. Malick, 'The Making of a Legend', pp. 11–12.

52. Brochure for Natyotsava 93.
53. Ibid.
54. Tanvir, *STQ*, p. 15.
55. Malick, 'The Making of a Legend', p. 9.
56. Habib Tanvir, 'Indian Theatre' [lecture on 6 March 2000 in Berlin] in *Nukkad*, p. 69.
57. Tanvir, *STQ*, p. 31.
58. Sameera Iyengar (ed.), *On the Road with Naya Theatre* (Mumbai: Prithvi Theatre Year-book, 2006), entry for 21 August.
59. Dalmia-Luderitz, 'To Be More Brechtian Is to Be More Indian', p. 221.
60. Her analysis finally suggests that 'Brecht's theatre was creatively appropriated' by Habib in a way that, eventually, 'the Brechtian elements in his theatre had merged totally with the rest' (pp. 222–227).
61. Habib Tanvir, 'In Conversation with Shampa Shah' in Neeraj Malik and Javed Malick (ed.), *Habib Tanvir: Reflections and Reminiscences* (Delhi: SAHMAT, 2010), p. 143.
62. Habib Tanvir, 'The World, and Theatre, According to Habib Tanvir' in *The Telegraph Colour Magazine*, 17 April 1983, p. 6.
63. Iyengar (ed.), *On the Road with Naya Theatre*.
64. Brochure for Naya Theatre's *Sajapur Ki Shantibai*, c.1979, undated.
65. See Chapter 8 ('Working with the Chhattisgarhis')
66. Iyengar (ed.), *On the Road with Naya Theatre*.
67. Dalmia-Luderitz, 'To Be More Brechtian is to Be More Indian', p. 227.
68. Habib Tanvir, 'Shakespeare in Translation: The Indian Context' [lecture on 26 February 2000 in Salzburg] in *Nukkad*, pp. 62–63.
69. Ibid.
70. Brochure, Naya Theatre presentation, Sri Ram Centre, February 14–16.
71. Habib Tanvir, 'Shakespeare in Translation: The Indian Context' [lecture on 26 Feb 2000 in Salzburg] in *Nukkad*, p. 63.
72. Ibid.
73. Kazmi, *The Times of India*, 8 March 1994.
74. Iyengar (ed.), *On the Road with Naya Theatre*.

CHAPTER TEN

CONNECTING WITH THE FOLK

Charandas Chor (1990s). The Lehenga Panthi Dance Party.
Photo courtesy Naya Theatre

As we have seen, Habib's interest in the cultural expression of the rural people—which we now commonly call 'folk'—took hold early. As a child, growing up in Raipur, he was surrounded by the Chhattisgarhi language, the songs, the colourful rituals and performance forms. His inclination towards leftist ideals, developed from his college days, led him to take an interest in people's culture; this was strengthened and further developed during his years in the IPTA, as he has clearly stated. Meanwhile, his love of language and literature drove him to explore dialects,[1] while his interest in music prompted him to collect folk songs. His years in the UK and Europe deepened his conviction that any original work in theatre had to grow out of local Indian traditions; and on his return, upon visiting his native Chhattisgarh, he rediscovered, with new eyes, the local performance form of the Nacha and the wonderful singers, dancers and actors who performed it. Several of them became part of his company, Naya Theatre.

We also know that Habib's theatre, although imbued with folk material and performed by folk actors, was never projected as folk theatre. He was clear about his being a modern theatre that incorporated, but did not replicate, the folk tradition. 'I'm not a revivalist. I do not want to do the folk play exactly as it is done.'[2]

What, then, was the nature of Habib's relationship with—his theatrical engagement with—folk material, in all its complexity? In this chapter, we will discuss his use of folk tales and folklore; music, song, ritual and dance will be dealt with in the next chapter.

Before we take up specific productions, let us take a closer look at his opinion on the rural (oral, folk, regional) culture that existed in India:

> It is not true that there is, on the one hand, sophisticated society and on the other hand a rural society which is totally unsophisticated. It is just two different sets of sophistications. I realized that their rites, their rituals, their harvest, their interests, their needs, their deprivations, all are connected with their cultural expression.[3]

This culture has its own store of knowledge, which the urban society makes the mistake of devaluing and ignoring:

> We neglected folk wisdom, the reservoir of traditional knowledge of panchayat administration, containing a vast mass of knowledge of our herbs and plants, cycle harvesting, of the native fertiliser system, of oral traditions of the epics, folklore, ballads, songs and rustic performing arts, of the adivasi manjhi system of social justice, jurisprudence—their system of taboos that safeguards trees, wild life and human rights.[4]

In an interview given in 1974, he talked of 'economic insecurity'—caused by an urban-centric focus which 'devalued the tiller in the development process', and privileged the corrupt middle-man—as a major factor leading to folk theatre being 'in a bad way'. Other causes, in his opinion, included 'the distortion of values resulting from a consumer-oriented industrial policy', 'an educational system which is both unimaginative and devoid of culture' and a mass media which promoted 'cheapness and vulgarity'. This combination of factors had had a 'devastating' effect on folk forms. 'Many forms have died. Others are in the process of dying. And yet others, struggling to come alive, are doomed to death almost before they are born.'[5] Ten years later, he was regretting the spread of 'many confused forms of theatre which on the face of it seem to stand for authentic expression and yet remain fake to the core'. The reason for this, he felt, was a realisation amongst the urban middle classes that the only way to 'portray our own unique reality' was through 'modes and methods indigenous to our own culture'. As a result, 'side by side with the folk theatre we have the pseudo-folk theatre'.[6]

Habib's own way of accessing and working with the folk took a different route. During his IPTA days in Bombay, he met 'a sprinkling' of folk artistes; when he visited the villages, he learnt a lot of songs through them, 'and when I looked at these folk arts, I learnt with new eyes'. On his return from Europe, he brought the folk artistes to the city to participate in his productions.

> Even that did not give me a proper vision. For years I used them only as performing artists. When I began going to the villages to have workshops and began mingling with them, only then I realized at long last that there is a lot to learn from them, not only to give to them, which is the usual attitude of the elite or middle class officials in rural amelioration projects. There is in fact more to take from them than to give.[7]

He realised that what makes the rural theatre different is

> the improvised dialogue of the folk theatre and its stock situations and plots, which remain nonetheless flexible, incorporating the latest local events and the changing social temper of the people and satirising topical happenings as they go along. This quality of the folk theatre is what makes for its perfect rapport with its audience. And if serious-minded theatre artists all over the world are at present engaged in devising new dramatic methods for establishing a closer relationship between the theatre and the people, then there is no reason why India, which already has a living indigenous theatre of this kind should not strive to make capital of it for the sake of its contemporary cultural requirements.[8]

He launched on a series of workshops, which yielded both insights and productions:

> Through the workshops with them I developed an integral view of the performing arts, which is, I dare say, not commonly advanced. Performing arts are considered 'high', to be pursued by themselves and are an end by

themselves. This is not true. In our case particularly, it is not true. For the people, who have a continuity, there was constant growth. It is not static, it is a growing culture and it exists. Since it exists, then we must do something worthwhile in the field of performing arts, then we must go back to the folk roots of the folk traditions in theatre. When I did that, I realized that imitation will not do. If I were to pick up things from the people and practise them it would be just as bad as aping the West.[9]

Habib took a range of approaches to the rich folk heritage he encountered. One was to showcase it with 'minimal' intervention, with the aim of bringing it to the attention of a broader—largely urban—audience ('I have presented it in the same manner as it is done in order to show what exists by way of rich forms in the villages.'[10]) This, for example, is what he did with *Arjun Ka Sarthi*. A second was to make a creative intervention in the content, structure, costumes, music, etc., with the aim of rejuvenating a once-rich tradition that had lost its freshness and vitality; examples of this were his Khayal production *Thakur Pritipal Singh* and the Chandaini production *Sone Sagar*. The third approach was to share knowledge of costumes, lighting and theatrical techniques with traditional artistes, in an attempt to build up standards and encourage them to enhance their own knowledge base, as, for example, at the Nacha workshop in Raipur in 1973.[11] And fourthly, there were the full-fledged Naya Theatre productions directed by him, based on folk tales—like *Bahadur Kalarin, Hirma Ki Amar Kahani* or *Ponga Pandit*. Here, the folk material and the folk actors combined with his directorial vision and direction to produce modern theatre.

After reviving *Agra Bazaar* in 1970 for the Sangeet Natak Akademi award festival (when he received the award for direction for 1969), with a cast consisting almost entirely of Chhattisgarhi actors, Habib continued to do theatre with them in Chhattisgarhi for the next few years:

From 1970 to 1973 I tried to work in their native language but not very creatively. I allowed them to do their stock pieces mostly in their own way. I merely touched them up, polished and edited them, and made them more presentable, more stage worthy.[12]

This phase lasted until the Nacha workshop that culminated in *Gaon Ka Naon Sasural.*

The year 1971 saw Naya Theatre present 'the truck-borne musical satire on elections'—*Indra Lok Sabha*.[13] The brochure evokes the medieval Italian commedia dell'arte tradition of travelling players who set up their temporary stages in public spaces to entertain the local audience and, in a more contemporary incarnation, the Century Theatre of Lancashire which 'toured the country in a caravan of 36 lorries'.

> The Naya Theatre with its Chhattisgarhi folk players goes to the people on the four wheels of a single truck, which not only transports actors and the stage equipment but on opening up also provides a proscenium stage ... complete with ceiling, backdrop, inbuilt lights and mike.[14]

The play takes up where the classic *Indra Sabha* ends, after the reunion of Sabz Pari and Gulfam.[15] These are the days of 'lok tantra' in Indra Lok; there is a clash between those who support Indra's reign and those who oppose it. However, the power to make or overthrow the government lies with Paltu the voter—he of the severed head, having had his head chopped off by a Naxalite in Calcutta. Paltu listens to both sides, tells his own story and, with Narad's help, comes to a conclusion about his vote. 'The idea of the play is to present our analysis of the present Indian political scene ... through humour and satire, ironical songs and situations, and make the electorate vote-conscious.'[16] The brochure recounts the daily experience of this truck-borne performance with a relish that vividly recalls the excitement of Habib's boyhood memories of the magic of theatre-going:[17]

> Every evening as the theatre rolls into one of the congested narrow bylanes of Chandni Chowk, the people mob the truck to see the works ... the local audience gathers round the truck instantaneously, and the crowds thus collected—about 3 thousand—is more than we can cope with for one per- formance. Within minutes, the truck changes into a full-fledged stage. The people are stunned by the spectacle. Next they wait for the lights, and the moment the functional stage is lighted up, a wave of cheer sweeps the street auditorium. The bazaar theatre, complete with a crowded audience, springs to life by the mere flick of a switch. The performance begins at 9 p.m. sharp and goes on for an hour and a half. Often the side curtains have to be tied up for the benefit of women and children peeping from balconies and perched on house tops.... The wayside tea and kabab shops do roaring business, for scores of people choose to simultaneously watch the performance and discuss the play over a cup of tea. The historical mediaeval lanes of old Delhi are at once transformed into an electrified Indian village.[18]

Simultaneously, a longer version was presented at the Fine Arts Theatre Auditorium, with additional songs, prose-poems and characters making up a 'fully developed satire on present-day politics'. The brochure continues,

'The production follows folk traditions in theatre, including elements of ad lib and utilization, with some change, of stock folk theatre situations.' The cast included Brij Lal, Devi Lal, Bulwa Ram, Lalu Ram, Babu Das amongst others, including Habib himself. Habib ends the brochure note with the statement: 'The theatre in Delhi has kept aloof from politics for a long time. We feel it our duty to bring it closer once again to the political questions of our day.'[19] Not everyone approved of this particular political move—as Javed Malick points out, his decision to mount this campaign play drew a fair amount of criticism, particularly from sections of the left.[20]

The same year saw him present a double bill consisting of *Arjun Ka Sarthi* and *Kushtia Ka Chaprasi*. The former was a 'dramatic ballad from Mahabharata sung and enacted by Puna Ram'.[21] Habib says:

> After working diligently on Pandavani, the *sampurna* or complete Mahabharata, and then, having a grasp of what they had to say and having studied Mahabharata over again, in the short form of Rajagopalachari, I got the hang of it, and devised a production. '*Arjun ka Sarathi*' was the name of a short piece of half an hour.[22]

The brochure establishes that his aim is to bring this rare folk form to a wider audience:

> In Chhattisgarh ... ballad-singers still sing the classical story of the Mahabharata. They are becoming rarer but they still exist ... they sprinkle the songs with dialogues and description in prose. They enact the story most artistically even while they are singing—ektara and khartal in hand, which they use both as musical instruments and stage properties.... We are presenting only a sample of this rare and unique folk theatre.[23]

Kushtia Ka Chaprasi was a half-hour skit described as a 'folk improvisation' consisting of stock comic situations and 'many collectively conceived events'.[24] Testifying to the resilience and adaptability of folk theatre, which easily adopts topical and contemporary references into its narrative, the brochure states that this farce was first presented to rural audiences as

> a satire against bureaucracy. In 1962, during the Chinese attack, they turned it into a satire about a Chinese spy. At the time of the 1965 Indo-Pak war, they introduced a Pakistani spy into the play and debunked him. Now we have adapted it to the situation in Bangla Desh ... the idea we are projecting [is] that the people shall win, no matter how protracted the war.[25]

Other folk plays shown in this period include *Jamadarin, Chheri Chhera, Kaghaz Ka Putli* and *Sadhu.*[26]

While working with folk forms, Habib has said:

> In my work, I have been careful not to tamper with the local forms in any drastic way. All I have tried to do is to go back in time and rid the folk forms of the vulgar hybridization of the past thirty to forty years and to move forward thematically in order to evoke a contemporary feeling in keeping with progressive views.[27]

A comment here: although he does not count such intervention as 'drastic' it is, nevertheless, a double-edged sword. Javed Malick lauds Habib's critical interventions:

> Tanvir does not romanticize the 'folk' uncritically and ahistorically. He is aware of their historical and cognitive limitations and does not hesitate to intervene in them and allow his own modern consciousness and political understanding to interact with the traditional energies and skills of his performers.[28]

The desire to restore the form to an earlier 'authenticity' is totally understandable, especially when one recognises that the form has had to incorporate 'popular' elements in response to a public taste which is being shaped by crass commercial entertainment. Yet, it is equally true that popular forms of folk entertainment have evolved continuously over the centuries in response to the current trends of the time. This is inevitable, and arguably it is what keeps them dynamic and contemporary. Hence the double-edged sword—interventions which seek to return a form to an earlier state may be counter-productive; at the same time, an expert like Habib, with an evolved aesthetic and dramatic sensibility as well as a true sensitivity to and understanding of the form, can help bring about an improvement in standards that can benefit the form. The key here would be 'sensitivity and understanding'—the right kind of guidance and exposing the artistes to older veterans and styles can offer them an alternative which they can then choose to adopt or not. Similarly, with the intervention in content: Habib says, 'Most of the folk artistes keep repeating mythological and historical themes which though excellent in themselves, are distorted by an emphasis on personal heroism and glamour. These had to be cleaned up and the focus brought back to the original.'[29] He wants to bring it in line with 'progressive views': ultra-rightwing, fascist and fundamentalist interventionists may seek to align it differently. In Habib's hands, the double-edged sword of intervention may not be harmful; in another's, it could.

It would be appropriate to pause here to consider Habib's own views on the need for, and nature of, such intervention:

> I have worked with folk forms in several regions—Orissa, Haryana, Rajasthan, Chhattisgarh etc. And I noticed, especially in Rajasthan, there was a kind of stagnation in their folk forms. It's like water, as long as it is flowing it works, the moment the flow stops, it stagnates ... if one can give it some kind of an outlet so it starts to flow again, it will cleanse itself of the impurities. You need a catalytic agent from time to time, you may need to work on the thematic aspects, or rethink the dramatic structure. But it is difficult to theorize or be more specific about this because it demands a great deal of sensitivity and intelligence to enable one to connect in a way that the stagnation can be removed.[30]

Habib himself was aware of the drawbacks of the wrong—or inappropriate—kind of intervention and, therefore, of the importance of being able to 'connect' before attempting it at all.

> Often government agencies, or other organizations or persons, intervene in folk forms without any understanding. Folk forms and songs should not be made mere vehicles of official propaganda but if intervention is made with empathy, in a manner so that their own concerns can be articulated in their own language and their own style, it can become a meaningful exercise.[31]

We have already discussed, in some detail, the Raipur Nacha workshop and the production that resulted in *Gaon Ka Naon Sasural*.[32] Soon after this, Habib held a workshop in Rajasthan, which was followed by other regional workshops with different local folk performance forms. Habib, speaking of these experiments, says:

> In all these productions the regional folk artists, illiterate most of them, participated. They all proved to some extent or the other the great capability of the folk forms of Indian theatre to imbibe and carry contemporary messages. Above all, they demonstrated that some of the traditions of improvised rural drama in India are so robust and imaginative that given an opportunity to develop on the right lines ... the validity of folk theatre forms for contemporary purposes will ... be vividly demonstrated.[33]

So one could claim that these workshops were an integral part of his theatre vision, which was to find a contemporary validity for traditional people's oral cultural forms.

Interestingly, at the Rajasthan workshop, he found that certain kinds of material did not suit certain forms.

> I had the story of a truthful thief from Vijay Dan Detha, who had collected it from Rajasthani folklore.... I tried to turn this story into a play. It did not work because I was trying to set it in the tak amrat khilari tradition. This Marwari tradition is an operatic tradition. The workshop had several strong, very talented singers, who could do the operatic form very well, but very few actors. The play I was trying called for very good actors.[34]

In a few days he realised that it would not work. 'There was only one good actor they had, a wonderful actor. Otherwise their whole strength lay in music ... the little scenes that they enacted had feeble acting.'[35] So he decided to change the text and the form they were to work with. He tried another story by Vijaydan Detha. 'It had a Rajasthani title which meant *Thakur Sahib ka rooth jana*. I called it *Thakur Pritipal Singh*.... This play worked while the thief story failed.'[36] The 'thief story', of course, was his seminal *Charandas Chor*, to which the Chhattisgarhi actors, with their evolved acting skills, did full justice.

Setting out to work in the Khayal style with the artist Ugam Raj Khilari from Borunda (Vijaydan Detha's native place), Habib began by viewing their performances. He watched *Amarsingh Rathore* and *Raja Harishchandra*, done in their traditional style. He found *Raja Harishchandra* to be a story with plenty of potential and possibilities, but felt that the performance was lacking in dynamism; there was no spark; he also found it rather sentimental. He decided that trying to rework a piece that was already set would be difficult; it would be better to begin with a new piece. So he spent some days working on the 'thief' story (entitled *Sachai Ki Bisaat*) but soon gave that up and turned to another folk tale recorded by Vijaydan Detha, *Thakur Ro Rusno*. This seemed more promising: 'It was full of comedy and humour and as the plot had the quality of a serial, it was more suitable for the circular structure of an opera rather than of a play.'[37]

The plot is about a whimsical and headstrong Thakur who is easily affronted. On one such occasion he leaves his village in a rage and refuses to return. His mother, at her wit's end, turns to the clever Chowdhury and requests him to fetch the Thakur back. The Chowdhury undertakes to do so and sets off in pursuit, following the Thakur from village to village till he lures him home with a stratagem. All's well that ends well.

The brochure makes a point of stating which aspects of the production are part of the traditional Khayal form and where there have been departures or additions. For example, it says that 'pure Khyal tunes and khyal meters are used for the songs' and that the manner in which some of the songs are sung are typical of the Khayal tradition. We know that Habib had approached 'a folk poet, Rahmat Dan Detha, to help write new songs and set them in the traditional forms of *khayal*'.[38] We also learn that the style of singing known in Rajasthani as Ter, which has vanished from the performance of other Rajasthani Khayal parties, has been introduced in this production, as in the song of Babu Saheb, the Thakur's mother. It was in conversation with Ugam Raj and some of the more senior members of his troupe, like Bhanwar Lal, that this rare style was discovered. Another interesting bit of historicisation is the tracing of the ritualised opening of a Khayal performance. It seems that during medieval times in most rural regions of the country, a sweeper would sweep and a *bhishti* (or water-carrier) would sprinkle the performance space or stage before a show began. Later this practice was incorporated into the Khayal form. Thirty or forty years ago, a Khayal performance would open with actors enacting the sweeping and sprinkling of water in a song and dance sequence. This production opens in the same way, followed by the traditional *vandana*[39] and the songs of introduction sung by the chief actors.

> During these introductory songs, the actor would turn round and dance his steps to the orchestra and kneel to it in salutation keeping in rhythm all the time. After this the main story would be unfolded in a kind of opera form which also includes some folk tunes and songs.[40]

There are some departures from the norm as well. Thematically a story like that of *Thakur Pritipal Singh* is 'perhaps not so true' to the Khayal tradition, which typically renders 'Pauranic tales enacted in melodramatic style with little food for thought'. In this tale, there was 'a hint of satire against feudalism'.[41] Another change is the introduction of the above-mentioned new songs, albeit in the traditional metres. A third, perhaps the most radical, is an 'element alien to the khyal tradition which has been injected into the fibre of the style'—this is the use of dialogue. The

> sprinkling of improvised dialogue in Thakur Prithipal Singh does not belong to the khyal tradition. But we considered this necessary to project our story

more clearly and hopefully also to help the khyal form get out of the stagnation into which it has currently fallen and find a new opening for further development.[42]

There was also a departure from custom with regard to costumes, which had an unexpected result. The story is best heard in Habib's voice:

> We chose printed cotton material for the angarkhas. When Hukum [sic] Raj saw the costumes, he simply refused to use them, saying that the audience would take umbrage and boo them off stage if they saw them wear these costumes. His reason was that the particular kind of print material was customarily worn by the sweeper castes! Now, they were beautiful costumes, but we understood his difficulty, so we made a compromise—they would wear their usual brocade costumes while performing in areas where this custom existed and use our costumes in the rest of the places.[43]

Amusing to read, perhaps, but containing a salutary lesson, a point to take note of: there are layers of subtext and signification so culture specific that they are almost impossible to know; the involvement of the artistes themselves is probably advisable while making decisions on the aesthetics of a traditional form.

The brochure insists that 'in directing the play we have made an effort to safeguard the traditional style and yet project through this newly told folk story a contemporary theme'.[44] Yet there are certain significant interventions made, in both form and content. When asked whether folk artists took easily to such changes, Habib responded, candidly, 'Oh no, not at all. We had to wage a regular psychological war in order to push our point home. But we could not impose it, we knew, and had to be extremely subtle and diplomatic about it.'[45]

Were such attempts to intervene—and refresh—traditional forms, to inject them with a new lease of life, either lasting or effective? It seems difficult to tell. Habib did enquire from Ugam Raj after about a year how the play was doing in the Khayal circuit and was told that there was not much demand for it. Yet, two years later, Ugam Raj said that the demand had improved significantly. Habib concludes that changes like this take time. 'It is not possible to make an assessment of this kind of thing. You cannot tabulate results as on the basis of statistics. It will take ten–twenty years to really know what kind of impact it has created.'[46]

On the heels of the Khayal workshop came one in Haryana, on the Swang form. It was held in Rai, under the auspices of the Haryana government. Prior to the workshop, Habib put in two months of 'exploration of the

Swang', which convinced him that this form, 'despite its apparent strength has become rather stagnant'.[47] What were the problems he pinpointed?

> It has become so informal that it has ceased to care for costume, grouping, dramatic tension, development and climax. The story reveals itself in a string of songs into which all virtuosity is instilled to the utter neglect of the story. They often dwell exhaustively on the various nuances of a particular situation through the medium of songs without effecting dramatic progression … the musical tension is often dropped by the bald little statements that usually inter-link the songs. And more often, there is a stalemate before the next song is allowed fully to emerge.[48]

However, he admits that the strong point of this form lay in its music. There were sometimes five or six songs for a single situation. The tunes were more classical than folk in feel and style, with a high pitch and intricate rhythms. And the audience, crowding the stage, seemed prepared to listen to the music all night. The stories, mostly sung, were all familiar—the audience appeared less interested in them than in a fresh voice or new orchestra. In fact, often the tale was not even completed in the course of the performance, but the audience did not seem to mind, treating it more like a concert than a dramatic performance.[49]

To Habib, the situation 'does not appear to ensure the Swang's survival'; he feels that 'the changing patterns of the rural work-a-day life caused by development and the comparative alienation of the village and urban youth from cultural traditions do not make for the best conditions for the perpetuation of the Swang in its present form'.[50] Nor can the present day performers compare to the pioneer Swangis of 60 or even 30 years ago, like Deep Chand, Lakhmi Chand, Mange Ram and Baje Nai. More contemporary composer-actors like Dhanpat Singh and Ram Kishan Vyas already perform a 'hybridised' version of the Swang.

Habib's strategy with the young Haryana folk actors in the workshop was to expose them 'exhaustively' to the Swangs performed by established Swangis as well as to other folk music traditions of Haryana. Thereafter, began a process of interaction and discussion 'to arrive at a critical selection of material and their blending'.[51] In terms of content, the major thrust was towards selecting sequences and collating them; the original three-to-four-hour-long performance was cut down to two hours by choosing 'suitable *ragnis*' to which were added folk songs interspersed with improvised dialogue. This was a major creative intervention.

The second important intervention was in the area of form and presentation. Traditionally performed in the round, the Swang stage or performance area was usually small, accommodating a cast of no more than 15 or 16 persons, with the orchestra seated in the middle and entries effected from centre stage. Attracted by the idea of the orchestra in the centre, Habib decided to retain that but, with designer Rajeev Sethi, set about redesigning the stage to accommodate sight lines which were hampered by the position of the musicians. First, the stage was made larger, 19 square feet. Rajeev Sethi created, in the centre, a 6' x 6' platform, about a foot higher than the main stage, which was 2' high. So the main stage was a sort of 3' wide apron surrounding four rectangular depressions about 3' x 6' and about 1' lower than the stage level, which accommodated the orchestra and the actors symmetrically around the central platform. These depressions allowed four pathways about 3' wide which led to the raised centre from the four sides of the stage. 'Thus, we managed to retrieve the vital stage centre for the actor's use without disturbing the central position of the Swang orchestra.'[52]

Keeping to the traditional number of performers (all male, as Habib had to accept perforce that women would not perform due to 'the force of the energetic dances and the strength and pitch of the songs'[53]), Habib ensured that they would fit, seated and half visible, into the four depressed rectangles from where they would enter and exit. There were more modulations introduced:

> We gave our characters further identification through costume and a colour scheme and used modern lighting, a cloth ceiling on top of the stage on four pipes for the sake of better acoustics, and microphones, all of which are absent from the traditional *Swang*, though it is always performed in the open.[54]

During the month-long workshop, Habib experimented more freely with a full-length production of two hours which they were to title *Jani Chor*. Conceived in the round, this had the musicians and actors seated at ground level on one side of the stage, while two pairs of raised platforms of differing heights with steps at the four corners of the stage in a symmetrical pattern allowed the actors to use the entire space. This piece had more dialogue, some *ragnis* from Dhanpat Singh's Swang, and a few community songs. More, it introduced balladeers from a totally different musical tradition: the Jogis of Haryana, street singers who roam about in pairs and sing accompanied by their *sarangis*.[55] Although unused to the stage, two pairs of Jogis performed as the chorus in this play.

Apart from the two pieces that were presented as an outcome of the workshop—*Shahi Lakarhara*, a Swang by Pandit Lakhmi Chand, and *Jani Chor*, 'a folk musical play' produced by Habib Tanvir—there were other positive results of the month-long interactive process. Such as 'interaction between groups of people drawn from various walks of life and from different cultural backgrounds'. Over hundred participants comprised largely of Haryana artistes—professional Swang parties, Jogis, government artistes from the districts, individual experts and village elders—along with non-Haryana artistes, experts and observers, attended.

> They were exposed ... to Haryana folk arts in addition to some non-Haryana theatre forms. There were discussions about *Swang,* Haryana folk-songs, dances, customs, rituals and the comparative values of folk legends such as those about *Bhartrihari* prevailing in Haryana and other states.... We ... watched old *Swangs* ... by professional parties of Ram Kishan Vyas, Tuley Ram and Dhanpat Singh respectively, and discussed their merits.[56]

The workshop, Habib felt, was an experiment aimed at opening 'a way for progress for the Swang' by demonstrating that 'there must be many more ways of re-moulding folk-theatre forms to our present day requirements' and an attempt to 'absorb a vital folk tradition into new theatrical forms before that tradition completely evaporates'.[57] For the participants, 'the roots of new ideas having been struck on the subliminal level' would, one hoped, 'germinate'; in the young, Habib was confident, they would be 'sure to shoot forth'.[58]

In April 1976, after a preliminary survey in February, Habib conducted a two-week Orissa Folk Performing Arts Workshop at Gopalpur-on-Sea in the Ganjam district of Orissa, on behalf of the Ministry of Education and Social Welfare, Government of India.

There were about 50 participants, including local performing arts troupes and artistes. Two folk forms were taken up at this workshop—Prahalad Nataka and Bharata Lila.

According to Habib, Prahalad Nataka is a folk form that verges on the classical—based on classical *ragas,* it is an operatic form with much dancing, in which movement is based on the musical rhythm.[59] Costume, make-up and masks follow a prescribed pattern. Since these facets are rigidly adhered to by practitioners, this form has acquired the characteristic of a classical performance form, without the impromptu improvisational qualities of folk forms.

In terms of form, the actors perform surrounded by the audience on three sides, at ground level. The fourth side is taken up by Hiranya Kasipu's throne, placed on a step unit about 9 inches high. The dancers perform complex dance movements up and down these steps.

Music creates and breaks dramatic tension in this form. Cymbals, *dholaks* (a kind of a drum) and chorus singers skilfully build up the rhythm and tempo, rising to a 'frenzied crescendo. The tension at this point is almost unsupportable beyond a brief moment. This over and we are allowed once again to be lulled by the low ebb of peaceful beats'.[60] These crescendos indicate a thematic climax, moment of high drama, or stylised, ceremonious entry. Altogether, the music creates a 'devotional feeling extremely contagious in its appeal'.[61]

In the course of watching performances of Prahalad Nataka by different troupes, Habib registered that the form was capable of great dramatic spectacle. Hiranya Kasipu would enter on a dummy elephant, with great pomp, and even a burst of fireworks adding to the display. A live cobra was used in the snake charmer scene in one production. Wrestlers were introduced as one of the ways to vanquish Prahlad. Actors wore dark glasses as part of their make-up. Having religious associations, the mask of Vishnu donned by an actor is seen as God's image. Before it can be revealed, a *puja* (prayer) has to be performed over it. After this ritual, the actor is in a trance-like state. 'So is Hiranya Kasipu just before this moment of supreme revelation for he knows he must merge with the Divine and therefore seeks his end eagerly.'[62] In the brochure note, he further added that the two actors were not supposed to come into close proximity; once there was a tragic incident when the actor playing God attacked the actor playing Hiranya Kasipu, causing him to die on the spot. This is an indication of the mystical fervour surrounding the Prahalad Nataka.

Due to the rigidity of the codification in this form, Habib did not try to make many changes. However, he did find a way of adding a political dimension: 'I made them present Hiranyakashap in the image of a dictator, and Prahlad's fight for freedom to worship other gods as a fight for a democratic form of government. This is what I tried to highlight in the play.'[63]

The second production—Bharata Lila—that came out of this workshop was much more up his street. He found it 'a less rigid and totally different form of theatre. Though essentially a musical form, it leans more on verbal expression'.[64] Here, the actors perform in the round, at ground level, making frequent sallies into the audience. The subject matter is from the *Mahabharata*—the story of Subhadra being given in marriage to Arjun. The tone is light, witty and satirical, with everything contributing to this overall effect—not just the improvised dialogue but also the songs, dances and gestures. There is a chief jester figure, the Dwari (in fact, an alternate name for this form is Dwari Nata).

The play in crux is a battle of wits between Dwari and Arjuna in which Subhadra, Shri Krishna's sister and occasionally Satyabhama his spouse also participate ... the target of attack is Arjuna and through him the Pandavas who are heartily debunked by all. For instance Arjuna's pride in the heroism of the Pandavas is made fun of by the Dwari who cites the example of their humiliating position in Virathnagar while in hiding.[65]

This is typical of the often irreverent and subversive approach of folk arts to the *shastra*s, of which, as Habib takes note, they display a comprehensive knowledge.

The repartees imply knowledge of the Shastras. Book chapter and verse are quoted in support of their arguments by each party not only from the Vedas but also from subsequent books written by other authorities ... wandering into new vistas depending upon the wit and knowledge of the participants.[66]

Habib finds that in this respect it can be called a secular form since 'much of its humour may be contemporary'.[67] Culling a half-hour sequence from the usual three- or four-hour long-performance, Habib presented this as a curtain-raiser to the Prahalad Nataka.

Habib noticed that the village audience were initiates in the form and consequently had high expectations of the performers, a demand to which the latter responded with a virtuosity that came from years of hard work and dedication to their craft. Sadly, economic remuneration was so insufficient that many of them could not sustain it, drifting off into other occupations which paid marginally better. However, there was a silver lining in the form of the use of child actors to play female and even male roles—Habib foresaw that they would grow up into able performers of the protagonists' roles, after being initiated into the form at a young age. He hoped that this presaged a future for these performance forms of Odisha.

These lengthy, intensive workshops with local folk artistes and troupes, to my mind, are a significant aspect of Habib's lifelong involvement with rural and people's culture, despite the fact that the productions did not become part of his regular Naya Theatre repertoire. Here he was putting into practice his professed belief in the role of the catalyst.[68] He was attempting to give back to the field in order to strengthen and revitalise it. He held strong views on the need for give *and* take between the urban artist and the rural folk culture:

There are several others who merely borrow some elements from the folk to embellish their productions for the urban audiences. I believe that imitation of any kind is bad—whether it is of the West or of the folk by urban—because you cannot produce meaningful theatre through imitation. It does harm, both to the urban imitators as well as to the folk forms which are imitated.... If one looks to the villages, one must not do so with the purpose of extracting something from them, or of exploiting them.... So, till the time you approach these forms only with the intention of taking from them, without giving anything in return, you cannot build a creative relationship.... It is important for both to interact with each other to make something of it.[69]

A slightly different kind of workshop experiment was done in connection with his short play, *Manglu Didi*, which was evolved in a workshop in Janjgir, Bilaspur, Chhattisgarh in 1984. It started with a challenge from a friend in the Madhya Pradesh government, Ajay Shankar.

[He] turned around and said to me that you sit there with your armchair criticism every time we get together, but what do we get? We get only second-grade writers to help us. Anyone like you only sits comfortably and criticizes; make yourselves available and we'll show you better results. He put it in such a nice manner that I accepted and I went. I produced *Manglu Didi*, a hilarious comedy about family planning.[70]

Before beginning his creative work, as was his custom, he did his research. He spoke to the doctors to identify the problem—they told him that in the villages it was the men who were against family planning initiatives, even though the women were willing. Next, he gathered the folk troupes or parties usually hired to do shows for government welfare programmes on health, family planning and so on. They told him frankly that they had come only because he had asked them—they either knew him personally or had heard of him—otherwise, since it was a government project, they would not have bothered, using some loophole to excuse themselves, because it was a waste of time for them, even though they were technically employed for the programme. They explained the way it worked on the ground:

They said, you see, they demand so many shows of a certain play and we get paid ... per show ... we fill up the list and show them that we've done it. But each time we do a government programme, there's no attendance, villagers just walk away, they don't want to see it, it's dull. They all insist on our own Nacha, so we perform a Nacha and we say we've done the programme on family planning.[71]

Habib began the creative process with exploring various folk tales and stories, and as they shared stories, he was told one that appealed. It was about a man and a woman who have four or five children to feed, which means they can't eat what they like. So they plot together—once the children are asleep, they'll make some *wadas* (dumplings) and eat some before putting some aside for the kids. Otherwise, as usual, they won't get any. So they start making the preparations but they find, one by one, all the things they need to cook the dish—the grinding stone and pestle, the oil, matches—are missing. After a hectic search, each item is discovered under the pillow of one of the children. They're all awake, having cottoned on to the plan, so the *wadas* are finally made—but they fight over them and finish them all.

Using this as the base, Habib started adding to the tale:

I made up a scene of the gods visiting the village, and they talk about child mortality and mosquitoes and unhygienic conditions and the laziness and sloth in the villages. So they come to examine what … is going on and see … a woman and a man … fighting over poverty and food. The fight is also comical … frustrated and in a rage, she blurts out that, 'if a sixth child is to come, may god will it that you have it instead of I.' And sure enough, his stomach begins to get bloated and he complains of some pain. Then there's a little scene about this—'take this *churan*' or 'go to the *vaid*'. And he says 'No, no, *churan* won't help, there's something moving inside, a ball, there's some kind of life inside'. She says, 'Could you be pregnant?' He says, 'I suspect I am.' 'In that case would you like to go to the doctor?' And he says, 'No, I feel rather affectionate towards it, I'm not going to get rid of it.' And then some visitors hear of it and he wants to escape them and puts on a saree to escape, but they catch hold of him and he's called Manglu didi (Manglu is a man's name), and they say you must get aborted. He refuses and a panchayat is called and the men press him to go in for abortion and he refuses and the women protest, saying that the child should be kept…. And when the men don't agree, the women strike against sex, men, relationships. So then starts another comedy—the men ask for their food or clothes, and when the village sarpanch is rebuking a man discovered to be going to meet his wife, which was forbidden … it appears that … the sarpanch is also trying to do the same thing and so on. Then the gods arrive and while Manglu has gone to the doctor and we're waiting to know what is to happen, the gods decide that there should be no child before eighteen years, and spacing between two children, all the scientific things that we know. I had read a lot about that first. In between the gods hear stories of how somebody died due to too many children too soon and so on, and they explain. Meanwhile, Manglu comes with a baby in his hand, he had delivered.[72]

Some of the workshop participants were apprehensive about whether the play would get accepted in the villages—the idea of a man getting pregnant was too radical for comfort. Habib tried to explain the scientific angle 'about change of sex being scientific, male pregnancy being scientific if you change your sex'[73] but they felt that it would be better if the man was found to have gas or a tumour, rather than a foetus, in his belly. However, the government official who had commissioned the project enjoyed the play so thoroughly that it was decided to go ahead with it—and true enough, it proved to be popular enough with its target audience.

Of course, Habib could not allow the issue to remain unproblematised and over-simplified, with the villagers being seen as the ones guilty of ignorance and backwardness and the government as entirely blameless. He made it a point to talk about the failures of the government as well—'lack of transport, inaccessibility of district level units, lack of *dais* and nurses and doctors and medical care. So the blame is shared.'[74]

Finally, he was satisfied with this play in terms of both form and content; he felt that 'the play was a genuine comedy, very entertaining and hilarious and it made sense, it was talking about family planning, in the end through the mouths of the gods; also because of the sanctity attached to gods in India in the villages, they carry much weight'.[75]

Let us now take a look at the major Naya Theatre productions based on folk material. We have already dealt with *Gaon Ka Naon Sasural* and *Charandas Chor* in detail. *Bahadur Kalarin* comes as an interesting departure from the above, being, as Habib described it, 'a stark tragedy'.[76]

Bahadur Kalarin was a Chhattisgarhi oral tale about incest between mother and son, which Habib found to be a very powerful Oedipal story. He 'was amazed to discover it as an oral tale in a village'. Given its tragic and intense nature, he says he 'was stuck for two years on how to tell the story, how to dramatize it'.[77]

Bahadur Kalarin is a wine-seller. She has a son from a king who is passing through, who seduces her, promises to marry her, but doesn't return. This son grows up and marries 126 girls before he declares to his mother that no woman he has known is as beautiful as her. The mother is appalled, but she hides her reaction and cooks him a very spicy, rich meal, which makes him terribly thirsty. She says there isn't any water in the house, and when he goes out looking for water, forbids the village to provide him with any. He comes back with a raging thirst, and she asks him to go and draw some water from the well. When, very weak, he tries to draw the water, she pushes him into the well and throws a rock on him, killing him, after which she kills herself.

This tale has mystic overtones. Habib points out that 126 is a magical number in folklore:

> [I]n Chhattisgarhi language it's called *chhe agar chhe kori,* which means six plus six times twenty, which is one hundred and twenty six. Their counting goes from twenty to twenty, not hundred, just like the French counting. This motif enters many legends and folktales.... And there're *murtis* in that village saying that this is the Kalarin. This is what the villagers believe.[78]

Habib was shown signs in the village as evidence of the Kalarin's actual existence:

> They showed me, in the village, where I heard this story, holes in the rocks, hundreds of them—'these are the holes made by the *bahus* who were married to Kalarin's son [with their pestles]. There are really some geological formations and they're just like the holes made by that ... the legend goes that she was a beautiful and very popular woman and she grew rich because she sold very good wine. People from far off villages came in bullock carts—and the grooves of the bullock carts were also shown to me, grooves on the rocks and lines on the road—to drink her wine, so that when she told the villagers not to supply water to her son they obeyed her.... The legend says that since she died, there came a plant by the side of the well, and a flower, multicoloured, which reproduced all the ornaments and colours which Kalarin was wearing when she died ... the villagers swear by it, they show me the well where she died, with a flowering tree.[79]

For this play, Habib wanted depth and emotional nuances in the depiction of characters; he wanted shades of grey. But this was not easy to achieve. When he followed his usual process of asking the actors to take on a role and improvise, he got stock black and white responses: 'The lover was bad, he let her down, the son was a scoundrel, a womaniser and a rogue—which didn't give me the play. Even before I'd introduced the more explicit Oedipal impulse into the play, these improvisations didn't help me.'[80] So he began to discuss motivation with them, trying to draw parallels with their own lives, to break through to a deeper empathy with the flawed characters. For example:

> I said look, the raja didn't tell lies to the girl, he genuinely loved her, he meant to come back, he got involved administratively, he didn't tell her that he had another wife at home, so why should you be surprised at all this? This is part of your life. You have two wives quite often.... So why make him into a scoundrel for that? So then I got better results, improvisations about some genuine love and conflict.[81]

Similarly, for the son he got them to think about how the boy may have had an actual psychological problem, finding that young women did not arouse him and that he was fixated on his mother.

> So I said, 'Now add to this, have you never known any incest?' thinking that they may not know of incest. Then they came up with many stories of incest, father and daughter, uncle and niece, father-in-law and daughter-in-law ... it may or may not be true, but they do live together and the folk story, the rumour, is that there's some sexual relationship between them ... it's not important whether it's true or not. It's important that people think so—that means that in their minds the possibility exists.[82]

This approach worked. He began to see a change in the way the actors played their roles. Fida Bai in particular, whom he praised for the maturity and subtlety of her acting:

> And then Fida Bai brought such sensitivity to the oiling of the hair and to the feeding of the meal to the boy, the sensitivity of the touching, the delicate way she did it, and the reaction of the boy when she touched his hair, and his eyes full of desire, before he discovers himself. And after his discovery, when she pretends, then again she gives him the meal and does the same things so that he remains deceived and feels happy and he's happy without sex, even when she's touching and being loving to him.[83]

Habib was delighted with the results: 'Then I got the wealth and the richness of the play and the texture which I wanted.'[84] He explains:

> The thing is that sometimes, like in this case, there is an awareness. But I have to make them aware of their awareness. They were aware of incest, but they weren't aware of the fact that incest can be analysed and dissected, reasoned out as an ailment, as a sickness.[85]

This is a perfect example of his psychological approach to actor training and preparation, a totally different experience from the Nacha training which does not require such in depth or layered understanding of motivation and behaviour. He had no doubt that the actors would grasp the ideas he was discussing:

> I would, even in the normal course of things, try to get the actor to relate himself to the reality around him, to his own experience; and knowing their experience as I do, I propel them towards that reality so that they can get the feel of what they are doing. And in this case, most of them being illiterate

was quite an advantage because I talked them closer to the text and to the root of the matter. Whenever I came across any stumbling blocks such as this, I'd make it a kind of classroom in which exchange could take place. They'd narrate to me stories of incest and I'd analyse incest and tell them my way of looking at it; at least one additional way of looking at incest from a scientific point of view, a doctor's point of view, an analytical point of view, as a disease. They have the mental equipment to grasp it and to produce it in their acting.[86]

In terms of form, there are two masterful instances of the use of song as a narrative device, where a longish stretch of the story gets aesthetically communicated through a single song and dance sequence. The first is the depiction of 126 brides:

I solved that through a tribal dance and one song in two minutes. The dance is going on and they're sleeping one after the other, two or three girls, and then just declaring one hundred and twenty six marriages. So it got simply done because by now I'd solved the problem of time and space and action easily.[87]

The second is when the mother forbids the villagers to give her son water: 'There's a song in which ritualistically I've shown the villagers condemning him, no water, not one drop to drink and he's becoming thirstier, in the middle of their circular dance.'[88] There is a final song at the end, sung by the mother after killing her son. 'The song is just a mother singing for the loss of her only son, only child.' Agonised, she whirls in a dance, and at the end, on the *sama*,[89] produces a dagger and she dies. Here, the song is used to emphasise the theme and deepen the poignancy of the moment.

Whereas *Bahadur Kalarin* is a psychological—Oedipal—tragedy, *Hirma Ki Amar Kahani*, also a tragedy, is a very political play, a story about tribals in Bastar. Here the folk material is not folk tale or legend, but tribal history. The play is based on the life of Pravir Chand Bhanjdev, erstwhile ruler of Bastar.[90] In it, Hirma Singhdeo Gangvanshi is the ruler of the tribal state of Titur Basna. The play deals with the clash between Hirma and the central government—a clash of values, priorities, attitudes towards development and friction over rival power bases and systems of governance. Presented in late 1985, it foregrounded the problematic tribal question, not least by underlining the complexities and ambiguities inherent in the situation. This ambiguity infuses the play. Hirma is a sympathetic and heroic figure as a fighter for tribal rights, but at the same time is capable of ferocious cruelty—his feudal attitudes are not downplayed by the playwright. Discussing this, Habib says:

> As far as I am concerned, the play was a kind of tight-rope dance trying to strike a balance between feudalism and democracy—feudalism which would appear to be rather undefendable and yet might show some unassailable benign qualities; and democracy which needs to be upheld, but which is also occasionally capable of carrying on a masquerade trying to conceal its fascist fangs underneath. I had tried to show a benevolent Raja of a tribe with some unaccountable personal kinks in confrontation with the democratic apparatus of the govt. which also carried more tyranny than the Raja was capable of. In the end, the king was liquidated rather treacherously.[91]

The collector, a friend of Hirma's, while understanding Hirma's viewpoint, is also a loyal representative of the government. The play moves inexorably towards the violent ending of Hirma's death—only to close with the popular conviction that Hirma still lives, even as a 'holy man' appears claiming to be him. Evoking Brecht, the play stirs up disturbing questions without offering any easy solutions.

Habib stresses the complexity of the issues thrown up by the play:

> The play does not, cannot, offer a solution. But I think it does present the dilemma in its naked form.... At the end, it is for you to answer the questions posed: Who is the victor? What is development? Does development mean the same thing for all societies, including the tribals?[92]

In his thoughtful review of the play, theatre activist Safdar Hashmi of Jana Natya Manch questioned the 'fundamental ambivalence in Habib Tanvir's stand on the tribal question'.[93] Habib comments:

> Safdar sensed the difficult theme, and he was equally keenly sensitive to my unresolved dilemma. Was I, in trying to decry one of the more abominable aspects of democracy, inadvertently and helplessly also tending to support a feudal regime despite some of its obnoxious manifestations? Had I then failed somewhere after all? I have no answer to the question suggested by Safdar in his review.[94]

Talking of his motivation in taking up this play, he said:

> It was part of my intention through this production to tell some elements … that there are two distinct camps and that I'm certainly not in the rightist

camp. Secondly, the theatre of debate and agit-prop that I did during my IPTA days still beckons to me. I had been wanting to use elements of that theatre for a long time. Then the problem of the tribals which I have taken up in *Hirma* is such that to deal with it only in a spectacular or festive manner, which is what most people today are doing, would have been to turn my back to it. The subject, the script I wrote and the numerous misconceptions that surround the problem made it more or less imperative for me to confront it politically.[95]

Habib's daughter, Nageen Tanvir, reminiscences about the process of preparing *Hirma*:

We were doing a workshop in Bastar in the Dantewara district … to incorporate the adivasis in the play. Most of the songs were written in the jungles of Bastar…. For instance, the last song in the play 'Thorik aankhein utha ke dekh, aakash ke rang hai neela' was composed in the village Jeeramtarai. We were staying in a mud hut and one evening, the sun was setting and Baba was lying on a charpai in the angan looking up at the azure sky and a quotation of C. V. Raman the scientist came to his mind—'You have only to look up and you will see that the sky is blue'—so poetically said. Baba immediately composed the first line, 'Thorik aankhein utha ke dekh, aakash ke rang hai neela'. He sat up and jotted the lines in Urdu in his work diary … the rest of the song followed … the song was fully composed within two or three days. The tune was composed by Baba himself. The tune of another song—'Yahi hamari mahatari, yeh dharti itni pyari'—which is sung during the vidhan sabha scene just before the interval—belonged to a Juthika Roy bhajan. I helped Baba in this song. It had five or six tunes. Baba, myself, Devi Lal, Amardas (the tabla player), Shankar (the clarinet player) and Ranu Bardhan were involved in the process of this particular song.[96]

The first show of *Hirma* was done in the open, in a railway stadium in Bilaspur, with the audience seated in the stands. According to Habib, it was performed with a cast of 70, including several tribal parties,

and they appeared to be enjoying dancing on the ground, on the grass, the sheer earth—and the dust being raised looked authentic, their feet felt firm and good, being used to earth. The actors who were playing the policemen, chasing people, enjoyed running and I enjoyed seeing them run, just run, about seventy feet.[97]

Later shows had to adjust to more conventional stages and performance arenas, but the sense of openness and space remained.

Another Chhattisgarhi folk form which Habib worked with was Chandaini—a form known as Lorikayan in Bihar—which tells the story of the lovers Lorik and Chanda.[98] *Sone Sagar*, presented in 1980, featured Naya Theatre actors Fida Bai, Bulwa Ram, Ram Charan, Mala Bai, Devi Lal amongst others.

Habib describes how he tracked down this little known folk form:

> Chandaini was a rare theatre form in Chhattisgarh till about seven years ago when we first contacted a lone old balladeer performing the story. At that time we discovered only two or three Chandaini groups. Recently, however, they have multiplied and now there are several groups of young artists staging Chandaini. They, however, remain confined to the districts of Raipur and Bilaspur.[99]

Just like the Pandavani performer with his *Mahabharata*, the Chandaini balladeer too takes more than 18 nights to unfold his story in full. There are other similarities—the main artist sings, narrates and dances with support from four or five instrumentalists and singers who provide the vocal refrain. However, in the case of Chandaini, as per the brochure note, 'the story being secular, oral and rarely known, the audience response to it differs'. Habib has an interesting insight here—he suggests that the secular nature of the tale results in a different expectation from the audience, resulting in a more exuberant song and dance style which casts its own spell on the audience so that they don't care if the tale is complete in all its details. In any case, different troupes do differ in terms of story details, although telling the same basic story.

Habib's production, needless to say, makes certain selections from the vast body of the narrative, guided by what he wishes to emphasise:

> In editing the rich sprawling legend, we had many choices. We have used our choice in projecting certain elements as against certain others and totally suppressed some aspects. For instance, the pastoral element ... suited our purpose, so we have integrated the cattle more closely with human characters. On the other hand, the element of magic appeared to divert us from our theme, so we sacrificed situations and characters representing this particular metaphoric element. In the process, the characters also underwent a change, and new situations and events got created. Fundamentally, however, our whole purpose has been to make a complex story clear in its narrative. In so doing, we became conscious of a dual purpose. Our other purpose was to inject some ambivalence into a story which in one sense is actually simple.[100]

In terms of the songs too, he states that he has not confined himself to using only Chandaini tunes, although they have been included in the production.

Ponga Pandit, and its earlier incarnation, *Jamadarin*, found its way into the Naya Theatre repertoire in 1970.[101] This was a popular Nacha *nakal* or comic skit prepared by veteran Nacha artistes Sitaram and Sukhram, which had been on the circuit since 1935 or so. It has been described as a 'hilarious attack on casteism'.[102] Habib had first seen it in 1958. At the time, Madanlal was playing the greedy pandit, Bulwa Ram the *jamadarin* (or female sweeper), and Thakur Ram the villager.[103] The story is about a shrewd *jamadarin* or sweeper who enters a temple, where she counters the contempt of the priest with the simple stratagem of touching each of the items which the pandit immediately pronounces 'polluted'; she ends up walking off with them all—including the idol—dismissing the priest as unnecessary since she doesn't need him anymore. According to Habib,

> This farce deals with major issues with great depth but also great simplic-
> ity. The subject shows up the greed of an avaricious pandit and the evils of
> chhua-chhuth or untouchability; above all the wonder of this play is that
> it shows that one can approach God directly, without resorting to any via
> medium—and does it through wit and humour, with a light touch.[104]

It is clear that this piece appealed to Habib as much for its subject matter as for its deft comic treatment. He felt that 'the goal of the theatre is not just to draw crowds or to achieve cheap popularity; it should, in fact, wean them away from cheap and vacuous entertainment towards a value based theatre. Our most important work is to re-establish the right values'.[105] Given this belief, a piece like *Ponga Pandit* suited him down to the ground; it was a creation of the people, it spoke of important issues of direct relevance to the people, and it was great theatre.

In a farcical twist worthy of the farcical nature of the play, this staple of the Nacha circuit, conceived by the Chhattisgarhi players themselves, drew the ire of the Hindu rightwing in the 1990s. Sudhanva Deshpande, writing in 2003, underscores the arbitrary nature of the attacks:

> *Ponga Pandit* is performed by dozens of Nacha companies all over Madhya
> Pradesh and Chhattisgarh, hundreds and thousands of times. For the past few
> years it has come under attack from the Hindu Right, in India and abroad.
> It is curious, sometimes it is attacked, sometimes not. Just before the recent
> spate of attacks and the disturbances actually began, Tanvir had toured 25

cities of Chhattisgarh in June and July with the same play and nobody raised any objection. But in Madhya Pradesh, the same play came under attack. It was disrupted at various points.[106]

Tracing the trajectory of the attacks, Habib recalls that in 1992, after the demolition of the Babri Masjid,[107] he held shows in Delhi at various colleges and elsewhere; in 1993, in Ayodhya itself, without any trouble. However, that same year, when he presented the play in Gwalior at a seminar on communalism, 'there was obstruction by the Sangh Parivar for the first time. Stones were thrown on the stage by a few hoodlums who were later chased away, after which the play completed its course'.[108] However, the ripples continued to spread—an article on the edit page of the *Indian Express* bracketed Habib Tanvir with Salman Rushdie, 'condemning the play as anti-Hindu'.[109] This was picked up by several other publications and newspapers. Repercussions were felt as far afield as England, where explanations were demanded of the touring Naya Theatre by the Sangh Parivar of England.

Habib's response to the hooliganism and violence, to the attacks on the play as anti-Hindu, was to persist with staging it, with the support of his troupe. He said, 'One must never ignore such allegations. If they can propagate lies, it is my job to counter those lies. Yes, by more such plays and by more such performances.'[110]

His play *Sarak* (meaning 'road') grew out of a workshop commissioned by the literacy section of the Department of Culture, Government of India. He decided that rather than follow the letter of the concept of literacy he preferred to address the spirit of it, which was *gnan* (consciousness and awareness). The workshop was held in Bilaspur, and the piece is an exemplary example of how he worked with improvisation, collaborating with his actors to develop a concept, contributing his direction, guidance, ability to provoke thought and helping them evolve a simple idea into a complex performance that communicates on several levels. Let us hear it in his own words:

> I told them to go to the next room and do some improvisation. Those were panchayat election times ... and there's a candidate and there's a village and he addresses them, asking them to vote for him and they make their demands. They say, make a road for us, bring us water, make a school for us. He becomes a minister and then he doesn't fulfil those demands. Somehow he has a heart-attack and dies and the contractor becomes the minister. Then I said, now let's talk about it.... And they said, it's rather dull ... rather clichéd—they used other words but they meant clichéd.... So I said, begin again and this

time, instead of asking the candidate to promise to make a road, ask him to break the road that you have, demolish the school, that you don't want any water, try and improvise right now. And they made their demands, promise us that you'll break the road, then we'll vote for you etc. And everybody present began to laugh. I said it's now becoming very funny, isn't it? They said yes. I said, now put some meaning into it, because fun without meaning has no meaning and no place in drama. So they started justifying why the road should be broken and they came up with a wealth of details.... Like: the weekly village market coming and disturbing our culture, foresters using the road and taking our rice or forest produce, our wealth going out because of the road, we getting exploited, deprived, our wildlife getting destroyed and killed by the road through which city tourists and foresters come and poach, and a million reasons, what happens to the animals, the birds, the wildlife, the trees and environment, to agriculture, to things of daily usage—hard liquor comes through the road, we don't want it, we brew our own wines and they're nourishing etc.—therefore break the road. So it became a satire on development and ... we're doing it now, successfully, and it's hilarious, right from beginning to end.[111]

In terms of form, Habib tried out different combinations to get the dramatic tension right. First he wrote it in three scenes thinking it might turn into a full-length play, but it was only an hour long. After doing several shows all over the country for Adult Literacy Day, the play was really tight and strong. They were getting good reactions to just the third scene alone. As the play was working so well, Habib decided to try the longer version with three scenes. He asked his actors if they thought it would have the same tension, and they thought it would. So after working on it some more, polishing and fine-tuning, they launched it in Ujjain. This version was a little under one hour long, with just one song, broken into three stanzas. But Habib was dissatisfied—he thought it should be brought back to its shorter form,

maybe just the third scene—no explanations about the breaking of the road, only some more elements taken from the other two scenes into the third, revising it drastically, cutting it and making it very terse. So this is the conclusion ... first we had a 25 minute play, now we have a 50–55 minute play, and I think we'll finally have a 40 minute play, and be content with that.[112]

This kind of restless perfectionism is typical of Habib—even with his older plays he has said that he tries to inject something new, something different or fresh, to break the sense of sameness or boredom that comes from frequent repetition.

In terms of content, he says that this play is a satire on development. In it he is

> trying to suggest that there're many paths to development, and that for the indigenous people, the tribals and others in the country, there must be different paths; that what is mainstream development for the whole country, in a regimented fashion, leads to underdevelopment for large sections of the people. This is the theme of the play.[113]

The concerns are the same as with his earlier play, *Hirma*, but whereas that was an intense tragedy, this is a hilarious satire.

No discussion of Habib's relationship with folk material and culture can be complete without taking into account his use of songs, music, ritual and dance. These will be taken up in the next chapter.

Notes

1. 'My literary interest brought me to … the dialects because I considered that to be the source for all great literature. Tulsidas, Mirabai, Kabir—all derived such strength from the people's dialects', Habib Tanvir, 'In Conversation with Anjum Katyal' in Neeraj Malik and Javed Malick (eds), *Habib Tanvir: Reflections and Reminiscences* (Delhi: SAHMAT, 2010), p. 132.
2. 'Habib Tanvir Interviewed' by Rajinder Paul [*Enact*, March 1974], in *Nukkad*, p. 87.
3. Habib Tanvir, 'Cultural Persuasions of Politics and Their Implications', VIII P. C. Joshi Memorial Lecture on 16 October 2000 at Jawaharlal Nehru University, New Delhi; included in *Nukkad*, p. 32.
4. Habib Tanvir, 'Sustaining Vitality', lecture delivered at the International Conference on the Vitality of India in the Regional and International Perspective, in Shimla in June 2004. Included in *Nukkad*, p. 58.
5. Habib Tanvir interviewed by Bindu Batra, 'Folk Theatre: What Is its place in India Today?' [*Youth Times*, 19 November 1974] in *Nukkad*, p. 82.
6. Habib Tanvir, 'The Crisis of Identity and the Question of Authenticity in Theatre', paper presented at the seminar on Perspectives of Contemporary Indian Theatre, organised by the Sangeet Natak Akademi on 17–19 December 1984, New Delhi. Included in *Nukkad*, p. 115.
7. Tanvir, 'Cultural Persuasions of Politics and Their Implications', p. 32.
8. Habib Tanvir, 'The Indian Experiment' [in *Enact*, Mar–Apr 1977] in *Nukkad*, p. 112.
9. Tanvir, 'Cultural Persuasions of Politics and Their Implications', p. 32.
10. 'Habib Tanvir Interviewed' by Rajinder Paul, in *Nukkad*, p. 87.
11. See Chapter 6 ('Naya Theatre and Other Milestones').
12. Tanvir, 'In Conversation with Javed Malick', p. 110.
13. This play was part of the 1971 Congress (I) election campaign. See Sudhanva Deshpande, 'Upside-Down Midas' in *Nukkad*, pp. 15–16. Javed Malick says, 'Tanvir's politics has had its share of controversy too. During the Lok Sabha elections of 1971, he wrote and produced a play called Indra Lok Sabha in support of Indira Gandhi's candidates

and … toured the production through the streets of Delhi', Javed Malick, 'Habib Tanvir: The Making of a Legend', *Theatre India*, November 2000 [in *Nukkad*, note 4, p. 12].

14. Naya Theatre brochure for Indra Lok Sabha, 1–7 March 1971, Fine Arts Theatre, Delhi.

15. The reference is to the classic Urdu opera style play by Agha Hasan Amanat, first staged in 1853.

16. Naya Theatre brochure for *Indra Lok Sabha*.

17. See Chapter 1 ('Growing up in Raipur, and Early Influences').

18. Naya Theatre brochure for *Indra Lok Sabha*.

19. Ibid.

20. See Javed Malick, 'Habib Tanvir: The Making of a Legend' in *Nukkad*, note 4, p. 12.

21. Naya Theatre brochure for *Arjun Ka Sarthi* and *Kushtia Ka Chaprasi*, 5–7, 11–14 October, Fine Arts Theatre, Delhi.

22. Habib Tanvir, *STQ*, p. 22.

23. Naya Theatre brochure for *Arjun Ka Sarthi* and *Kushtia Ka Chaprasi*.

24. Ibid.

25. Ibid.

26. Naya Theatre brochure for *Raja Chamba Aur Char Bhai*, undated.

27. Habib Tanvir interviewed by Bindu Batra, p. 82.

28. Javed Malick, 'Habib Tanvir: The Making of a Legend', p. 11.

29. Habib Tanvir interviewed by Bindu Batra, p. 82.

30. Habib Tanvir, 'In Conversation with Shampa Shah' in Neeraj Malik and Javed Malick (ed.), *Habib Tanvir: Reflections & Reminiscences* (Delhi: SAHMAT, 2010), p. 146.

31. Ibid., p. 149.

32. See Chapter 6 ('Naya Theatre and Other Milestones').

33. Habib Tanvir, 'Journey into Theatre' in Tata Chemicals Booklet, 1976, in *Nukkad*, p. 101.

34. Tanvir, 'In Conversation with Javed Malick', p. 112.

35. Tanvir, *STQ*, p. 25.

36. Tanvir, 'In Conversation with Javed Malick', p. 112.

37. Tanvir, 'In Conversation with Shampa Shah', pp. 146–147.

38. Tanvir, 'In Conversation with Javed Malick', p. 112.

39. A form of salutation or invocation.

40. Brochure for Naya Theatre's *Thakur Pritipal Singh* (on 30–31 March and 1 April 1976) and *Gaon Ka Naam Sasural, Mor Naam Damad* (on 2–4 April 1976) at Triveni Garden Theatre.

41. Habib Tanvir, 'In Conversation with Shampa Shah', p. 148.

42. Brochure for Naya Theatre's *Thakur Pritipal Singh*.

43. Habib Tanvir, 'In Conversation with Shampa Shah', pp. 146–147.

44. Brochure for Naya Theatre's *Thakur Pritipal Singh*.

45. Habib Tanvir interviewed by Bindu Batra.

46. Habib Tanvir, 'In Conversation with Shampa Shah', p. 148.

47. Director's Note, 'Approach to Production', Naya Theatre brochure for *Shahi Lakarhara* and *Jani Chor*, 1976, p. 1.

48. Ibid., pp. 1–2.

49. Ibid.

50. Ibid., p. 2.

51. Ibid.

52. Ibid., p. 3.
53. Ibid.
54. Ibid., p. 4.
55. In Indian classical music, this is a bowed, stringed instrument with a short neck.
56. Note, 'Swang Workshop at Rai', Naya Theatre brochure for *Shahi Lakarhara* and *Jani Chor*, 1976, p. 9.
57. Director's Note, 'Approach to Production', pp. 4–5.
58. Note, 'Swang Workshop at Rai', p. 9.
59. This is based on the legend of Hirankashyap and his son Prahlad and can be read as a struggle over the right to individual freedom of worship.
60. Director's note, Naya Theatre brochure for *Prahalad Nataka*, 21, 28, 30 April in Orissa, 19–20 May in New Delhi, 27 May at Sangeet Natak Akademi, Bhubaneswar.
61. Ibid.
62. Ibid.
63. Habib Tanvir, 'In Conversation with Shampa Shah', p. 148.
64. Director's note, Naya Theatre brochure for *Prahalad Nataka*.
65. Ibid.
66. Ibid.
67. Ibid.
68. See Chapter 6 ('Naya Theatre and Other Milestones').
69. Habib Tanvir, 'In Conversation with Shampa Shah', p. 145.
70. Tanvir, *STQ*, p. 37.
71. Ibid.
72. Tanvir, *STQ*, p. 38.
73. Ibid.
74. Ibid.
75. Ibid.
76. Ibid., p. 11.
77. Ibid., p. 31.
78. Ibid., p. 32.
79. Ibid., pp. 33–34.
80. Ibid., p. 32.
81. Ibid.
82. Ibid.
83. Ibid.
84. Ibid.
85. Ibid., p. 35.
86. Ibid.
87. Ibid., p. 33.
88. Ibid., p. 34.
89. The first beat of a rhythmic cycle in traditional Indian music and dance.
90. Habib Tanvir, 'A Dilemma of Democracy', Preface to *The Living Tale of Hirma*, translated by Anjum Katyal (Kolkata: Seagull Books, 2005), pp. 1–3.
91. Habib Tanvir, 'Janam Comes of Age' in Sudhanva Deshpande (ed.), *Theatre of the Streets: The Jana Natya Manch Experience* (New Delhi: Jana Natya Manch, 2007), p. 72.
92. Habib Tanvir, 'A Dilemma of Democracy', p. 4.
93. Safdar Hashmi, 'Habib Tanvir's Latest Play: Hirma Ki Amar Kahani', 1 December 1985 (courtesy SAHMAT, The Right to Perform), included in *Nukkad*, p. 200.
94. Tanvir, 'Janam Comes of Age', p. 72.

95. Quoted in Safdar Hashmi's review, 'Habib Tanvir's Latest Play: Hirma Ki Amar Kahani', in *Nukkad*, p. 200.
96. 'Ranu Bardhan, a well-known sitarist and Shanti Bardhan's younger brother, has worked on a lot of Chhattisgarhi folk tunes with Baba'—Nageen Tanvir, personal communication, April 2011. Unpublished.
97. Tanvir, *STQ*, p. 29.
98. Habib finds it 'significant that the former title [Chandaini] celebrates the heroine and the latter [Lorikayan] the hero.' This signals a difference in emphasis—in Chandaini the woman emerges as the central character, in Lorikayan, the man is the protagonist. Lorikayan employs Bidesia as the predominant style of singing; Chandaini has its own characteristic style and tunes. Director's Note, Naya Theatre brochure for *Sone Sagar*, undated, c.1980.
99. Director's Note, Naya Theatre brochure for *Sone Sagar*.
100. Ibid.
101. Sameera Iyengar (ed.), *On the Road with Naya Theatre* (Prithvi Theatre Yearbook, 2006), entry for 17 June.
102. 'Trauma of Our Times', *The Hindu*, 27 August 1993, in Iyengar (ed.), *On the Road with Naya Theatre*.
103. Director's Note, Naya Theatre brochure for *Sadbhavna Yatra*: Two Plays; *Lahore and Ponga Pandit*. Undated. Translated by Anjum Katyal.
104. Ibid.
105. Habib Tanvir, 'In Conversation with Shampa Shah', p. 145.
106. Iyengar (ed.), *On the Road with Naya Theatre*. For details of the attack, see Sudhanva Deshpande, 'Habib Tanvir under Attack', *Economic and Political Weekly*, 38 (35), 30 August–5 September 2003.
107. Destruction of a disputed religious site in Ayodhya by Hindu Rightwing activists, a watershed in Indian history.
108. Iyengar (ed.), *On the Road with Naya Theatre*.
109. Ibid.
110. Ibid.
111. Tanvir, *STQ*, pp. 36–37.
112. Ibid., p. 37.
113. Ibid.

CHAPTER ELEVEN

MUSIC, SONG AND DANCE

Dance and live music were always an integral part of Habib Tanvir productions.
A scene from *Charandas Chor* (1982). Photo courtesy Avinash Pasricha

Songs were perhaps the first kind of folk material that Habib incorporated into his theatre. We know that songs and music were a major interest from a very young age. He mentions learning Chhattisgarhi folk tunes even as a child and has often acknowledged his debt to the IPTA for exposing him to the wide variety of folk music in India. His first major play, *Agra Bazaar*, included songs; thereafter, the presence of live music and songs, often accompanied by dances, was a staple of his theatre style.

Before we turn to specific examples of usage, it is useful to understand the nature of his approach to folk songs. Apart from finding them musically attractive, he had a strong anthropological interest in them as well and often went out of his way for a new musical insight:

I've constantly explored the temple for my songs, tunes, and other things. In Dongargarh, there was Began Bai, a priestess who taught me about religious music. I was so inspired with her knowledge and I stayed in the dharamshala for days immersing myself in the music.[1]

His own Chhattisgarh region was very rich in folk tunes: 'The songs were in the fields, at harvesting time, in the mandir, during rituals, in childbirth, good, authentic songs, death songs, marriage songs, all these existed in society, but on the rustic stage little of it was reflected.'[2] Habib realised that the disappearance of a traditional way of life was taking the songs with it—fewer and fewer people still remembered, let along sang, the old songs. He undertook to save as many from extinction as he could, and also to revive the old songs by incorporating them into his productions. He taught his troupe these songs, locating them at workshops, from older artistes, from wherever he happened to come across them.

> For instance, when the well-known folklorist, Komal Kothari, invited me to participate in a workshop in Rajasthan, we took up a *khayal* in this way. We found an old folk artiste who remembered how it was sung thirty years ago and with some persuasion made the actors sing it in that way.[3]

Devi Lal Nag, who played the harmonium and formed part of the Naya Theatre musicians' group, recalls learning folk tunes from across the country—'a Haryanvi tune and also a Gujarati one in *Mitti Ki Gadi*: "Jaa re jaa re ab jaa re andhakar"'.[4] In fact, Habib's theatre ended up as quite a treasure trove of ethnic heritage music. Devi Lal elaborates: 'Many of the village musical forms—Sua, Dalia, Karma, Jawanra, Gaura, Panthi and Chameni—have entered Habib Sahib's theatre.'[5]

Apart from collecting traditional songs, Habib would also combine folk tunes or write fresh lyrics to existing melodies or interweave traditional words and choruses with newly written verses.

> Sometimes, I also modify the music to make it blend. For example, I changed the rhythm of the tabla in one folk song. In another I changed the tune a little. Sometimes I have used the Chhattisgarhi tunes like an orchestra … in *Agra Bazaar*, the song *Baja re baja* occurs within another song *Jor Baldeoji ka mela hai*. Here the audience already knows that … the lyrics are not important, only the sound matters. The song is being sung while the child's cart is being pulled along. So the attention of the audience is focused on the sound and the rhythm.[6]

He found that there was a musical correlation between the traditional melodies of different regions and that they could at times quite easily be woven together to form fresh tunes. He said, 'Rather than concern myself with purity, I have often tried to blend various kinds of music … it is not purity alone which can produce such harmonious effect … you mould and create a harmony of your own.'[7] In fact, purity or *shudhhata* was not important to him:

> Time and again I've noticed that the blend is harmonious, despite what the purists might say about *shudhhata*, one goes by the inner harmony one feels, confidently. There's no such thing as *shudhhata* alone creating harmony, and blending or mixing producing disharmony. This is a fallacy … if our ears are pleased and we trust our own aesthetics, well then fine, we can trust the *darshak* to receive it. In between comes the pundit. The *darshak* takes it, you feel happy and the pundit objects, so who is wrong? The pundit is wrong.[8]

Nageen, a trained singer who was closely involved with the music of Naya Theatre productions, reminisces about how obsessed her father would get with the musical aspect of a play:

> When Baba worked on music he spent days, weeks on a particular song. He made us repeat one single line several times until we got it just right (like the traditional ustads). To make [the artistes] mug up the lyrics of the songs was an uphill task since they used to memorize by rote…. Baba worked very hard when new lyrics were written to traditional tunes. Things became more difficult for the artistes when Baba composed his own tunes, to which their ears were not attuned … for days and weeks work on just music would take place. Devi Lal was asked to compose music between the antaras on his harmonium. This process too took days. Even when by himself, Baba would keep humming the tunes and try to fit in the words.[9]

Clearly music was, to Habib, a very important aspect of the overall production, requiring at least as much attention as the acting or any other aspect.

In *Agra Bazaar*, songs are already being used to make a philosophical comment on the action on stage (the fakirs' songs) as well as part of the narrative (the vendors' songs). Tellingly, Habib does not see the songs as extrinsic to the essential dramatic unfolding of the play as fillers or interludes; on the contrary, they are as intrinsic to his directorial intent as other aspects of the structure. He grapples with how to interlock the narrative flow and the songs:

It was necessary to take this story to its logical climax. In the course of working out this problem, yet another difficulty got sorted out which had to do with the aesthetic and semantic impact of the music. I had already arranged the vendors' songs into one sequence. The three songs are sung one after another in quick succession. Each has a different tune. To make the transition from one tune to another dramatically effective, a musical bridge was needed. I obtained this bridge by using a Chhattisgarhi folk song as a recurrent orchestra. The problem now was that these songs were immediately followed by the 'Aadminama' which had an entirely different tune. The poem could not be shifted anywhere else because it provided a perfect ending for the play. What helped was the scene that I had written as the culmination of the story of the rivalry between the Police Constable and the Rake which shows how through duplicity, falsehood, brute force and misuse of his position, the Police Constable has the Rake arrested on trumped-up charges and thus achieves a victory over him. To solve my musical problem I placed this brief scene between the vendors' songs and the last chorus (the 'Aadminama'). This solved my problem regarding the musical transition as well as completed the story.[10]

He is already using folk melodies and hybrid musical elements: 'The songs in the play were mostly set to the tunes that I had either heard during my childhood or had composed for my own poetry. Only the tune of "Banjaranama" was composed by Khalili of Bhatinda.'[11]

Europe brought Habib to Brecht and a deeper understanding of the role music could play in theatre. According to Brecht:

Music must strongly resist the smooth incorporation which is generally expected of it and turns it into an unthinking slavery. Music does not 'accompany' except in the form of comment. It cannot simply 'express itself' by discharging the emotions with which the incidents of the play have filled it.... Music can make its point in a number of ways and with full independence, and can react in its own manner to the subjects dealt with; at the same time it can also quite simply help to lend variety to the entertainment.[12]

Combined with his own inclination to include music--especially folk melodies—in his productions, the Brechtian approach to music showed the way to very inventive and creative uses of music in all subsequent Habib Tanvir productions. He contrasted the Brechtian employment of songs and music with the way it was done in folk theatre:

Today, the folk theatre in India, by and large, will have songs and music in a very fine or didactic way of preaching and teaching, to say that such and such a thing is bad and you must give it up. It is a little ornament of a song or a dance, or a reformative kind of a performance or to comment on it in a very straightforward manner to suggest that this is bad: adultery is bad and therefore you must be faithful to your wife or whatever. On the other hand, Brecht does not have this kind of preaching. Brecht uses music … in a very, very incisive way, a thought provoking way. He will have one song in a play and another song contradicting it so that between the two forces you can arrive at your own conclusion.[13]

So, although he used the folk songs and melodies intensively in his productions, he did not use them in the folk manner; instead he followed Brecht in this aspect:

Charandas Chor … has a song which goes—Suno, suno sangwari, Bhai mor Charandas chor nai hai. It means, listen friend, Charandas is not really a thief, there are bigger thieves in society. Charandas is really a good man; he steals from the rich and gives it to the poor, so on so forth. In another song one woman is addressing another woman—look, a thief is coming, hide your things, he is a great thief, he can steal anything, protect yourself.... This is direct borrowing from Brecht, not of the songs but of the technique. You can just go along with the character and sing it from one point of view, then have another song from another point of view and let the people think about it.[14]

Javed Malick sees the songs in Habib Tanvir's plays as exemplars of the 'rich interaction between Tanvir's urban, modern consciousness and the folk styles and forms'.[15] He holds up *Kamdeo Ka Apna Basant Ritu Ka Sapna* and *Sajapur Ki Shantibai* as examples of this:

In these plays, he has worked close to the original text and written songs which reproduce the rich imagery and humour of Shakespeare's poetry and the complex ideas of Brecht. Despite this fidelity to the original texts, not only has Tanvir given his poetic composition the authenticity and freshness of the original but has also fitted his words to native folk tunes with remark-able ease and skill.[16]

Given that the singers of these songs were folk artistes, this suited them perfectly.

Typically, a Naya Theatre production will open with a song, sometimes accompanied by dance; songs will punctuate the production and usually close it as well. A live orchestra, sometimes consisting of just two or three musicians, will perform on stage, usually sitting on one side in full view of the audience. Musically the melodies are strong, vigorous, haunting.

Philosophical, metaphorical, oblique—the words are linked to the content
in different ways.

They can open up a whole new dimension to the narrative and bring up
important themes which may not be immediately obvious in the action.
Habib gives us an example of this:

> I had used the refrain 'Charandas, Yam se chori to mat karbey' (literally,
> 'Charandas, do not ever steal from Death'), in the Panthi song, because
> I wanted it to work on the audience's mind subliminally, allowing them
> something like a premonition of the death that comes at the end of the play.
> The sado-masochistic aspects of the Panthi dance, which accompanies this
> song, also suggest what is to come. The spectators may not be conscious of
> all this but these images, I believe, work on their minds and prepare them
> for the approaching death.[17]

They often add a layer of interpretation or ambiguity to what one is
seeing on stage. For example, the tongue-in-cheek comment on gurus who
exploit their disciples' devotion in this song from *Charandas Chor* (where
the 'due' is dual, of course—not just the respect and recognition but also
the guru *dakshina* or fee):

> Is it salvation you want? Just
> Give the guru his due.
> All learning is a sham till you
> Give the guru his due.
> Nothing will work for you till you
> Give the guru his due.
> Watch good things happen to you, once you
> Give the guru his due.[18]

At other times they offer a social critique, as in the *Charandas* song:

> There are so many rogues about, who do not look like thieves,
> Impressive turbans on their heads, softly shod their feet,
> But open up their safes and you will surely see,
> Stolen goods, ill-gotten wealth, riches got for free.[19]

The fakirs in *Agra Bazaar*, functioning as a sort of chorus, sing songs of
comment on social issues. Their opening song provides an introduction
to the socio-economic condition of Agra, establishing the milieu against
which the play unfolds:

Poverty has destroyed what was once a lovely city,
Every street woebegone, every mansion arouses pity;
A garden needs a gardener in order to grow and thrive,
But Agra waits in vain for a tender, caring eye.[20]

Friction in the bazaar between rival vendors is punctuated by the fakirs singing about the effect of poverty on the human psyche. One of the songs has the refrain 'Only the poor know the pain of poverty'.[21] Later, they sing about how 'All the world loves a flatterer/God loves one too',[22] just after a sequence where the 'literati' indulge in some mutual praise. Another fakir song comes straight after money matters are discussed between an aspiring-to-be-published poet and the bookseller:

Money is what the rich desire
Money is what the poor require
Of power and glory money's the sire,
Makes the world spin and go haywire;
To colour and beauty money gives birth,
The penniless have no value, no worth.[23]

The criticism of worldly wealth and greed is reiterated in the fakirs' post-interval song which begins the second half of the play: 'Why do you wander restlessly, why this envy and greed/Death'll follow wherever you go, a truth you better heed!'[24]

In *Charandas Chor*, too, the show opens with a song praising Truth and the guru—thereby introducing the main theme of the play:

Our guru does teach us
That truth is so precious,
Only a handful can
Uphold the truth.[25]

Hirma also opens with a song which presages the tragic trajectory of the play: 'For the sake of that ring, a throne was lost ... not just a throne, a country was lost ... not just a land, life itself was lost ... not just life, bhagwan was lost ... devotion and worship itself was lost.'[26]

Habib also uses songs to move the narrative along—for example, in *Bahadur Kalarin*, in the two scenes when he needs to show multiple marriages and when the boy is being denied water by one villager after another.

Closing songs are also very typical of Naya Theatre productions. In *Agra Bazaar*, the chorus sings about humanity —about how 'Man is the best of the best that we have/and the worst and the meanest too is man'—bringing to an end a play about a poet who dedicated his art to the common man. In *Charandas Chor*, the chorus comes on to sing about a simple man who has become a hero by force of his own convictions:

> An ordinary thief is now a famous man,
> And how did he do it?
> By telling the truth.

Habib talks of how he got the kind of lyrics he wanted for his plays from the folk poets he worked with:

> I got some local folk poets to compose songs ... almost dictating the theme to them. Our folk poets are so adept in writing songs that preach, moralistic songs. There are sometimes inspired songs that I love, songs with beautiful images, allusions, subtlety and so on. But they do not write perverse or cynical kind of songs reflecting my kind of consciousness or, if you please, complexity. So I told them that their songs should not say, 'lying is bad, drinking is bad' and so on. They should instead state that these things are a habit and habits do not go away easily; and that the liar cannot give up lying and the drunkard drinking.[27]

Most of Habib's plays incorporate not just folk songs (or folk-style songs) but also folk dances and rituals; for example, the *panthi* dancers and Satnami ritual in *Charandas Chor* or the Gauri–Gaura ritual. Often, as Brecht says, the purpose is quite simply to 'help to lend variety to the entertainment'. By bringing in these sequences Habib achieves several things at once: he showcases the richness and vitality of a folk culture that is rarely seen outside its own cultural context or by urban audiences; he adds an aesthetic dimension to the production by bringing in a different flavour and texture; and he controls the pace of the narrative by introducing these 'breaks' in the flow of the play. He has said, when asked why he inserts ritual in his play that he finds it good theatre as 'its magic is felt'.[28] It is this instinct for the performative, for dramatic impact, that gives Habib's theatre its inimitable appeal.

One may ask, how is this interjection of rituals and dances by folk groups different from directors who employ 'ethnic' sequences as a form of exotic spectacle? The major difference comes from the fact that the whole play is being performed by folk actors in their native tongue, with folk-flavoured live music on stage—the rituals and dances fit right in. They do not stand out as 'exotic' or 'imported' elements.

Habib's love of music, folk ritual and dance and his intelligent use of them in his theatre created a unique style. Nageen quite rightly observes that 'music was an integral part of the Naya Theatre productions, without which the plays would have seemed stark and incomplete'.[29]

Notes

1. Habib Tanvir, 'In Conversation with Javed Malick' in Neeraj Malik and Javed Malick (eds), *Habib Tanvir: Reflections and Reminiscences* (Delhi: SAHMAT, 2010), p. 121.
2. Habib Tanvir, *STQ*, p. 25.
3. Habib Tanvir, interview with Bindu Batra, 'Folk Theatre—What Is Its Place in India Today?' *Nukkad*, pp. 82–83.
4. Devi Lal Nag, 'Naya Theatre ke Abhinctaon se Bath Cheet' (Talking to the Actors of Naya Theatre) in *Nukkad*, p. 143. Translated by Anjum Katyal.
5. Ibid.
6. Habib Tanvir, 'In Conversation with Sangeeta Gundecha' in Neeraj Malik and Javed Malick (eds), *Habib Tanvir: Reflections and Reminiscences* (Delhi: SAHMAT, 2010), pp. 154–155.
7. Ibid., p. 108.
8. Tanvir, *STQ*, p. 36.
9. Nageen Tanvir, personal correspondence, 31 Mar 2011, unpublished.
10. Habib Tanvir, 'Preface to the Revised Edition: Some Excerpts' in *Agra Bazaar*, translated by Javed Malick (Kolkata: Seagull Books, 2006), p. 18.
11. Ibid., p. 19.
12. Bertolt Brecht's 'A Short Organum for the Theatre' ('Kleines Organon für das Theater') is a theoretical work written in 1948 and published in 1949. See John Willett (edited and translated), *Brecht on Theatre: The Development of an Aesthetic* (London: Methuen, 1964), pp. 179–205.
13. Tanvir, 'Indian Theatre' in *Nukkad*, p. 68
14. Ibid.
15. Javed Malick, 'Habib Tanvir: the Making of a Legend', in *Nukkad*, p. 11.
16. Ibid.
17. Habib Tanvir, 'In Conversation with Javed Malick', p. 118.
18. Habib Tanvir, *Charandas Chor* (Kolkata: Seagull Books, 1996; reprint 2004), p. 64. Translated by Anjum Katyal.
19. Ibid., p. 84.
20. Tanvir, *Agra Bazaar*, p. 29.
21. Ibid., p. 38.
22. Ibid., p. 43.
23. Ibid., p. 62.
24. Ibid., p. 64.
25. Tanvir, *Charandas Chor*, p. 55.
26. Habib Tanvir, *The Living Tale of Hirma* (Kolkata: Seagull Books, 2005), p. 9. Translated by Anjum Katyal and Prabha Katyal.
27. Tanvir, 'In Conversation with Javed Malick', p. 118.
28. Tanvir, *STQ*, p. 22.
29. Nageen Tanvir, personal correspondence, 31 March 2011, unpublished.

CHAPTER TWELVE

THE POLITICAL HABIB TANVIR

The last production—*Raj-Rakt* (2006). L-R Amar Singh, Udai Ram, Himanshu Tyagi.
Courtesy Naya Theatre

> I was convinced that I had something to say. And for what I had to
> say, in aesthetics, in the performing arts, as well as what I had to say
> socially, politically—the medium … was the theatre.[1]

This realisation motivated Habib to dedicate his life to theatre in the early
1950s, choosing it over his other early love, cinema. Theatre, to him, was
'connected with all aspects of life' and 'the performing arts … a profoundly
spiritual activity in the true spirit of Bharat Muni's Natya Shastra'.[2] Over
the next half century and more, he would produce theatre—whether satires,
rollicking comedies or intense tragedies—marked by what he had to say and

by his own values and beliefs. This is what one could call the political aspect of his work, and it showed itself in both form and content. One theatre scholar claims that he 're-invented the idea of the "political" in theatre'.[3] Let us look back over his life in theatre to come to an understanding of the political dynamics of the man, the artist and his work.

Habib's politics—progressive, people-centric, democratic and secular— were essentially left-leaning. This belief system was built up from the time Habib was introduced to a circle of left-oriented litterateurs in college in Aligarh. In fact, his memoirs contain an amusing anecdote in this regard, about his friend and constant companion Usman:

> Many years later Usman revealed to me that before I reached Aligarh he had received a letter from Nagpur from Comrade Mushtaq which went, 'A very bright young man from our city of Raipur is going to Aligarh. He is making his way to communism through literature. Take care of him.' It was as if from that very minute Usman had left everything and had devoted himself wholeheartedly to my education…. This was the same Usman alias Athar Parvez who was instrumental in getting me to stage *Agra Bazaar*.[4]

Whether he eventually 'made his way to communism' or not, Habib definitely aligned himself with a progressive, and on the whole, left-oriented value system. During his time in Bombay, his involvement with the PWA and IPTA deepened this inclination, which was always closely interwoven with poetry, literature and the arts, particularly music and theatre. While reflecting on the political street theatre form, he recalls:

> We during the IPTA days of Bombay in the late forties had attempted some kind of street plays in a very primitive way. In those days, however, our music squads were more significant, in the political sense. In all political public meetings of the CPI, the IPTA music squads, Hindi, Marathi, Gujarati and Konkani used to sing political songs before political leaders delivered their speeches. However, apart from proscenium stage plays, we also used to present skits and short plays in working class chawls in Parel, in narrow verandahs in 3rd or 5th or 7th floor of a chawl, where workers with their families would gather on one side or peep through the doors and windows of their dwellings.
>
> One such play was *Shanti Doot Kamgar*, a kind of poster play if you like, that I had written under the inspiration provided by the Chinese example.
>
> During the civil war in China in the mid-forties, the communist activists would visit restaurants, and other public places, cook up some kind of quarrel between themselves, and when people's attention was sufficiently

drawn to them, one of them would scramble up on top of a table and deliver an agitational speech summoning support for the cause of the Red Army.

We thought up a similar play about world peace. An actor puts up a poster at the gate of a factory. Another actor playing a policeman takes objection to the poster. In the squabble that ensues due to the argumentative policeman, a domestic fight is kicked up between the poster man and an actress, his wife, who happens to wander into the scene. And when a crowd gathers due to this happening, a third actor gets up on a table and delivers a speech.[5]

Javed Malick says:

Tanvir's active involvement with IPTA in the 1940s not only renewed his early interest in the folk culture but also gave it a new political significance and dimension. IPTA's slogan 'People's theatre stars the people' prompted many to link their art to plebeian cultural forms and traditions as opposed to the culture of the ruling classes.[6]

It leads one to wonder whether Habib's choice of Chhattisgarhi actors may not have been guided by this IPTA principle.

We already know that it was the IPTA experience that helped shape his abiding interest in, and value for, folk cultural forms. Dialects, and the language of the common man, attracted him strongly; he was equally drawn to folk songs, folklore and rural cultural expressions in which he found a sophistication and visual drama that appealed to his sense of theatre. I agree with Javed Malick when he says,

His interest in folk culture and his decision to work with and in terms of traditional styles of performance was itself an ideological choice as much as an aesthetic one, whether Tanvir himself was fully conscious of it as such or not. There is a close connection between his predilection for popular traditions and his left-wing disposition. His involvement with the left-wing cultural movement … meant a commitment to the common people and their causes.[7]

Indeed, his choice of actors, the language of his theatre and the material he chose to present, all testify to a political stance that was committed to the common man and his culture. Sudhanva Deshpande says:

If there is one theme that runs consistently through all his creative output, from *Agra Bazaar* and even earlier … it is the celebration of the plebian. The culture, beliefs, practices, rituals of the Chhattisgarhi peasants and tribals, their humour, their songs and their stories, all this is what has given his theatre its incredible vitality.[8]

To that I would add that it was not just the Chhattisgarhis; he also involved himself in tribal and rural culture of other parts of India, as his workshops in Rajasthan, Odisha and Haryana indicate.

It is perhaps this 'celebration of the plebian' that leads Javed Malick to state that

> in Tanvir's major productions the real protagonist ... is the ordinary people. This protagonist is sometimes latent, operating on the deeper, subtextual level (or, if you like, in the interstices of the episodic structure), and sometimes not so latent. In either case, it is almost always there somewhere.[9]

The clearest example of this would be *Charandas Chor*, where the thief is a very ordinary man who in turn champions the downtrodden; but even in plays where the leading characters are members of royalty (as in *Hirma* or *Raj-Rakt*), it is the common man who is the real subject—and concern—of the drama.

Javed Malick observes that Habib's work in the theatre, 'in style as well as in content, reflects this commitment [to the common people] and can be seen as part of a larger (socialist) project of empowerment of the people'.[10] This rings especially true when one recalls the sense of agency and confidence developed in his actors due to the wide exposure, critical acclaim and honour they got as artistes on their international tours. They talk with pride about the recognition and respect they received from audiences and critics alike; they also appreciate the expansion of their knowledge horizons through their involvement with Naya Theatre.[11] Habib also attempted to build the capability of local artistes through his regional workshops, not just in terms of form and content but also in technology (as in the simple lighting techniques he demonstrated at the Raipur Nacha workshop).

In the preceding chapters we have seen that there is no play by Habib—from the most farcical skit to the darkest tragedy—that does not contain sharp and thought-provoking social comment or subversive elements of some sort. What is the target of these critiques and attempts at subversion? He identifies capitalism as the cause of the unsatisfactory socio-economic situation he sees around him. In 2004, delivering a talk, Habib, already over 80 years old and with a lifetime of cultural activism behind him, questions:

> And what did we see of the development resulting from capitalism? Technology taking over science and leaving science behind; the globe polluted

and denuded ... wars for petrol, for water, for market, for weapons of mass destruction; wars for fundamentalist reasons; wars based on state terrorism, racist, ethnic wars; wars in Africa, Asia, East Europe, Latin America ... wars, wars, wars.[12]

He rues the blind aping of the Western model of capitalist-driven development and progress which has led to India losing a precious opportunity to 'find patterns of development suited to the native genius of the developing Third World ... to create our own patterns of growth and seek paths of survival'.[13] In an explosion of disillusioned anger, he raves:

We sold our soul to the devil of technology, to the devil of globalisation, consumerism, liberalization, free market, obscene advertising, poisonous satellite television, allowing 13 percent of owners of cellphones and automobiles to shine in obscene opulence and leaving the vast masses of people, the adivasis, the dalits, peasants and farmers and urban lower middle classes in the darkness of poverty, leaving millions to fall below the poverty line, thousands to commit suicide, in the last five years multiplying the numbers of rural and urban unemployed—the very people of agrarian India, whose production sustained this kind of 'Shining India'.[14]

He goes on to despair over art and culture being reduced to 'sale as consumer commodities', the pauperisation of tribals and the demolition of their community sense, the neglect of intellectual property rights pertaining to natural produce, the annihilation of indigenous performing arts. He then turns his wrath on the forces of fascism—'the monopoly of the majority community alone'—which caused the killing and targeting of specific communities, 'revealing not only ethnic and caste cleansing but also the ugly aspect of economic benefits accruing from fascist attacks'.[15] He ends by stating:

I have simplified the division of culture. I have divided it into just two: the culture of the oppressor and the culture of the oppressed. You have to decide which side you are with—the oppressors or the oppressed?[16]

This is the voice of an artist who has spent his life siding with the culture of the oppressed; an artist who attacks the evils of the capitalist system and supports a more people-oriented economic and political policy.

An important political aspect of Habib's theatre lies in his quality of raising questions and foregrounding issues that the audience is then left to think over. Issues like the power of the State to crush defiance despite it coming from an honest man (*Charandas Chor*); appropriate development goals and strategies for tribal society (*Hirma*); State and religion as rival power centres (*Raj-Rakt*); untouchability (*Ponga Pandit*). In the Brechtian manner, Habib problematises such situations and issues, thereby aiming to politicise his audience who are made to think them through. In this way, he targets leading social and political evils of the day, earning the reputation of being 'the enemy of parochialism, of bigotry, of fundamentalism and of the kind of development that crushes the poor,' as Sudhanva Deshpande says, going on to list the plays that address these concerns.[17]

In an article entitled 'My Subversive Allies in Theatre' Habib Tanvir begins with the assertion, 'I have always believed that art must be subversive if only to survive' and claims that 'my folk actors have remained natural allies with me in the process of unfolding a certain kind of subversive theatre'.[18] He goes on to say that 'dance, folk music and songs also served this process of subversion for they were not in general vogue and often had a critical content'.[19] Certainly the lyrics of his songs were full of subversive comments—from 'Food prompts people to worship and pray' (*Agra Bazaar*)[20] to the fakirs' song in *Hirma*:

> This world is theirs, they can make their own pleasures
> Yes, it's all theirs, the whole world and its treasures
> They make the poor, they both rob and they feed
> For us, the poor, God is what we need
> Life without God is nothing at all
> For us, life with no God is nothing.[21]

Here, we see how he brings up complex and controversial issues through the deceptively simple medium of song. He is talking about how basic concerns of survival (food) drive people to seek solace in religion; about power relations between the haves and the have-nots; about the helplessness of the poor in a world where the rich hold the power to both rob and feed them and about how, stripped of worldly goods, the underprivileged often turn to God for compensation and relief. Subversive, indeed.

It is this strong thread of critical commentary running through his theatre that causes Javed Malick to describe Habib's vision as 'utopian'. He feels that Habib's work has

> a tendency towards what may be described as a Utopian horizon—akin to what the German Marxist philosopher, Ernst Bloch, refers to as 'the hope principle'. It signifies a desired, but empirically unavailable, state of happiness,

the idea of an egalitarian rearrangement of society which critically reflects on and offers a radical alternative to the prevailing social order.[22]

Certain sociopolitical issues preoccupied Habib more than others. An inequitable social system was one; casteism another; religious fundamentalism yet another. He was unhesitatingly active in protesting against fascist and violent acts like the murder of Safdar Hashmi and, thereafter, the fascism of the militant religious right. He accepted the social responsibility of the public intellectual, speaking out and standing up against anti-democratic and violent acts and forces. Sadanand Menon writes:

> By the early 1990s Habib was very much at the forefront of the cultural resistance movement of artists in the wake of the murder of Safdar Hashmi by political goons.... He became an inseparable part of the secular mobilisation and literally channeled his entire creativity to providing much needed artistic and cultural oxygen to the secular front.[23]

Sudhanva Deshpande sees a fresh 'radicalisation' in Habib in the mid-1980s:

> [H]e underwent his second radicalisation from the mid-1980s onwards (the first being in the 1940s, when he joined IPTA), as the new, liberalised economy in the Rajiv Gandhi-Narasimha Rao years steamrolled the poor, and the rise of the Hindu Right threatened to alter the basic structures of Indian democracy. From about 1985 onwards, virtually every one of Habib Tanvir's plays is political—Hirma ki Amar Kahani and Sadak, both on 'development' and tribals; Moteram ka Satyagraha, Baagh and Jis Lahore Nahi Vekhya Voh Janmya hi Nahi on communalism; Dushman (Gorky's Enemies in Safdar Hashmi's adaptation), an out and out anti-capitalist play; Zahareeli Hawa on the Bhopal gas tragedy, Raj Rakt on violence and non-violence. And after the demolition of the Babri Masjid, when the Sangh Parivar began targeting Naya Theatre's Ponga Pandit, the play became among his most performed. In fact, the way he faced up to those attacks, often vicious and physical, without once considering compromise, is a lesson in public commitment and courage.[24]

With regard to social issues, however, Javed Malick points out that gender inequality and patriarchy, though burning issues of our times, were not taken up by Habib with any particular emphasis.[25] There are plenty of strong women characters in his plays, but the issue of gender discrimination is perhaps dealt with only in *Manglu Didi*, in which he does take up the whole question of women's right to reproductive agency.

Arguing that Habib 're-invented' the political in Indian theatre, Sadan- and Menon contrasts Habib's approach to politicisation of the text and the audience with the prevalent modes of the time:

> As someone familiar with 'radical' playwrights, actors and directors of the Indian stage, I was forever excited with the manner in which Habib could reconfigure the idea of the 'political' through the minutest of gestures or linguistic and tonal inflections of speech, without any of the self-conscious radicalism of fist or flag-waving and declamatory sloganeering. Forever, Habib remained a refined storyteller who, in each retelling of a story, could find fresh and creative ways in which to mine it for a contemporary, current nuance, and re-politicize it.[26]

One could quote the sharp indictment of inequitable 'development' in *Sarak* or the biting sarcasm-laden lyrics of the fakirs' songs in *Agra Bazaar* in support of the above. Menon goes on to admire how Habib 'slid in to' a space dominated by a strident theatre of 'oppositional' politics with 'a distinctly different comprehension and conceptualization of the pedagogic/political in theatre'.[27] He feels that Habib developed his work in two distinct areas:

> one, to reclaim the space for a new suggestive, allusive content more common to folk ballads and to a whole range of humorous and irreverent performances drawing upon the spirit of resistance embedded in native wit and irony. The other area was the rejection of the proscenium space in favour of a more fluid and unregulated theatrical space which contributed immensely to the participative character of his productions.[28]

Prasanna, leading director and socially committed theatre activist, talks of how Habib, in his work with 'traditional' theatre forms, 'revealed to us a strong and vibrant protest tradition lying underneath. He thereby established that Indian protest need not be imported from the West'.[29]

All Habib's political and ideological beliefs and actions led him in one direction—that of an inclusive theatre, one that was not premised on imitation and exclusion but incorporated the tribal, the rural, the folk, the subaltern, in a fundamental and meaningful way while addressing important contemporary social and political issues, to form a truly original, indigenous theatre for today's India. Prasanna says: 'Habib Tanvir showed us the path. It is a difficult path, but a path compatible with the socio-cultural situation in India ... a more integrated and ... people-friendly production style ... both traditional and contemporary ... flexible enough to be produced anywhere in India. It retains the narrative and yet breaks it.'[30]

To me, Habib exemplifies the ideal of the Indian artist. He drew freely, with both knowledge and respect, on all the streams, religions, cultures and classes that make up our heritage, from the 'highest' to the most marginalised. His art, which was aesthetically of the highest quality, appreciated by critics and popular with laypersons, was imbued with his social consciousness, his progressive, people-centric politics and a thoroughly secular, non-sectarian sensibility.

To end with a tribute from Prasanna, 'Habib inspires'.[31]

Notes

1. Habib Tanvir, *STQ*, p. 9.
2. Habib Tanvir, 'Sustaining Vitality', lecture at the International Conference on the Vitality of India in the Regional and International Perspective, in Shimla, June 2004; in *Nukkad*, p. 58.
3. Sadanand Menon, 'Reinventing the Political in Theatre' in Neeraj Malik and Javed Malick (eds), *Habib Tanvir: Reflections & Reminiscences* (New Delhi: SAHMAT, 2010), p. 45.
4. From the English translation of Habib Tanvir's Urdu autobiography, chapter titled 'Aligarh', translated by Mahmood Farooqui (Forthcoming).
5. Habib Tanvir, 'Janam Comes of Age' in Sudhanva Deshpande (ed.), *Theatre of the Streets: The Jana Natya Manch Experience* (New Delhi: Jana Natya Manch, 2007), pp. 68–70.
6. Javed Malick, 'Refashioning Modernity: Habib Tanvir and His Naya Theatre' in Neeraj Malik and Javed Malick (eds), *Habib Tanvir: Reflections & Reminiscences* (New Delhi: SAHMAT, 2010), pp. 16–17.
7. Javed Malick, 'Habib Tanvir: The Making of a Legend', in *Nukkad*, p. 10.
8. Sudhanva Deshpande, 'Upside-Down Midas' in *Nukkad Janam Samvad*, April 2004–March 2005, p. 16.
9. Javed Malick, 'Introduction to Habib Tanvir', *Charandas Chor*, translated by Anjum Katyal (Kolkata: Seagull Books, 1996/2004), p. 12.
10. Malick, 'Habib Tanvir: The Making of a Legend', in *Nukkad*, p. 10.
11. 'Naya Theatre ke Abhinetaon se Bath Cheet' (Talking to the Actors of Naya Theatre) in *Nukkad*, pp. 136–191.
12. Tanvir, 'Sustaining Vitality', p. 59.
13. Ibid.
14. Ibid.
15. Ibid., pp. 59–60.
16. Ibid., p. 60.
17. Sudhanva Deshpande, 'Upside-Down Midas', p. 16.
18. Habib Tanvir, 'My Subversive Allies in Theatre', *Frontline*, 22 August 1997 (in *Nukkad*, p. 113).
19. Ibid., p. 114.
20. Habib Tanvir, *Agra Bazaar* (Kolkata: Seagull Books, 2006), p. 34. Translated by Javed Malick.
21. Habib Tanvir, *The Living Tale of Hirma* (Kolkata: Seagull Books, 2005), p. 43. Translated by Anjum Katyal and Prabha Katyal.

22. Malick, 'Introduction to Habib Tanvir', *Charandas Chor*, p. 12.
23. Menon, 'Reinventing the Political in Theatre', pp. 51–52.
24. Sudhanva Deshpande, 'Habib Tanvir and his Red-hot Life' in Pragoti, 2009, http://www. pragoti.org/hi/node/3456, accessed on 27 May 2012.
25. Malick, 'Habib Tanvir: The Making of a Legend', note 5, p. 12.
26. Menon, 'Reinventing the Political in Theatre', p. 45.
27. Ibid., p. 46.
28. Ibid., pp. 46–47.
29. Prasanna, 'The True Significance of Habib Tanvir,' in Neeraj Malik and Javed Malick (eds), *Habib Tanvir: Reflections & Reminiscences* (New Delhi: SAHMAT, 2010), p. 28.
30. Ibid., p. 29.
31. Ibid., p. 30.

APPENDICES

Appendix 1: List of Plays by Naya Theatre and Habib Tanvir[1]

Year	Play	Group	First Show Venue	Author
1948	*Shantidoot Kamgar (H)*[2] *(short play)*	IPTA, Bombay	Bombay Mill gate, Parel	Habib Tanvir
1953	*Jaalidar Parde (U) (short play)*	J J School of Arts, Bombay	Bhartiya Vidya Bhavan, Bombay	Adaptation of Soviet play by Habib Tanvir
1953	*Shatranj Ke Mohre (U)*	IPTA, Bombay	Prem-chand Day, Hyderabad	Dramatised by Habib Tanvir from Premchand's story [Directed by Dina Pathak]
1954	*Agra Bazaar (U)*	Jamia Drama Society, Delhi	Jamia open air theatre, Delhi	Habib Tanvir
1954	*Kartoos (H) (short play)*	School children of Faridabad	Faridabad Fort	Habib Tanvir
1954	*Doodh ka Gilas (U) (short play)*	Children	All India Radio, Delhi	Habib Tanvir
1954	*Parampara (H) (short play)*	Jamia children	Jamia, Delhi	Habib Tanvir
1954	*Chandi Ka Chamcha (U) (short play)*	Jamia children	Jamia, Delhi	Habib Tanvir

(Appendix 1 contd.)

(Appendix 1 contd.)

Year	Play	Group	First Show Venue	Author
1954	*Har Mousam Ka Khel (U) (short plav)*	Jamia children	Jamia, Delhi	Habib Tanvir
1954	*Aag Ki Gend (U) (short play)*	Jamia children	Jamia, Delhi	Habib Tanvir
1954	*Gadhe (U)*	Children of Shiv Niketan	Open air, Delhi	Habib Tanvir
1955	*Mirza Shohrat Beg (U)*	Jamia Drama Society, Delhi	Jamia, Delhi	Adaptation by HT of Moliere's *The Bourgeois Gentleman*
1955	*Khudkhushi (U) (short play)*	Monologue by Habib Tanvir	Aligarh Muslim University	Dramatisation by HT of a story by Dostoevsky
1958	*Mitti Ki Gadi (H)*	Hindustani Theatre	AIFACS Hall, Delhi	Adaptation by HT of Sudraka's *Mrichhakatikam,* transl. by Qudsia Zaidi and Noor Nabi Abbasi
1959	*Phaansi (U) (short play)*	Naya Theatre	Sapru House Hall, Delhi	Adaptation by HT of an English play
1959	*Tambaku Ke Nuksanat (U)*	Naya Theatre	Sapru House Hall, Delhi	Translation by HT of a play by Chekov
1959	*Saat Paisy (H) (short play)*	Naya Theatre	YWCA Hall, Delhi	Dramatisation by HT of a Czech story [Directed by Monica Misra]
1960	*Rustom-o-Sohrab (U)*	Naya Theatre Delhi	Sapru House Hall, Delhi	Aga Hashr Kashmiri
1961	*The Good Woman of Szechwan (E)*	College Drama Teachers' Work-shop	Pachmarhi, MP	Bertolt Brecht

(Appendix 1 contd.)

(Appendix 1 contd.)

Year	Play	Group	First Show Venue	Author
1961	*The Taming of the Shrew (E)*	Unity Theatre, Delhi	AIFACS Hall, Delhi	William Shakespeare
1961	*The Importance of Being Earnest (E)*	Lady Irwin College/St. Stephen's College	Lady Irwin College Auditorium, Delhi	Oscar Wilde
1964	*Servant of Two Masters (E)*	New Delhi Polytechnic for Women	Polytechnic Auditorium	Carlo Goldoni
1964	*The Shoemaker's Prodigious Wife (E)*	College Drama Teaehers' Workshop	Mysore	Federico Garcia Lorea
1967	*Lady Windermere's Fan (E)*	Lady Irwin College, Delhi	Lady Irwin College Auditorium. Delhi	Oscar Wilde
1968	*Merey Baad (U)*	Naya Theatre, Delhi	AIFACS Hall, Delhi	Habib Tanvir (play on Ghalib)
1968	*The Signet Ring (E)*	St. Stephen's College	AIFACS Hall, Delhi	P. Lal's translation of *Mudrarakshasa* by Visakhadatta
1969	*Shatranj Ke Mohre (U)*	Naya Theatre, Delhi	Jamia	Revised version of earlier play
1970	*Kushtiya Ka Chaprasi (H), Arjun Ka Sarthi (C), Gauri Gaura (C)*	Naya Theatre, Delhi	AIFACS Hail, Delhi	Written by Habib Tanvir, Pandavani by Puna Ram Nishad. Temple ritual songs (Triple bill)
1970	*Agra Bazaar (U)*	Naya Theatre, Delhi	AIFACS Hall, Delhi	Revised version of earlier play
1971	*Indra Lok Sabha (C) (short play)*	Naya Theatre, Delhi	Chandni Chowk, Delhi	Habib Tanvir

(Appendix 1 contd.)

(Appendix 1 contd.)

Year	Play	Group	First Show Venue	Author
1971	*Sutradhar (H)*	Naya Theatre, Delhi	Gandhi Memorial Hall, Delhi	Habib Tanvir
1972	*Raja Chamba Aur Char Bhai ((!)*	Naya Theatre, Delhi	Kamani Hall, Delhi	Habib Tanvir
1973	*Gaon Ka Naon Sasural Mor Naon Damad (C)*	Naya Theatre, Delhi	Moti Bagh, M.P.	Habib Tanvir
1974	*Sampoorna Mahabharat (C)*	Pandavani, Puna Ram Nishad	Open air, Karol Bagh, Delhi	Workshop production
1974	*Char Nai* (and 3 plays) *(C)*	Folk theatre workshop, Bhilai	Balod, Durg, M.P.	Presented by HT from folk stories
1974	*Ganga Jamuna* (and 3 plays) *(C)*	Folk theatre workshop, Bhilai	Balod, Durg, M.P.	Presented by HT from folk stories
1974	*Thakur Pritipal Singh (R)*	Ugam Raj Khiladi	Borunda, Rajasthan	Dramatised by HT from Vijaydan Detha's story
1975	*Charandas Chor (C)*	Naya Theatre, Delhi	Kamani Hall, Delhi	Dramatised by HT from Vijaydan Detha's story
1976	*Shahi Lakarhara (Ha)*	Folk theatre/ Naya Theatre workshop, Rai	Sonepat, Haryana	Lakshmichand
1976	*Jani Chor (Ha)*	Folk theatre/ Naya Theatre workshop, Rai	Sonepat, Haryana	Based on improvisations
1977	*Uttaramacharit (Hn)*	Naya Theatre, Delhi	Kalidas Samaroh, Ujjain	Translation of Bhavabhuti's play
1977	*Prahalad Nataka and Bharata Lila (O)*	Folk theatre workshop, Orissa	Behrampur, Orissa	Presentation by Habib Tanvir

(Appendix 1 contd.)

(Appendix 1 contd.)

Year	Play	Group	First Show Venue	Author
1977	*Chundaini (C)*	Folk theatre workshop	Ber Sarai, Delhi	Chhattisgarhi folk ballad
1977	*Bhagavaddajju-kam (H)*	Naya Theatre, Raipur work-shop	Ravi Shan-kar Univer-sity, Raipur	Translation of Sanskrit drama by Mahendra Vikram Varman
1977	*Jamadarin (C)*	Naya Theatre, Delhi	Delhi streets	Chhattisgarhi Nacha play
1978	*Sajapur Ki Shantibai (C)*	Naya Theatre, Delhi	Triveni Delhi	Translation by HT of Brecht's *Good Woman of Schezuan*
1978	*Bahadur Kalarin (C)*	Naya Theatre, Delhi	AIFACS Audito-rium, Delhi	Habib Tanvir
1978	*Mitti Ki Gadi (C)*	Naya Theatre, Delhi	Kamani Hall, Delhi	Translation by HT of Sudraka's *Mrichhakatikam*
1978	*Duryodhan (C)*	Naya Theatre, Delhi	Mavalankar Hall, Delhi	Bhasa trilogy
1979	*Four Plays (C)*	Asian the-atre work-shop, Anang, Mahasamund, M.P.	Mahasam-und, M.P.	Presentation of improvisations of four stories from four Asian coun-tries
1980	*Shah Badshah (H)*	IIT, Delhi	IIT Audito-rium, Delhi	Balraj Sahni's adaptation of Gogol's *Govern-ment Inspector*
1980	*Devi Ka Vardaan (C)*	Naya Theatre, Delhi	Open air, Vasant Vihar, Delhi	Dramatisation by HT of folk tale by Vijaydan Detha

(Appendix 1 contd.)

(Appendix 1 contd.)

Year	Play	Group	First Show Venue	Author
1981	*Lala Shohrat Rai (C)*	Naya Theatre, Delhi	Shri Ram Centre, Delhi	Adaptation by HT of Moliere's *The Bourgeois Gentleman*
1981	*Sone Sagar (C)*	Naya Theatre, Delhi	Kamini Hall, Delhi	Habib Tanvir
1984	*Nand Raja Mast Hain (H)*	Workshop production, Raipur	Medical College Auditorium, Raipur	Adaptation of Manoj Mitra's *Rajdarshan*
1984	*Mangloo Didi (C) (Short Play)*	Folk theatre workshop, Janjgir	Janjgir, Bilaspur, Chhattisgarh	Habib Tanvir
1985	*Hirma Ki Amar Kahani (H)*	Naya Theatre, Delhi	Railway Auditorium, Bilaspur	Habib Tanvir
1988	*Ek Aur Dronacharya (H)*	IPTA, Bhilai	Bhilai School, Durg	Shanker Shesh
1988	*Moteram Ka Satyagraha (Hn)*	Jana Natya Manch, Delhi	Pyare Lal Hall, Delhi	Dramatisation by Safdar Hashmi and Habib Tanvir of Premchand's story
1989	*Dushman (Hn)*	NSD Repertory Company, Delhi	Kamam Hall, Delhi	Adaptation by Safdar Hashmi of Gorky's *Enemies*
1989	*Case No. 432 (H)*	Naya Theatre, Delhi	Shri Ram Centre, Delhi	Habib Tanvir
1990	*Jis Lahore Nai Dekhya Wo Janma Hi Nai (U)*	SRC Repertory Company, Delhi	Shri Ram Centre, Delhi	Asghar Wajahat

(Appendix 1 contd.)

(Appendix 1 contd.)

Year	Play	Group	First Show Venue	Author
1992	*Dekh Rahe Hain Nain (U)*	Naya Theatre, Delhi	Shri Ram Centre, Delhi	Habib Tanvir (adapted from Stefon Zweig)
1992	*Bagh (H)*	Naya Theatre, Delhi	Shri Ram Centre, Delhi	Translation by Vikalp of play by Sisir Das
1993	*Kamdev Ka Apna Basant Ritu Ka Sapna (U)*	Naya Theatre, Delhi	British Council Garden, Delhi	Translation by HT of Shakespeare's *Midsummer Night's Dream*
1994	*Sarak (C)*	Naya Theatre, Delhi	Talkatora Garden Theatre, Delhi	Habib Tanvir
1995	*A Broken Bridge (E)*	Chicago Actors' Ensemble	Chicago Church, Chicago, USA	Habib Tanvir
1995	*Daddy Ka Ghar (H)*	Naya Theatre, Delhi	Ber Sarai, Delhi	Habib Tanvir
1996	*Mudrarakshasa (H)*	Naya Theatre, Delhi	Kalidas Samaroh, Ujjain	Translation by Habib Tanvir
1998	*Kissa Thela Ram Ka (H)*	Children's workshop, Raipur	Town Hall, Raipur	Rajesh Ganodwale
1999	*Ek Aurat Hipetia Bhi Thi (U)*	Jana Natya Manch, Delhi	Ashoka Road, Delhi	Habib Tanvir
2000	*Sun Bahri (C)*	Naya Theatre, Bhopal, Raipur workshop	Sapre School, Raipur	Habib Tanvir (play on awareness of leprosy)
2001	*Veni Sanhaar (H)*	Naya Theatre, Bhopal	Kalidas Samaroh, Ujjain	Translation by Radha Vallabh Tripathy of Bhatta's Sanskrit play

(Appendix 1 contd.)

(Appendix 1 contd.)

Year	Play	Group	First Show Venue	Author
2002	*Zehreeli Hawa (H,C,E)*	Naya Theatre, Bhopal	Bharat Bhavan, Bhopal	Translation by Habib Tanvir of English play *Bhopal* by Rahul Varma
2003	*Mujhe Amrita Chahiye (H)*	Students of Lady Shriram College	LSR College Auditorium, Delhi	Yogesh Tripathi
2005	*Visarjan (H)*	Naya Theatre and Rangakarmee	Madhusudan Manch, Kolkata	Translation of Tagore drama into Hindi by Usha Ganguli
2006	*Raj-Rakt (H)*	Naya Theatre	Rabindra Sadan, Rabindra Utsav, Kolkata	Adaptation of Tagore's *Visarjan* and novel *Rajarshi* by Habib Tanvir

Notes

1. Appendix list based on List in *Nukkad*, pp. 195–198.
2. Key: C-Chhattisgarhi, E-English, H-Hindi, Ha-Haryanvi, Hn-Hindustani, O-Odiya, R-Rajasthani, U-Urdu.

Appendix 2: Awards, Honours and Milestones

1923	Born 1 or 23 September, Raipur
1940	Matriculation from Laurie Municipal High School, Raipur
1943–1944	Bachelor of Arts, Morris College, Nagpur
1944–1955	Master's course, Aligarh Muslim University
1945–1946	Assistant Editor, *Film India,* Bombay
1945–1947	Programme Producer, All India Radio, Bombay. Editor, Textile Journal, Bombay
1945–1952	Editor, *Box Office,* a Bombay film weekly. Acted in nine features, wrote songs and dialogue for films, made advertising shorts, Famous Films, Bombay
1946–1953	Actor/Director, IPTA, Bombay; active member of the PWA
1954	Co-founded Hindustan Theatre, Delhi
1955	Trained in acting at Royal Academy of Dramatic Arts, London
1956	Trained in play production at Bristol Old Vic Theatre School, UK
	Trained in drama teaching at the British Drama League, London
	Associate of British Drama Board, Londo
1956–1958	Travelled in Europe, watching and studying theatre
1958–1959	Return to Delhi, production of *Mitti Ki Gadi*
1959	Started Naya Theatre with Moneeka Misra
1962–1963	Theatre observation tour in the US through Institute of International Education, New York
1964	Producer, TV Centre, New Delhi
	Birth of daughter Nageen.
1964–1972	Worked at Soviet Information Centre, Delhi. Wrote on drama and film for the *Statesman, Patriot, Link, Mainstream*
1969	Sangeet Natak Akademi award for theatre
1972–1978	Nominated Member of Parliament, Rajya Sabha
1973	Shikhar Samman, Madhya Pradesh government award for drama
1980	Visiting Professor, Jamia Millia University, New Delhi
1982	Fringe First award for *Charandas Chor*, Edinburgh International Drama Festival
	Awarded Padmashree by the Government of India
	D. Lit., Indira Kala Music University, Khairagarh

1982–1984	Jawaharlal Nehru Fellow
1982–1985	Visiting Professor, Pandit Sundarlal Sharma Chair, Ravi Shankar University, Raipur
1983	Academy of Arts and Literature award, Delhi administration
1985	Nandikar award for drama, Calcutta
1986	Visiting Professor, M. S. University, Baroda
1990	Kalidas Samman, Bhopal
1995	D. Lit., Rabindra Bharati University, Calcutta
1997	Sangeet Natak Akademi fellowship, Delhi
2000	Maharashtra State Urdu Akademi Award for plays and poetry, Mumbai
2001	Aditya Vikram Birla Kala Shikhar Award for literature, Mumbai
2002	Awarded Padmabhushan by the Government of India Bhavabhuti award for literature, Hindi Sahitya Sangh, Bhopal Chakradhar Samman, Chhattisgarh government, Raipur
2002–2003	Held Sombhu Mitra Chair, National School of Drama, Delhi
2003	D. Lit., Vidyasagar University, Midnapur, West Bengal D. Lit., Guru Ghasidas University Bilaspur, Chhattisgarh
2004	D. Lit., Kalyani University, West Bengal
2005	Moneeka Misra passes away on 28 May
2006	National Research Professor Award, Government of India Officer of the Order of Arts and Letters, The French Republic
2007	Visiting Professor, Mahatma Gandhi Hindi Vishwavidyalaya, Wardha, Maharashtra.
2008	Desikottamma award, Vishwabharati University, Santiniketan, West Bengal
2009	Habib Tanvir passes away on 8 June
2010	Lifetime Achievement Award, Government of India, Delhi (posthumous)

SELECT BIBLIOGRAPHY

Books and Articles

Agarwal, Pratibha (ed.). *Habib Tanvir: Ek Ranga Vyaktitva*. Calcutta: Natya Shodh Sansthan, 1993.

Bennett, Tony, Lawrence Grossberg and Meaghan Morris (eds). *New Keywords: A Revised Vocabulary of Culture and Society* (Malden, Massachusetts: Blackwell Publishing, 2005), p. 116.

Bhargava, Bharatratna. *Rang Habib*. New Delhi: Rashtriya Natya Vidyalaya (NSD), 2006.

Brecht, Bertolt. 'A Short Organum for the Theatre' ('Kleines Organon für das Theater'), in John Willett (ed. and translated), *Brecht on Theatre: The Development of an Aesthetic*. London: Methuen, 1964.

Dalmia-Luderitz, Vasudha. 'To Be More Brechtian Is to Be More Indian: On the Theatre of Habib Tanvir', in Erika Fischer-Lichte, Josephine Riley and Michael Gissenwehrer (eds), *The Dramatic Touch of Difference: Theatre, Own and Foreign*, Forum Modernes Theater, Schriftenreihe Band 2, pp. 221–235. Tubingen: GNV Gunter Narr Verlag, 1990.

Dharwadker, Aparna Bhargava. *Theatres of Independence: Drama, Theory, and Urban Performance in India*. Iowa City: University of Iowa Press, 2005.

Iyengar, Sameera (ed.). *On the Road with Naya Theatre*. Mumbai: Prithvi Theatre Yearbook, 2006.

Jana Natya Manch. *Nukkad Janam Samvad: Focus on Naya Theatre* 7/23–26. New Delhi: Jana Natya Manch, April 2004–March 2005.

Kaifi, Shaukat. *Kaifi and I: A Memoir*. New Delhi: Zubaan, 2010.

Lal, Ananda (ed.). *The Oxford Companion to Indian Theatre*, pp. 472–473. New Delhi: Oxford University Press, 2004.

Malick, Javed. 'Habib Tanvir: The Making of a Legend', *Theatre India*, 2 (November): 93–102, 2000.

Malik, Neeraj and Javed Malick (eds). *Habib Tanvir: Reflections & Reminiscences*. New Delhi: SAHMAT, 2010.

Mee, Erin. *Theatre of Roots: Redirecting the Modern Indian Stage*. Kolkata: Seagull Books, 2008.

Natarang Pratishthan. *Natrang*, 22, 86–87, July–December 2010 [Special edition on Habib Tanvir].

Payne, Michael and Jessica Rae Barbera (eds). *A Dictionary of Cultural and Critical Theory* (Chichester, UK: John Wiley and Sons Pvt. Ltd., 2005), pp. 553–555.

Ram, Bulwa. '25 Years with "Babaji"', *The Telegraph* Colour Magazine, Kolkata, 17 April 1983, p. 6.

Rea, Kenneth. 'Theatre in India: The Old and the New: Part III', *Theatre Quarterly*, 8 (32): 47–66, 1979.

Segal, Zohra. *Close-Up: Memoirs of a Life on Stage and Screen*. New Delhi: Women Unlimited, 2010.

Tanvir, Habib. 'Mera Mrichhakatika ka Prayog—Ek Adhuri Kahani', *Natrang*, 1 (1), 1965.

———. 'Hashyakan ki Samasya', *Natrang*, 1 (2), 1965.

———. 'My Life in Cart', *Enact*, October 1967.

———. 'Brecht for One Producer', *Enact*, March 1968.

———. 'Producing Lorca', *Enact*, April 1968.

———. 'Parsi Theatre ke Natak: Aaj ke Vatavaran Me', *Natrang*, 3 (6): 74–76, 1968.

———. 'Shivpuri's Rajhans', *Enact*, January–February 1973.

———. 'Theatre Is in the Villages', *Social Scientist*, 2 (10), 1974.

———. '"It Must Flow"—A Life in Theatre', *Seagull Theatre Quarterly*, 10 (June): 3–38, 1996.

———. *Charandas Chor*. Kolkata: Seagull Books, 1996/2004.

———. *The Living Tale of Hirma*. Kolkata: Seagull Books, 2005.

———. 'Hindi Rang-Andolan', *Natrang*, 14, 74–76, 2005.

———. *Agra Bazaar*. Kolkata: Seagull Books, 2006.

———. 'Janam Comes of Age', in Sudhanva Deshpande (ed.), *Theatre of the Streets: The Jana Natya Manch Experience*, pp. 63–77. New Delhi: Jana Natya Manch, 2007.

Other Media

Charandas Chor (1975/156 mins/Hindi), directed by Shyam Benegal, produced by Children's Film Society of India, starring Smita Patil, Lalu Ram, Madan Lal, Sadhu Meher, Habib Tanvir, Sunder and others.

Dancing at 80—Habib Tanvir and Naya Theatre (2003/29 mins/Hindi), directed by Mahmood Farooqui.

Deshpande, Sudhanva. 'Habib Tanvir and His Red-hot Life', *Pragoti*. http://www.pragoti.org/hi/node/3456, accessed on 27 May 2012.

Gaon Ke Naon Theatre, Mor Naon Habib (2005/75 mins/Hindi and English), directed by Sanjay Maharishi and Sudhanva Deshpande.

Tanvir ka Safarnama (2007/78 mins/Hindi and English), directed by Ranjan Kamath.

Zaidi, Shama. 'Beyond the Fourth Wall', Outlook india.com http://www.outlookindia.com/article.aspx?250267, accessed on 27 May 2012.

INDEX

ABOUT THE AUTHOR

Anjum Katyal has been involved with theatre publishing for decades as an editor, writer, translator and critic. As Chief Editor of Seagull Books, Kolkata (1987–2006), she was responsible for their New Indian Playwrights series, which featured post-Independence Indian playwriting in English translation, as well as several theatre studies titles. She was Editor of *Seagull Theatre Quarterly* (1994–2004), the only national theatre journal of its time, which focused particularly on the voices of practitioners. She has translated Habib Tanvir's *Charandas Chor* (Charandas the Thief) and *Hirma ki Amar Kahani* (The Living Tale of Hirma) as well as Usha Ganguli's *Rudali* (Funeral Wailers) and stories by Mahasweta Devi and Meera Mukherjee; she is currently translating Habib Tanvir's *Bahadur Kalarin*. As Editor of *Art and the City* (www.goethe.de/artandthecity), a web magazine on the contemporary arts, she has commissioned and edited pieces on contemporary theatre in urban India.

Apart from theatre in particular, she has worked on publications on Indian arts and culture and been involved in organising several exhibitions of contemporary art, as well as writing catalogues for exhibitions by Chittrovanu Mazumdar, Somnath Hore, Manu Parekh, Madhvi Parekh, Reba Hore and Nasreen Moochhala. She has a background in education and teacher training. A published poet, she also sings the blues and reviews and writes on theatre and the visual arts.

She is presently Consultant (Publications) with Maulana Abul Kalam Azad Institute of Asian Studies (MAKAIAS), a research institute based in Kolkata. She is also a Consultant with Oxford Bookstore.

Katyal is currently writing a book on Badal Sircar (SAGE Publications, Forthcoming).

Year - 2012
Pages - 178
Stock - 1
Ded Price - Rs 1,095
Point Rem - ?
sugg. Price - ?